CH00704984

I NS

2 0318326 5

WATERHOUSE AT LARGE

WATERHOUSE AT LARGE

Keith Waterhouse

Illustrations by Michael Heath

Michael Joseph
LONDON

First published in Great Britain by Michael Joseph Ltd
44 Bedford Square, London WC1
1985

British Library Cataloguing in Publication Data

Waterhouse, Keith
    Waterhouse at large.
    I. Title
    828'.91407   PR6073.A82

ISBN 0-7181-2652-1

Typeset in Bembo by Alacrity Phototypesetters, Weston-super-Mare, Avon
Printed and bound by Billing and Sons Ltd, London, Guildford and Worcester

CONTENTS

Most of the shorter pieces collected here are from my twice-weekly column in the *Mirror*. The other material is culled from contributions of mine to: *Company*; *Cosmopolitan*; *Expression!*; *Good Housekeeping*; *Highlife*; *Moneycare*; *Observer Magazine*; *Over 21*; *Punch*; *Sunday Express Magazine*; *The Sunday Times*; *Telegraph Sunday Magazine*; *The Times*; *The Times Educational Supplement*; *TV Times*; *Vogue*; *Yorkshire Magazine*; *YOU Magazine*.

One or two pieces have appeared in previous collections now out of print: *The Passing of the Third-Floor Buck*; *Mondays, Thursdays*; *Rhubarb, Rhubarb*.

'The Parents' Charter' in Chapter 6 is the only article of mine, so far as I know, to have been previously published as a tea towel.

K.W.

1

UNDERNEATH THE LAMPLIGHT

PLEASE TO REMEMBER

PLEASE TO REMEMBER

If my exhaustive inquiries this weekend are anything to go by, Bonfire Night is almost a thing of the past.

Of all the people I questioned, neither had any plans to have a bonfire tonight or attend a bonfire tonight. I even came across one deprived little lad who had never heard of Guy Fawkes. I have reported his parents to the borough children's officer.

Nor, in my neighbourhood, could I find any evidence that the anniversary of gunpowder, treason and plot will be celebrated to any marked degree. Someone usually sets fire to the community centre around this time of year, so that gives us a bit of a blaze, but it's not quite the same without baked potatoes and treacle toffee.

I can think of three main reasons why this pleasant tradition seems to be dying out. One is that today's children are so bone-idle – no better not say that, it makes me sound like Rhodes Boyson.

Try again; today's children are so mollycoddled, spoonfed and spineless that they cannot be bothered getting the ingredients of a bonfire together. I don't blame them – they're so used to having everything done for them, they probably think there's a Council Bonfire Warden who delivers ready-sawn branches in a plastic bag (there probably is).

The second reason – at least as far as city kids are concerned – is that you can't get the wood. Half the fun of a bonfire is building it, and if there are no trees within a five-mile radius, it's difficult.

At one time before they were chopped down to make way for adventure playgrounds, there were woods within walking distance of most housing estates. Or perhaps I should say within running distance, as that was the method of perambulation most favoured after being spotted by the park ranger.

Collecting bonfire wood where I came from was known as *chumping*, a dialect word whose origins have long gone up in smoke. Chumping was more than a chore, it was a ceremony. When half a dozen urchins returned from a raid on the Clerk of Works' Depot dragging a ton of seasoned roof joists on the end of a rope, the whole street turned out to watch. But for the runny noses and the police car, it was like that Victorian painting they produced on Christmas cards, 'Bringing home the yule log.'

Chumping always culminated on November 4, which in the North was known as Mischief Night. This was when junior terrorists were traditionally licensed to throw lighted jumping crackers through old ladies' letter boxes without fear of reprisal. The real point of Mischief Night, however, was de-chumping. De-chumping consisted of finding the largest stockpile of wood owned by the smallest boys, and relieving them of it. The power struggle on November 4, as marauding gangs criss-crossed the street requisitioning or repossessing the choicest logs and branches, made the Balkans look like the Home Counties.

The evening of November 5 always commenced with Mrs Cooney's court of inquiry. Mrs Cooney was the local busybody whose house habitually resembled the Old Bailey as – acting as judge, prosecuting counsel, jury and executioner – she cross-examined us on our latest misdemeanours. Mrs Cooney always took it upon herself to restore all bonfire materials to their rightful owners. Her decision was final.

When all these territorial disputes were settled, the huge pyres were lit. There was one in every back garden and soon the scene was reminiscent of the English coastline when the news spread of the approach of the Armada.

After the last banger had banged, the last sparkler had fizzled out, and the last crumb of parkin (gingerbread to you southerners) been disposed of, we would sit around the embers boiling lead. This singularly pointless exercise consisted of putting a toy soldier in an Oxo tin and holding it over a fire with pincers until it could be poured out like mercury. I have the scars on my leg to this day.

This brings me to the third and last reason why Bonfire Night is in decline, which is that it has been taken over by social workers, who were rightly scandalised at unattended children being in possession of explosives. It is not much fun standing behind a roped off enclosure while the meals-on-wheels lady lights a catherine wheel, and so November 5 ceased to be a red letter day. Now that councils have very little money to spend on fireworks, there are fewer communal bonfires than ever.

The right for youngsters to have their hands blown off is not one I would argue very passionately. Even so, Bonfire Night is the one single occasion in the calendar when we celebrate anything to do with our own history. It is sad that in the lifetime of everyone reading this column, it will have been meddled out of existence.

Where have all the grannies gone?

Where have all the grannies gone? I mean the genuine, original, twenty-two carat articles who wore black shawls and cameo brooches, sat in rocking chairs and smelled of camphor, and who – if you were good – would hobble to a dark cupboard with the aid of a silver-knobbed cane and dole out goodies from a bottomless jar.

Don't fob me off with any of your modern substitutes, who shop in supermarkets, watch television and are fetched in cars to have Sunday tea in high-rise flats. They may be grannies in the sense that their sons and daughters have grown up and produced offspring; they may delight in their grandchildren and offer gratuitous advice on their upbringing; they may very well sport grey hair and sweet smiles; but they are not stamped 'granny' all the way through.

True grannies were never seen in shops. They were never seen anywhere except at funerals. They did not visit their grandchildren: their grandchildren visited them. They would not have watched TV even if there had been TV to watch – partly because it would have been new-fangled, mainly because it would have been worked by electricity.

True grannies would have nothing to do with electricity.

True grannies were gas-driven.

Now there are grandmothers to be seen in boutique or bingo parlour – some of them wearing trouser suits – who admit, and indeed boast, that they were born in the twentieth century. This is an error. True grannies, by their very definition, belong to a bygone age.

I count myself still a youngish man: but the grannies I knew in my childhood were all Victorians.

They remembered, first hand, events that were already in the history books, such as the death of Livingstone, as well as events that never made it into my century like the fearful petroleum accident on the Abergele railway. They celebrated strange festivals that certainly did not appear in my Wolf Cub diary: Plough-Monday, Quinquagesima Sunday, Lammas Day and the Dog days.

Their own grannies, so they told me, had worn black in mourning for Horatio Nelson.

I should explain why I speak of these grannies plurally or in the corporate sense.

The fact is that, in my neighbourhood at least – and I suspect in many others – grannies were regarded as communal property. If you had a granny, you shared her with your friends.

A small child paying an unsolicited call upon his granny, in the hope of receiving a halfpenny or a sweet as a fair swap for listening civilly to a lecture about his manners, or general appearance, might be accompanied by as many as eight or nine casual acquaintances. They would hover on the threshold like so many supernumary Red Riding Hoods, hoping that when the goodies jar was produced, they would be invited to dip in.

Conversely, and on a reciprocal basis, any granny felt free to make use of the pool of child labour available in the district. A net curtain pulled aside and a bony figure rapping at a window pane meant that you were expected to present yourself at the double, even to a total stranger – to run an errand, do a bit of washing up, or capture an escaped parrot.

Nor were adults immune from this granny power. I have seen grown men, hurrying to some urgent appointment in pub or billiard hall, who have been beckoned by a parchment hand and despatched back down the street to fetch a newspaper. I have seen young mothers on their way to evening surgery with their sickly babies, who have been stopped in their tracks with a recipe for a dandelion poultice. I have seen rent collectors, tallymen, council officials, census takers, Parliamentary candidates, men from the water board, Income Tax collectors, bailiffs and similar intruders fleeing like chastened schoolboys from the wrath of grannies.

They sat, these grannies, in parlours that were far removed from the uncluttered council house living-rooms I knew. To enter one was to enter another world: of family Bibles and antimacassars, stuffed animals, wax fruit in glass cases, knick-knacks, framed homilies or proverbs, water colours, sepia photographs in bamboo frames, cushions embroidered with some patriotic motif.

The fly invited into the spider's web would recognise the feeling of trepidation that we had when calling upon granny. She was a terrifying figure, a straight-backed, uncompromising sub-agent of God who could find out your sins before you had even committed them. But somehow a reassuring one. We believed in her, trusted her wisdom, relied on her. It was a granny era, when a grannyarchy ruled over a granny empire.

And it has all gone now. Grandmothers may stock up with Smarties and Mars bars for their impish young visitors; they may hoard snapshots of christenings and baby's first smile; they may have a cure for whooping cough that would not be approved by the National Health; and grandmothers they may be, but they are not grannies. The magic is over. The secret is lost. The mould is broken.

Sociologists explain it by dusting down their theories about the break-up of community life. The close-knit terraces have gone down, the tower blocks have gone up. Families have been dispersed. Granny no longer lives around the corner. How can there be granny-power when granny has to take the 173 bus and change at the Angel, Islington, before she can tell her daughter that the baby, although superficially in good health, is clearly sickening for German measles?

The explanation has something in it but I am more inclined to put the blame on the break-up of the nineteenth century. The grannies of my day were so foreign to the times I was growing up in that they could have come from another planet. They were the last messengers of an age that has now disappeared.

THE KALAMAZOO EGG-WHISK

The great department stores, like the great luxury liners which in many ways they resembled, are not what they were. Every month or so in this or that town some locally-famous name puts the 'closing-down sale' stickers in its window. Now even the mighty Woolworth's itself is feeling the pinch.

It would be as pointless to mourn the passing of their great days as to shed a tear for the extinction of the dinosaur, but I shall miss them when they are gone, or so modernised and rationalised and generally tarted-up that they are department stores no longer within the meaning of the Act.

One of the great pleasures of my childhood was being taken on occasional Saturday morning shopping trips around the department stores of Leeds. 'Shopping' is perhaps a misnomer, since we rarely bought anything beyond a bag of Woolie's broken biscuits. Indoor window shopping would be more accurate.

The expedition always followed a pre-ordained route: Woolworth's, Marks and Spencer's then Lewis's, the vast shopping cathedral which dominated the city centre and happily still does. There were – are – two other department stores but they were reckoned to be too upmarket for the likes of us and even now, such was the awe engendered by these hoity-toity establishments, I would be diffident about crossing their marble thresholds.

Woolworth's, which I regarded as an all-year round Christmas grotto, then of course had its policy of everything at threepence and sixpence, or giving it away as we would say if it happened now. It was an interesting hobby, almost as absorbing as collecting cigarette cards, to wander through the store finding new examples of the ingenuity by which goods quite clearly costing half a crown or five and ninepence were contained within these price limits – a kettle and its lid, for example, would be sold as separate items, as were the components of the cricket set I coveted: bat sixpence, stumps threepence each, bails threepence, ball sixpence.

It was in Woolworth's that I nurtured my first vocational ambition, which was to become a shoplifter. The displays of goodies looked so tempting and the purloining of modest quantities of them seemed so easy. Luckily I was not big enough to reach the counter, let alone dip into it.

About Marks and Spencer's as it was then I have little recollection except that no sooner had we passed through its swing doors than my mother would invariably commence to relate the story of how Mr Marks had started his great enterprise with a penny bazaar in Leeds market – a saga that lasted all the way through children's clothing, lamps and electrical fittings, toys, crockery, soft furnishings and hardware, and out into the street again. I never tired of hearing this story, which for me had the magic of Grimms' Fairy Tales.

But enjoyable though these jaunts to Woolworth's and Marks and Sparks always were, they were but a prelude – mere trips round the lighthouse before the cruise on the Queen Mary. It was Lewis's that was the star attraction.

Built, I should think, in the late 'twenties or early 'thirties,

Lewis's was in my estimation the most modern building on the face of the earth. Everything about it dazzled with streamlined up-to-dateness, from the gleaming chrome of its purring escalators to the shining bronze of its silent lifts, from the pristine tiles of its American soda fountain to the burnished glass of its Ladies' and Gentlemen's Hairdressing Establishments.

In the fluorescent-lit basement, young women in white smocks demonstrated the latest household gadgets, usually, like the soda fountain, American in origin. To watch a girl from Pudsey with a permanent wave and a Clark's Business College accent (which meant she would claim to be from Padsy) demonstrating an egg-whisk patented in Kalamazoo was almost as good as sitting through a Judy Garland and Mickey Rooney picture at the Paramount de-luxe cinema across the road.

My greatest desire was to get lost in Lewis's, for there was said to be a wonderful room on the top floor crammed with battery-operated toys and rotogravure comics, where lost boys and girls were fed Knickerbocker Glories while waiting to be claimed. While I never achieved this goal, in a sense I was lost every time I set foot in the place – lost in wonderment at this brightly-lit, futuristic Aladdin's Cave of electric chandeliers and American egg-whisks.

WHERE THE WHEELS WENT

Other things are happening in other places. One of the things happening in a place called Barnsley is that the home-made go-karts, trolleys or bogies which have brought joy and concussion to generations of youngsters, are an endangered species because of the shortage of materials.

It is not that they cannot get the wood but that they cannot get the wheels.

I have this on the authority of one of my readers, Mrs Jean Hall, who writes from the Barnsley province of Ardsley that up there in King Coal's dominion the sport of hurtling downhill on these makeshift kamikaze outfits still leaves Space Invaders trailing as a runner-up attraction.

Of course it does, love. The vein of good sense that runs under the Yorkshire sub-soil is at its richest in Barnsley, where they dig it out in nuggets with pick-axes. They would no more swop their old street games and pastimes for a mess of electronic bleeps than they would trade in their rabbit-gravy-smothered, dustbin-lid-sized Yorkshire puddings for frozen pizzas.

I suppose, though, that for those of a Space Invaders and frozen pizzas disposition who may have their headphones tuned in to this column this morning, I had better explain what a go-kart, trolley, bogie or what-you-will is (the name differs not only from region to region but from street to street).

It is a primitive racing-car, propelled by boot-power, on which the driver lies or sits according to whether he prefers to break his head or his shins. It is made of wood, and steered by rope, and has a braking distance of shortly after you land in the duck-pond. It is an exhilarating and terrifying method of getting from Point A to Point Aaaarrggh!

But there is a problem. Wheels, lack of. Since, in the course of normal wear and tear, they tend either to buckle or spin off over the horizon, never to be seen again, they have to be constantly replaced. Jean's son has reported that they are getting more and more difficult to find, and she asks me if I can shed light on this grave and unhappy state of affairs.

I have made my enquiries and I can. If you will just step out into the street for a moment, Jean, I will point the finger of scorn at the culprit.

No, it is not the prying social worker wishful of corralling the kids into a supervised adventure playground with only safety-tested scooters to ride on. It is not the sinister Japanese lodger who is secretly cornering all the wheels so that bored youngsters will turn to Pacman and suchlike video diversions. It is not the rag-and-bone man.

There is the villain, madam. Yes – there in the pram. I name the guilty baby.

Note carefully, Jean, the style and dimensions of the vehicle wherein that deceptively cherubic infant is dribbling. I have described it as a pram, but the description is wrong. It is more of a pushchair, isn't it? A stroller, I believe the technical expression is.

Look closely at the wheels. Observe their circumference. If the four of them were made of smoked glass they would barely add up to two pairs of sunglasses.

Now that is not how babies used to get themselves about back in the golden age of gurgling. At one time they refused to ride around in any perambulator smaller than the Coronation coach. I don't know how wide your street is, Jean, but I bet when two of these primadonna prams of old met face on, one of them had to reverse.

They were prams and a half, they were. They had the gleaming coachwork of a chauffeur-polished Daimler. They had the chromium accoutrements of a sea-going yacht. They had the tassels and trimmings of a tent of Araby. They had the springs of an LNER main-line tank engine. And they had wheels. Oh my, did they have wheels!

I have spoken of Barnsley Yorkshire puddings the size of bin lids. These were wheels the size of Barnsley Yorkshire puddings.

They were perfect for your go-kart, trolley or bogie. They could have been custom-made for the job. You found them on rubbish tips, begged them from junk yards, bartered them from ex-babies, or in extreme and desperate circumstances tipped your little sister out of her pram and made off with her means of propulsion.

Them was wheels, them was, and they are as difficult to come by now as buttercups on a pit-heap. But they are still to be found, Jean, so tell your lad to keep looking. And just one word to him from a former go-kart champion before he sets off on his next knee-grazing speed trials: *Wheee!*

FLEAPIT JOYS

It is well known that memory plays you tricks. I don't mind that: I can take a joke like anybody else. I have just found out, however, that my memory has been deliberately misleading me for more than half a century.

All this time I have had in my mind a vivid recollection of my first visit to the Tivoli cinema, Leeds, on the Saturday of its opening week.

I was four years old. The film was Our Gang in *The Trail Of the Lonesome Pine*. The prices were fourpence, sixpence and eightpence, and we sat in the fourpennnies. A large orchestra – either Henry Hall's or the band of the Coldstream Guards, I never established which – played the popular hits of the day in the interval. I remember it well.

Yet here in front of me is documentary proof that memory has been sniggering up its sleeve. I was not four years old, I was five. The film was not *The Trail Of The Lonesome Pine*, it was *Gold Diggers Of 1933*. The prices were not fourpence, sixpence or eightpence, they were fivepence, sevenpence and ninepence, so we must have sat in the fivepennies. The massed Henry Hall-Guards band shrinks, before my very eyes, to a nine-piece ensemble.

My memory, I can tell it here and now, has not heard the last of this. I will have a word with it later. For the moment, however, I would like to linger with my adjusted recollections of those old fleapit days of mine, for the belated accuracy of which I am indebted to an enchanting little book by one Robert E. Preedy, which a kind friend has sent me.

A scholar of note, this Mr Preedy, who has rightly divined that specialisation is the key to learning. Where other academics toil over the broad and bewildering canvas of eighteenth-century constitutional history or the causes of the Seven Years' War, Mr Preedy has shrewdly taken for his subject the cinemas of the city of Leeds in their heyday. His thesis, appropriately entitled *Leeds Cinemas Remembered*, will be treasured by all the millions who remember the cinemas of Leeds. (Or don't, in the case of a certain memory not a million miles from this column.)

The Tivoli, I learn, was the sixty-fourth cinema to open in Leeds in an era when more people went to the pictures than presently have hot dinners. There was to be a grand – nay, a de luxe – total of sixty-eight silver screens dotted about the city before the decline set in and the Tivoli was relegated to bingo after being subjected to the indignity of showing *I Was A Teenage Werewolf* as its closing feature in 1960. Nowadays there are only fifteen cinemas for a population of three-quarters of a million.

I was about to say that all this is supremely useless information but of course, if the learned Mr Preedy were to go on Mastermind he would wipe the floor with the opposition, unless they happened to be authorities on the cinemas of Bradford or Manchester.

Mr Preedy, the Electra Picture Lounge in Jubilee Terrace opened on November 9 1916 and closed on Saturday March 9 1957. How many did it seat? Six hundred and sixty – 509 in the stalls and 151 in the balcony. The architects were Mosley's of Wormald Row and the closing film was *Private's Progress* starring Ian Carmichael. *What was the slogan of the Palace Picture Hall, owned by the Armley Rink Co. Ltd?* The most healthy and comfortable hall in the district, with a breathing area of 500 cubic foot per patron.

How many other – I've started so I'll finish, Mr Preedy – how many other Leeds cinemas can you name? The Assembly Rooms, the Crescent, the Gem, the Golden Cross Electric Theatre, the Kings Lighthouse, the Imperial, the Miners Institute, and the Palace Picture Hall, the –

I really must stop this. This column is under instructions to appeal to a wide audience and there must be at least four or five of you out there who were never familiar with the Shaftesbury Luxury Cinema, in whose back row I squandered so much of my youth in the nearest thing to a blissful trance this side of Hollywood. What does it matter, therefore, that an unusual feature of the place was reported thus when the Shaftesbury opened in 1929: 'Something novel in the way of seating accommodation is supplied by the provision of wide chairs for two. One presumes that the two-seaters are there to supply a long-felt want?'

Remembering keenly the long-felt want referred to, I suppose I can hardly blame my memory for being a little hazy on exactly what films we saw together in the fleapits, picture palaces and super cinemas of Leeds. As a lady recalls in Mr Preedy's book: 'We always seemed to have such fun. One Saturday I fell out with my current boyfriend, Sam, and on the insistence of my best friend, said I would go out with George. George was sitting about six seats away and it took him nearly half the film before he sat next to me. I was all of ten years of age.'

Such, such, were those dear old fleapit joys.

THE HAUNTED GRAVEYARD

Down in Brighton this Bank Holiday weekend, I spent a happy hour in the last penny arcade in England.

It is on the end of the Palace Pier and although it costs thirty new pence to get in, they give you five old copper pennies of Saturday-pocket-money vintage (and you can buy as many more as you wish, at the reasonable exchange rate of 5d for 10p) with which to play the machines.

Thus you can have a go at What the Butler Saw (or even, if you want to be a devil, What the Butler Didn't See), the test-your-strength machine, the Hercules Developer electric shock machine, the Laughing Sailor, the mechanised Pharoahs' Tomb – and all for a fraction of what you would have to pay for one round of Space Invaders.

There are machines in this penny-in-the-slot paradise that I have not clapped eyes on since I was a regular dropper-in on Dreamland, that truant-officer-haunted, watch-committee-condemned sink of coin-operated iniquity that was once a hissing and a by-word in the Sodom and Gomorrah postal district of Leeds.

It was as a long-lost pal that I greeted the All-Win Reserve Ball Machine in its handsome oak cabinet. Place coin in slot, press chromed trigger, and steel ball whizzes round and round then drops into one of a row of holes labelled 'win' or 'reserve.' There are NO LOSERS. And the winner stands to bet his penny back, plus free ball.

I was a wrist-flicking champ on the All-Win machine in my teens – many is the evening it has financed my obsessional but doomed efforts to wrest a packet of five Black Cat out of the maws of the Goliath wheel-operated grab crane – and I am here to tell you that I have lost none of my skill. In no time at all I had increased my five old pence to twelve old pence, or one old shilling.

But the grab crane still refuses to cough up. I had three frustrated, tantalising tries at releasing a Mars bar from glass-cased captivity before remembering why we nicknamed our

Dreamland grab crane Pauline. Pauline was a girl at school who promised much but delivered nowt.

The Allies Victory Ball machine I recognised as another old adversary. Built presumably as the amusement arcade trade's contribution to the war effort, the Allies Victory was mechanically programmed to sound the All-clear siren if, by fluke or miracle, you failed to lose your penny to Old Adolf. Or so it was claimed. I never heard the All-clear sound in Dreamland in 1943 and I didn't hear it in Brighton in 1983. I was another fourpence down before moving on in disgust to the Crying Baby machine.

The Crying Baby is a kind of obverse development of the Laughing Sailor. It features a waxen image of a harassed father nursing a colic-smitten baby. Put your penny in the slot and the figures become animated – particularly the baby, which emits scream upon scream fit to wake up the dead in the Haunted Graveyard machine (who otherwise will rise from their coffins only if their bones are crossed with copper).

All innocent, simple fun – as innocent and simple, you might think, as a village idiots' outing. Yet wandering around this clanking grotto was an experience of pure enchantment – not only for me, a notorious sucker for the pleasures of times past, but clearly for all the other punters present, old and young alike.

I watched two punkish youngsters playing a race game where you each wind a handle as fast as you can to jerk your cardboard horse past the winning post. They were as fascinated as if it were the very latest in push-button, new-diagonal-ricochet-feature video gadgetry. Then they moved on to the Prisoners At Work machine. Put in your penny and three cell doors swing open, to reveal convicts picking oakum, sewing mailbags and breaking rocks. Hardly a match for *E. T.* at the Brighton ABC but the pint-sized audience was riveted.

For myself, I squandered my remaining fourpence on the Airship Profit-Sharer (it doesn't say with whom it shares the profits – certainly not me); The Bumper Pintable; the Don't Blush peepshow; and the slot-machine that gives you a Photo Of Your Future Mother-in-law.

Strolling back down the pier I passed one of those zapping hell-holes which pass for amusement arcades in this electronic era. Those two same punks were now exterminating Martians by the million and they looked bored stiff.

IF I HAD A MILLION

There have been, alas, no sightings yet of my tall story from the granny-in-the-boot factory about the naked woman wedged in a roll of lino on a layby on the A23.

However, this really did happen to a friend of a friend of a friend a few days ago. His son came home from school with the announcement that he was helping to collect a million Mars bar wrappers which would finance a trip to Disneyland for a sick child.

The years rolled back – to 1936 when I was collecting a million bus tickets to send a sick child to Blackpool.

Never having been to Blackpool at the time, it did selfishly occur to me that if you could get there for a million bus tickets I wouldn't mind muscling in on the act myself. I made discreet inquiries as to where you took your million bus tickets when you had collected them (I had already accrued about fifty, so I was practically half-way there). Nobody, I need hardly say, had the faintest idea.

The million-bus-ticket myth, or variations of it, is the childhood equivalent of the granny-in-the-boot epic, which itself has many variations (one version reaching me from Cornwall has it that granny expires while on a picnic, her nearest and dearest shove her in the boot until they have finished their sandwiches, as mythology demands, whereupon the car rolls over a cliff and they are charged with murder).

There are, of course, many others. I particularly used to relish the grisly moral tale of the lad who ate ice cream straight after a fish and chip tea. He died instantly, his innards congealed like lard.

But it is the million-bus-ticket yarn that is the all-time children's favourite. It is handed down, embellished and updated, from one generation to the next like some Icelandic saga.

In their book *The Lore and Language of Schoolchildren*, Iona and Peter Opie have a version going as far back as 1850, when a rumour swept the land that a certain young lady living in Derbyshire was to be incarcerated in a convent by her eccentric father unless she procured a million postage stamps by a certain date. Another supposed incentive for amassing a million postage stamps – a substantial reward from the Post Office – goes back almost to the year Rowland Hill invented the penny black.

The Opies list many other variations. A million cigarette cards, a million milk-bottle tops, a million toffee papers, a million bus tickets that have to end with a lucky seven, and so on. Sometimes the purpose was charitable – to send a poor person to hospital or on a seaside holiday perhaps – but more usually it was to earn for the hoarder personally a fat prize.

It says something for our over-maligned youngsters of the present day that their motive for collecting a million Mars bar wrappers or iced lolly sticks or whatever is invariably selfless. Often it is a kidney machine they imagine they are collecting for, sometimes an expensive operation in the United States for a child with a rare disease. It is never, ever, for a bag of money to squander on sweets and riotous living.

In all the years I have been hearing the million-bus-ticket myth, in its many manifestations, I have never once come across a juvenile collector who questioned for an instant what anyone would want with a million bus tickets or milk-bottle tops or why they were deliberately keeping a sick child at death's door until this pointless Herculean labour was completed.

Nor have I heard of the magic million target ever being reached. About a hundred, I'd guess, would be the average mark before a fresh rumour sweeps the playground to the effect that a ball of string six feet in circumference will secure a stay in a Swiss clinic for a badly-shaken granny recovering from being locked in a car boot.

As to the hold the story has on successive generations, it would be a flint-hearted child indeed who did not believe in the crock of gold at the end of the rainbow – which is what the million bus tickets, in essence, represent.

Child psychologists may have a more complex explanation but I am afraid their expert advice comes expensive. Send me a million copies of this column, however, and I will gladly secure it.

THE PINDROP MAN

An assembly of headmasters – a concept as grisly, to those of us with long memories, as a convention of hangmen or a jamboree of hooded crows – has voted to end the school morning assembly.

At their annual conference, the National Association of Head Teachers came out in favour of changing the law whereby schools are compelled each day to herd all their charges into a hall smelling of chalkdust and make them sing the praises of the Great Headmaster In The Sky.

The idea is to have more freedom in handling the needs of children of different religions and cultures than the one that gave us 'We plough the fields and scatter.'

Fair enough. But there is a danger here not only of throwing out the baby with the bathwater but of throwing the bath itself on the rag-and-bone cart.

Religious instruction is only one function of the school assembly. Another is to give those assembled a sense of unity, of belonging to the school and the school belonging to them, as against just tagging along with one of a number of education units housed in the same building for administrative convenience.

The army parade serves much the same purpose. Indeed, my own recollection of school assembly is that it was pretty well interchangeable with an army parade – in the glasshouse. If, as it sometimes threatened to, the demented yelling of our genial headmaster had blasted the roof off our assembly hall, we should have had a barrack square ready-made.

Daily assembly was an exercise in orchestrated terror. From the moment we shuffled into that parquet-floored compound in single file like old lags in 'Each Dawn I Die,' to the moment we trooped out in a state of subdued relief like lifers unexpectedly granted parole, we were in a state of knee-buckling apprehension.

We invariably kicked off with 'All Things Bright And Beautiful' in which the whole school had been drilled to the precision of the Von Trapp singers. Old Pop, as our headmaster was known, always made his entrance during the second verse. It was his signature tune, his 'Bring Me Sunshine.'

The apoplectic double of Captain Mainwaring, he would

waddle furiously down the central aisle to a piping accompaniment of 'Each little flower that opens, each little bird that sings' as if he had just discovered a cache of fag-ends in the bogs or an escape tunnel under the dinner hut.

The hymn reaching its tremulous 'Amen,' Old Pop would then favour us with his Glare. Old Pop's Glare was famous. Every one of us, by holding his breath, puffing out his cheeks and bulging his eyes could imitate it. He looked like a frog which has discovered something disgusting in its pondweed.

Old Pop's Glare would continue until he could hear a pin drop. If Old Pop could not hear a pin drop, he would announce formally that he wished to hear a pin drop. He would add that it was all the same to him if we all stood there until five in the afternoon, but hear a pin drop he would.

It was not only pins dropping but hearts thumping you could hear at the end of this opening harangue. Having cowed us into submission – not that we took much cowing – he would then try to lull us into complacency with a few routine announcements about milk monitors, the inadvisability of leaving wet running shoes on the radiators, and so on.

Old Pop had nobody fooled. We listened in trepidation, waiting for him to clear his throat. When Old Pop cleared his throat, it was time for the morning bloodbath.

'A Boy. From This School. Has Been Seen. Spitting. At A Tram Stop.' You believed him. No one doubted that Old Pop had a network of spies across the neighbourhood. There followed a scathing lecture on the hygienic and aesthetic undesirability of expectoration. Or, as it might be, smoking. Or Smut. Or eating chips in the street.

On any given day there might be half a dozen of these hellfire mini-sermons, each one accompanied by fearsome threats. Old Pop would then treat us to one last Glare of utter contempt and loathing, and dash out of the hall as if suddenly seized by the need to vomit.

There would be a corporate sigh of relief as loud as the North Wind, and we would repair to our classrooms light of heart in the knowledge that the worst of the day was over. That was school assembly, that was. Don't revoke it – revive it.

A GOOD PLACE TO KEEP A PARROT

A few days ago I put my thumbprint on the mortgage papers for my new house, and in so doing I signed away a small ambition.

Feet-first Cottage, as I have christened my latest and last abode on account of my determination not to move on again until I am carried out, is a nice house as houses go.

It has the usual offices. It has hot and cold running water. It has wall-to-wall floorboards.

But – it does not have a front room.

All my life I have wanted a front room. Whenever I have had the gypsy-like urge (every seven years or so) to strike camp and try pastures new, I have promised myself: 'This time I'll have a front room.'

And now – but I see a good half of my audience looking baffled.

The younger end of the market are asking themselves what the silly old fool is rambling on about this time. What, they wish to know, is a front room when it is at home and what does a front room have that a back room doesn't?

Let me elucidate.

Years ago, when that concrete moonscape you see out there was a herringbone pattern of closely-packed and sooty terraces, there were more front rooms in this land than there are now corrugated iron windows – which is saying a lot.

Our grandparents called them parlours.

Any house that boasted two downstairs chambers – even if one of them was only the kitchen – reserved the classier of the two as the parlour.

In the kitchen-cum-living-room you ate, read your evening paper, had your hip-bath, tripped over the dog, cuffed the children, cleaned your boots and blew pipe-smoke over the blancmange.

In the parlour you played the harmonium.

The parlour was also where you entertained your relatives to cold meat suppers, stuck picture postcards in your photograph album, played Charades and Consequences (which is why they are called parlour games) and listened to the wind-up gramophone. A limited range of other sedate activities was also permissible, so long as you wore your jacket.

When the front room was the parlour it was used regularly if selectively. When the parlour became the front room – that is, when the last of the Victorians popped their clogs and the kitchen wireless replaced Happy Families as a source of amusement – it was used only on red-letter days or by special dispensation.

The front room was open for business on Christmas Day and Boxing Day, and on selected Sundays if company was expected. It was used for the lying-in-state of a departed grandfather, and for the ham tea afterwards. It was used as the starting-gate for weddings and christenings, when the sideboard would be unlocked and sherry dispensed.

In the exceptional circumstance of there being an aspiring brainbox in the family, the front room might be unsealed to allow him to do his homework in peace. The daughter of the house and her young man, if they could prove that his intentions were honourable or anyway serious, were also granted access. (Being allowed to do your courting in the front room was the next best thing to being sewn in a blanket.)

Otherwise, the front room remained for the most part chill and empty, smelling of Mansion polish and last year's turkey giblets, while up to half a dozen people might be crammed in the limited living quarters at the back.

It was a daft institution and what killed it off was not only demolition but television, for where front rooms survive they now have the telly in the corner and families lounge about on the uncut moquette for all the world as if they were in their own homes.

One thing England had while the front room lasted, and that was a sense of decorum. Also, it was a good place to keep a parrot.

I, sob, sob, never had a front room as a child and I always envied those who had access to this grotto of antimacassars, decorative firescreens, framed sepia photographs of soldiers with drooping moustaches, and souvenir pottery with the coats-of-arms of seaside resorts. I have hankered after a front room ever since but have never lived in the right-shaped house – and now it is too late.

It's a good thing I never bought a harmonium.

THOSE OLD BASIN BLUES

There used to be a little periodical, a monthly ragbag of jokes and cartoons with the extraordinary title of *A Basinful of Fun*.

I was reminded of it by a letter from Mrs Annie Fenn of Leeds this week, conveying the mournful intelligence that they have filled in the basins.

The basins were a series of shallow quarries in the middle of an enchanted forest – well, more of a little wood, really – which was the training-ground for my boyhood apprenticeship as cowboy, outlaw, smuggler, apeman, castaway, detective, engine driver and such-like career opportunities.

Where *A Basinful of Fun* comes into it is that it never occurred to me at the time that there was anything unusual about such a title. The basins were such enormous fun that it seemed altogether natural and proper that someone should wish to name a jokebook after them.

How these four or five mini-craters came into being I had and have no idea, though theories were legion. One was that they were old mine workings, another that they had been caused by bombs dropped from a stray Zeppelin in World War One, another that they concealed hidden gold looted from a treasure ship that had foundered on the Leeds and Liverpool Canal.

By far the most plausible, or anyway the most popular, explanation was that they had been formed by rockets landing from Jupiter.

Sometimes, when the August sun filtered through the trees, we would catch a glint of metal in one of these basins and dig feverishly for the concealed spacecraft. In this way we unearthed many rare objects such as old sardine tins and, once, what was either a time-worn Abyssinian coin or a tap washer.

The basins were all things to all boys. To bike riders, they were the speedway track or the Wall of Death. To owners of chariots in the shape of a plank on four pram wheels, they were a Roman Coliseum. To the underprivileged deprived of any form of transport except an imaginary bucking bronco, they were the foot-hills of Arizona.

My own especial delight, as the wounded colonel in command

of the First Leeds Mounted Aerial Marine Infantry, was to find the basins occupied by the kids from the Catholic School. If our council school platoon were present and correct in sufficient numbers, we would fight the Battle of Mons.

(No doubt my correspondent Mrs Fenn, being of a younger generation, took part in the D-Day landings on the basins when she would have been allowed to be a nurse.)

In winter, the basins filled up with water when they became the Atlantic or the Mississippi River. In high summer when their clay surface was baked hard and stippled with little cracks, they were the Sahara Desert or the moon.

There was never any single moment when any of us saw them simply for what they were – a few small depressions in the middle of a wood.

Back to Mrs Fenn and her letter: 'My friend and I (both in our thirties with an assortment of kids) make our annual pilgrimage every July to where we – and you – were brought up. Always we hear the call of the basins. We swoop down into them making the ancient animal noises known only by our tribe, watched by the younger generation who stand in wonder. Once this ancient ritual is accomplished we are refreshed and invigorated enough to face another year.

'Anyway, imagine our surprise this year when we turned the corner where the basins should be in sight and saw a ploughed field there instead. I thought I'd better write to inform you of their passing.'

Indeed, yes. It is distressing news, but it had to be broken, otherwise I should have had an even nastier shock. For by coincidence I was up in Leeds myself this week where somebody wanted to take my photograph in some of the old haunts, and I as near as dammit headed for the basins. Heart attack material that could have been, to find crops growing where Mars, the Grand Canyon and Lake Geneva used to be.

I did, however, drive past a deserted adventure playground. It didn't look anything like the foothills of Arizona to me.

Walking Tall on Bread and Dripping

Of my childhood friends, one is now a lecturer in speech and drama, one is a writer like myself, one finished up in Borstal and was never heard of again, and one killed himself in his late teens. The rest, I believe, are leading sane and industrious lives in the engineering or tailoring trades.

The only generalisation I can offer from this is that most people drift along with the tide but a few do not; those who do not must either sink or swim.

That seems to suggest that some of us were more keenly aware of our environment than the others, and that we were making a conscious effort – crooked or otherwise – to get out of it. I have no recollection of any such insight.

I was born in Leeds in the Depression year of 1929. It was not until the war, when my mother had three sons sending home their Army pay, and luxuries such as a regular egg ration were coming into the house for the first time, that I realised I had spent my early childhood in the most acute poverty.

My father, an unsuccessful costermonger, had died when I was quite small. Most of our furniture had gone to the bailiffs, or back to the hire purchase company. But that was not unusual in our street. For many years I thought an orange box covered with wallpaper was the standard form of bedside table, that a wardrobe was a curtain slung across a corner of the room, and that fitted lino was the perquisite of the rich.

Bread and dripping was my favourite meal, so I had no objection to having it for breakfast and tea. The lunchtime stews I found unremarkable, not realising that each one was a culinary and economic miracle.

My mother brought up five of us on what she could screw out of the Board of Guardians, so it was a great day when my eldest brother started work. As a fourteen-year-old adult bringing in a wage packet, he was entitled to a nourishing supper when he got home. The problem on the first evening was that there was no money in the house. However, a prolonged search revealed an unused three-halfpenny stamp. We persuaded the Post Office to buy it back from us and invested the proceeds in a tin of sardines. I have a vivid memory of the whole family crowding around the scullery table – which had been covered in fresh newspaper for the occasion – to watch my brother eating his first grown-up meal.

Such highlights apart, it seemed to me that our life was average and commonplace. I accepted that people like us did not go on holiday, except to the Poor Children's Camp, and that the Means Test man had the right to search the house and order us to sell any trinkets of the smallest value. My mother would outwit him by hiding cheap ornaments under the coal.

We were not a political family, and while my mother told me stories about how the other half lived in the big houses where she had been in service as a girl, I was never taught to question the system that had caused these inequalities. Nor were any of my friends, although their experiences were much the same as mine.

Where they and I differed from some of the other children was that we were supposed to belong to 'respectable' families. We were not allowed to eat bread and jam in the street or to play near the fever drains; there was a black list of uncouth homes we were not supposed to enter, and – what was most important – we wore shoes rather than boots or clogs.

If one of us had grown up to be a sociologist, he could have written a good thesis on Social Precedence as Classified by Footwear in a Working Class Community.

At the top of the tree were the shoe-wearers. They tended to join the Boy Scouts, pass exams, belong to the public library, wear spectacles, and go into office jobs. There were many sub-divisions between the shoe-wearers themselves. I remember one shoe-wearer having a birthday party, the first event of its kind I had ever come across outside fiction. Confidently expecting an invitation, I was not in the least put out to be told that his mother wouldn't have me because I was too dirty.

Next came the boot-wearers, the solid middle stream. Keen street footballers, avid comic swappers, good at metalwork and woodwork, but not at scripture or geography, they became skilled craftsmen. Then the clog-wearers: tough guys, usually with shaven heads; not interested in school work; formed gangs; smoked a lot; usually went into heavy industry.

And at the bottom of the scale were the wretched little pariahs who were allowed to run around in tattered plimsolls in all weathers. They suffered from impetigo, played truant, stole lead from the church roof, drank condensed milk straight from the tin, and finished up in dead end jobs.

The divisions were not economic ones. Some of the shoe-wearers were among the poorest families in the street, while most of the plimsoll-wearers had both parents working full-time (which accounted, I suppose, for the children's disgraceful appearance and high truant record). The difference I think was this: while the boot- and clog-wearing factions were mostly controlled by the male breadwinner, the shoe-wearing families seemed to be dominated by the mother.

This was either because, as in my case, the father was dead, or, as in most others, because the mother was simply the stronger personality of the two. And, as I've said, what these mothers had in common was that they considered themselves 'respectable'. They believed in 'keeping themselves to themselves'. And above all, they wanted their children to 'get on'.

For most shoe-wearers, 'getting on' merely meant a job at an office desk rather than at a factory bench – but in our street it was regarded as a giant step. I've found that in other walks of life where people have 'got on' in the most spectacular ways, there has usually been a strong mother figure somewhere in the background.

As to our methods of 'getting on', the two of us who became writers were lucky because our trade required no formal training, and we were able to learn it while we did routine clerical jobs to earn a living. The one who became a lecturer had a harder time – fifteen years in an insurance office before he was able to throw it all up and get into a college of further education. The boy who went to Borstal was simply unlucky. Many young men who are 'getting on' go through a period of dishonesty, if only to prove how clever they are, and he was unfortunate enough to be caught before he'd grown out of it. Otherwise he would have been a chartered accountant by now.

The chap who killed himself had 'got on' to the point at which he – and everyone else – realised he had a remarkable intelligence. But he had no idea what to do with it. I remember him one night at a meeting of the local film society gravely asking the visiting speaker from London whether he didn't agree that film made of celluloid was superior to that made from baked clay, owing to the flexibility of the former. The next day he was dead.

ALADDIN'S CATALOGUE

Always, it started as a rumour, rippling from one end of the street to the other, usually on the strength of the postman having been spotted humping a squarish, heavy parcel to No. 27.

Then there were reported, but unconfirmed, sightings. Mrs So-and-So had been seen with it. Mrs What's-her-name was supposed to have had it last. Mrs Whatsit was believed to be next in line for it.

Finally, it was definite, and the news flashed through the neighbourhood: *'The catalogue's here!'*

Paul Revere, galloping from one New England hamlet to the next yelling: *'The British are coming, the British are coming!'* might have caused some excitement back in 1775. But no more, I suspect, than the stir created by the arrival in those same hamlets, less than a century later, of the pioneering Montgomery Ward catalogue. And certainly no more than the buzz that went up and down our street the day the catalogue finally came.

It was (and still is) 1000 pages thick. For some families I could mention, it was the only reading matter that came their way from one year's end to the next. But in the first exciting week of its arrival, they were allowed no more than a tantalising two hours flat (a whole evening in the case of a few favoured customers) to leaf through it.

The system was that the catalogue thudded twice a year (spring/summer, autumn/winter) on the doorstep of the lady at No. 27, who was the authorised agent and collector.

It then went the rounds of all her customers – that is to say, every one of her neighbours, barring the solitary, leprous outcast at No. 41, who one year had returned the catalogue with half its pages defaced by childish crayon scribblings – until everyone had seen it and handled its glossy pages. Thereafter, the kitchen of No. 27 became a kind of public reading room, where the catalogue could be consulted and pored over.

In due course, our mothers and big sisters made their selections, and, in the fullness of time, their mail order parcels began to trickle in. But for us small fry, the delivery of a steady stream of winter coats, handbags, enamelled breadbins, collapsible beds, blankets, carpet-sweepers, fire-irons, parchment lampshades, barometers, teasets, and – a bizarre choice on the part of No. 36 during a brief period of affluence – electric waffle irons, did not quite match the excitement of the actual catalogue that had generated this miniature consumer boom.

The main attraction, for us, was the Toys and Games section – especially in the autumn/winter edition, which any connoisseur of catalogues knows is the bumper Christmas number. The tallest and spottiest of us might sneak a few covert glances at Ladies' Foundation Garments and Stockings, but even these sex maniacs could not resist the Toys and Games section for long – especially since (hands ritually scrubbed, no food or drink allowed in near vicinity) we were allowed only fifteen minutes' goggling before the catalogue was claimed by the woman next door.

The Toys and Games section was like a petrified Christmas grotto. Every comic annual, boxed game, electric train, dressing-up outfit, construction kit, musical instrument, model soldier, doll, clockwork car, conjuring set, rollerskate, football, kite, jigsaw and three-speed bicycle ever manufactured was there in glorious colour. (Or was it, in those days, glorious black and white? Glorious pictures, anyway).

As the catalogue was removed from our clamouring reach, we pleaded for Meccano and Monopoly and Hornby. And by and by a mysterious parcel arrived and was spirited into the airing cupboard, and we understood that Father Christmas's standing arrangement with the catalogue firm still held good.

There was one other section that grabbed the attention of us junior browsers, and that was Sweets and Confectionery. With such a feast of selection boxes and drums of Turkish Delight and ½lb bars of chocolate and trays of toffee and tins of *Batons des Voyageurs* (whatever they might have been) to drool over, we would never understand why our parents preferred to waste their precious two hours staring at pictures of wooden clothes horses and japanned tin coal scuttles.

Yet stare they did, and choose they did, and order they did, when the lady from No. 27 came round with her book and tape measure. For she insisted on checking dress sizes personally, to avoid the risk of one of her clients putting on a little around the midriff between ordering and taking delivery of a spring frock, then to claim they'd sent her the wrong size.

I'm told that mail order sales are now running at £2 billion a year, and I'm not surprised. For the spending in our street alone must have accounted for a substantial slice of that sum – and that was before World War Two. In those days, you could buy a canteen of cutlery, a basket-weave linen chest, a two-piece costume with matching blouse, and a home perm set, and still have enough left over for a pair of roller skates or a box of chocolate creams if you were susceptible to pestering.

The secret, of course, the open sesame to this parcel post Aladdin's Cave, was that you paid 'by the week'. A pound note for a British-made nickel-plated electric toaster – then much in demand as the perfect wedding present – was hard to find, but a bob a week over twenty weeks wasn't too bad. So spring/summer and autumn/winter alike the catalogue did a brisk trade in our street.

I believe a spot inventory would have proved that a good fifty per cent of all goods and chattels in our homes, not to mention the clothes on our backs, came from the mail order warehouse. Since that is over five times the present national average – catalogue shopping now accounts for ten per cent of all non-food sales – I think that entitled us to an extra discount, but I don't think we ever got one. But the lady at No. 27 got her commission, which included – or so it was said – one of those enormous presentation tins of assorted biscuits that were such a mouth-watering feature of the catalogue each year.

Or perhaps they were an annual present from a grateful management – or maybe she bought them herself. Anyway, the tin of biscuits was always on her sideboard, and anyone who dropped in to consult her catalogue was offered a ginger nut or a plain rich tea.

It was a far more civilised, and less exhausting, way of shopping than traipsing round the stores in town. The only trouble was, when small urchins knocked on the door of No. 27 to say they were thinking of choosing a birthday present for their mothers, and was there anything in the catalogue under threepence, they were sent away with a flea in their ear. And no offer of a biscuit.

With such cavalier treatment of its future customers, I'm surprised the mail order business is still so healthy some four decades later.

TEA ON SUNDAY

'Sunday tea was the peak. By six on that evening the middens up the back had a fine topcoat of empty salmon and fruit tins.'

Thus Richard Hoggart, in *The Uses of Literacy*, remembering the Sunday teas of his Leeds childhood. And of mine. He does not go into further detail, but I know his Sunday teas were exactly the same as mine, for all Sunday teas between Trent and Tweed were exactly the same as mine. It was an immovable feast, an immutable rigmarole.

You ate off thin bone china with gold-leaf rims, from a white damask or Irish linen tablecloth which had been given as a wedding present and which otherwise spent its week in a sideboard. Paper doilies were much in evidence, as were the Apostle teaspoons and any item of tableware the household might possess which was chromed or electro-plated.

The centrepiece of the groaning board was a two-tier cake stand featuring a geometrically arranged display of sliced slab cake or 'fancies' on the upper deck and malt loaf on the lower. You could not have cake until you had eaten a piece of malt loaf. You could not have malt loaf until you had got through your quota of bread and butter.

This was no hardship for on Sundays the bread was not only cut into triangles, which to my fastidious mind put it almost in the 'fancies' class itself, but it was spread with best butter as yellow as buttercups. I can still feel the tickle in the throat induced by this Sabbath upgrading from Maggy Anne or dripping.

There would also be a bowl of salad in season, jars of piccalilli and pickled beetroot, bottled mayonnaise and two kinds of sauce. There might be optional extras in the way of plates piled high with currant teacake, vases of celery, side dishes of cheese and potted meats. But all this was mere garnishing for the *pièce de résistance*, which, as Hoggart recalls, was as often as not tinned salmon – the pink middle cut, swimming in vinegar and sometimes containing tiny bits of bone.

Like him, I still relish it more than fresh or smoked salmon. But the following course, the tinned fruit – usually pineapple chunks or slices, served with thin tinned cream or packet custard – I have lost my taste for. Nor, even then, did I care much for the tea – pale, sweet and milky – which was swigged in prodigious quantities all through the meal (weaker by far than the robust mashings with which we washed down our everyday fare). But of course it would never do to drink out of half-pint pots at Sunday tea.

You partook of this feast either at home or away – that is, you entertained your relations, or your relations entertained you, on a kind of tacit rota basis. The more the merrier seemed to be the principle. No matter what quantity of aunts and cousins descended, the tinned salmon, the 'fancies' and the weak tea seemed infinitely expandable, like the loaves and fishes. Only occasionally was Sunday tea taken simply *en famille* – when, even though all the formalities were nevertheless observed down to the last paper doily, there would be a feeling of anticlimax, like spending Christmas in a bed-sitter.

But it had to be relations or nobody; under no circumstances would you sit down with friends (I do recall, however, being invited by a prosperous schoolmate who lived in a private semi to come in and watch him eating his Sunday tea, an experience he thought I would enjoy. I took him up on it, and, though it was rather disappointing that he had tinned salmon like ours, I was fascinated to observe that his pineapple chunks were served up with jelly. The rich, I thought, are different from us – they get two puddings).

I never quite worked out how the various relatives knew when it was their turn to visit – how this or that aunt, turning up out of the blue once a year from a distant township, never seemed to clash with geographically nearer kinsfolk who came round every two months or so; nor how we never chanced to be out enjoying reciprocal Sunday hospitality when a tribe of cousins hungry for malt loaf arrived from far away.

No one was on the telephone in those days, and, though you could send off a postcard at breakfast time and it would reach its destination by teatime, this service did not extend to Sunday teatime. Nor were return fixtures prearranged – the nearest I ever heard to a firm replay date was the injunction: 'Don't leave it so long next time', as aunts bloated with weak tea put on their hats. These Sunday expeditions – very often heroic treks involving two or three changes of tram – seemed to be spur-of-the-moment affairs, decided on after dinner as an alternative to falling asleep with the newspaper over one's face.

Perhaps it was all governed by some corporate migratory instinct, of cousin being drawn towards cousin, grandmother towards daughter, sister towards brother, by the faint vinegary tang of tinned salmon wafting irresistibly on the Sunday afternoon breeze.

However they came to have their feet under the table, my recollection is that there were never enough chairs to go round. The available furniture was apportioned according to rank; the dining chairs to heads and dowager heads of households, the bedroom chairs to heirs and heiresses apparent, and the end of the sofa, the kitchen stool and, on occasion, the laundry basket and an upturned orange box to lesser fry.

Sunday tea could be an elbow-to-elbow affair when we had a full house. Inevitably, on these crowded occasions, a fragile teacup would be caught by a sleeve button as a visiting pleni-potentiary reached for a lemon curd tart or slice of seed cake. The chomping procedure would then be frozen while a saucer was placed under the affected portion of the tablecloth and salt sprinkled over the spillage. This was so regular an interruption that it seems, looking back, to have been a part of the ceremonial itself.

I have put my recollections of Sunday tea in the past tense as if the institution no longer existed. Nor does it, for me, living now in the effete south, where tea is a thing of chintz armchairs, nests of side tables and thinly sliced cucumber sandwiches. But Sunday tea as I knew it is still robustly alive and well 'twixt Trent and Tweed, though the marauding hordes of relatives now tend to warn one another that they are on their way. And they are lucky to be offered tinned salmon.

PLAYING THE GAME

I arrived at my council elementary school on a Leeds housing estate a precocious four-year-old and left it a precocious fourteen-year-old.

In the intervening years I was intolerable. I went through my schooldays convinced that I was the cleverest boy in the school – which, if cunning is another word for cleverness, I was.

I was astounded and hurt if I did not come top in examinations, for I was a brilliant and audacious cheat. For conventional studies I had no time at all. My only aim was to demonstrate my superiority over all those who were ill-starred enough to be my teachers, whom I arrogantly regarded as morons. It is astonishing that I survived.

I was allowed to join the infants' class two terms early by reason of having harassed my mother to distraction by prematurely reading books. A self-taught four-year-old among a class of five-year-old illiterates is off to a head start. No wonder I was insufferable.

I won my first school prize at the age of six. Our teacher, a Miss Pease, turned up on the first day of term with a ceramic salt, pepper and mustard set in the form of a donkey and fruit-cart. I don't know how she came by it or what possessed her to offer a cruet as a suitable prize for children barely weaned off rusks. But offer it she did. It was to go to the boy or girl judged by Miss Pease to have been the best-behaved during the term. I determined to have it.

So did all the other children in the class (so maybe it was not such a bizarre choice after all). But I was smarter than they were. I reasoned that being of such tender years they would quickly forget why they were behaving so nauseatingly well, and would lapse into their old ways. I, however, would remember. Instead of wasting my energies being indistinguishably well-behaved along with everyone else, I would continue routinely creating havoc until the last couple of weeks of term, by which time all my classmates would have fallen by the wayside. I would then bring myself to Miss Pease's attention with a quick spurt of angelic behaviour, and so win the prize. The ploy worked. I bore the donkey-and-cart cruet home with smug pride and it stood on my mother's mantelpiece for twenty-five years.

Moving up to the junior school was an unsettling experience, for the junior school had male teachers, many of them said to be of a violent disposition, and I was not sure that they were to be bamboozled as easily as the ladies in lilac smocks I had led by the nose in my spectacular career in kindergarten.

I decided to put the issue to the test at the earliest opportunity. Positioning myself outside the junior school staff-room, I chalked on the wall in six-inch-high letters the legend KW IS A FOOL. And then waited for a teacher to emerge. As it happened, it was the headmaster himself who came out first. Quailing inwardly, I regarded him unblinkingly as he stared distastefully at my graffiti.

'Is that your handiwork, boy?'

'No, sir.'

'Don't lie to me, laddie! You still have the chalk in your hand!'

'But sir!' I piped up, all injured innocence, pointing to the KW in KW IS A FOOL. 'Those are my own initials. I'm not likely to call myself a fool, am I?' Thwarted by this piece of warped logic, the headmaster strode off without another word. Brandishing my chalk, I turned back to my handiwork and thickly underlined it for good measure, assessing correctly that he wouldn't remember whether it had been underlined or not.

In junior school I learned how to win at exams. The more spectacular the crib, I found, the less likely it was to be detected. Teachers were always on the look-out for history dates scribbled on thumb-nails or on bits of stamp-hinging wrapped around inkwells. They were not on the look-out for history dates meticulously copied out to resemble a school timetable and then pinned to the class notice-board – which happened to be next to my desk. I put no little effort into cheating at exams – far more than I ever did into swotting up for them – and I regret to say that I have never felt the slightest twinge of guilt at thus beating classmates academically abler than myself.

My most famous coup was to cause an end-of-term geography paper to be 'lost', so that I had to sit the examination again. By that time, of course, I had mugged up the answers. But to allay suspicion I was careful not to get every one right, so that I came not top, but third. Such subtle manoeuvres, while doing little for the soul, must at least have been useful for exercising the intellect.

More fruitful, I believe, than learning the principal rivers of Australia.

I think I will draw a veil over my three years in senior school. I was bolshie, cocky, overwhelmingly conceited and a considerable pain in the neck, especially to my English teacher, with whom I used to argue insolently about syntax. Probably to his relief, I discovered the delights of playing hookey. A playground fall had resulted in my having to report to the City Infirmary for a series of X-rays, and I had had the foresight to retain the last of my official appointment cards demanding my presence on Friday at 3pm. But it didn't say which Friday. Over a period of two years, brandishing my grubby exeat, I would periodically skip Friday afternoon English classes and take myself off to the pictures.

Years later, when as a reporter on the local paper I went back to my school to cover some function or other, I confessed to my English teacher.

'Yes, I know,' he said. 'You were seen more than once going into the cinema.'

'Then why didn't you do anything about it?'

'We didn't want to cramp your style,' he said. And it wasn't until then that I realised my teachers knew more than I thought about teaching.

UNDERNEATH THE LAMPLIGHT

I had a nasty shock the other day. I went back to the street where I was brought up and found that the lamp-post was missing.

There was a lamp-post there all right, a concrete clothes-prop fizzing pale-blue mercury and bathing the neighbourhood in shadowless light – very efficient, and for those within its pale orbit undoubtedly the next best thing to having a council house in the Sea of Tranquillity.

But the lamp-post I remember, *the* lamp-post – a squat, cast-iron pillar painted bright green, surmounted by a hissing gas-lantern that flickered behind four square window panes like a stranded lighthouse – was gone for ever. This is my requiem for it.

You must understand that it was more than a source of light.

Our lamp-post was, to begin with, a highly functional object. Protruding from its iron neck was a stout metal bar, the official purpose of which was to support the ladder of the man who came to mend or clean the gas-mantle.

This metal bar was perfect for tying bits of rope to, swinging from, doing somersaults over, throwing pieces of slate at, or merely dangling from by two puny arms while your friends counted slowly to a hundred and you felt that you were on the rack.

Because of its basic usefulness to us the lamp-post was the pivot of our community. It was our maypole, roundabout, assault course, market place, moot and general headquarters.

It was the wicket for our cricket matches, one side of a goal mouth, the base for rounders and a complicated game called 'Relieve-oh!' which rarely got further than a shrill quarrel about its devious local rules.

We played marbles under our lamp-post, tested our conkers against its hollow, clanking base and shinned up it to light Woodbines and sparklers, or merely to experience the heady smell of singed hair.

The fraternity of our lamp-post, like an officers' mess or a gentleman's club, had a rigid system of protocol. No one was admitted to membership under the age of three; no one from other streets was allowed except as a guest; cry-babies, boy scouts and anyone wearing glasses were rigorously blackballed.

Ladies' night was on Fridays, when the girls of the street, hungry for adventure, hung about under that shining orb like tiny Lili Marlenes.

Our lamp-post was the venue for all the main social events of the year.

In high summer we sat beneath it poking tar bubbles in the road with long sticks or trying to prise up the lid of the storm-drain that was supposed to give you scarlet fever.

In November we assembled around it to count our fireworks and decide whether the Big Banger or the Jumping Cracker should be poked through Old Mother Teaker's letter box.

At Christmas we used it as a boundary post to divide the carol-singing concession between those whose voices had broken and those who could still bring a fine treble to the first two lines of 'Away in a manger'. But the social attraction of the year in our street was the Button Fair, and this was invariably staged beneath our lamp-post. This always followed the annual bank holiday fair that was held on an acre of waste-ground nearby; having lost all our pennies on the roll-'em-down stalls we would hurry home and chalk up our own stalls on the pavement, using buttons for money.

Different kinds of buttons had different values: a trouser button was the lowest denomination, a jacket button was worth two trouser buttons, an overcoat button was worth three, and a cloth-covered button snipped surreptitiously off your sister's best coat was worth four or even six for a big one.

Sometimes urchins from other streets tried to gatecrash the Button Fair with handfuls of shirt-buttons snitched from their mothers' work-boxes, but these were rejected as being worthless foreign currency.

If you had comics to swop at any time of the year, you stood under the lamp-post with your rolled-up merchandise tucked into your stocking; eventually a fellow-trader would come out with his stock of *Radio Funs* or *Knock-Outs* and haggle with you – one *Knock-Out* for two American Dick Tracey comics (they were a drug on the market at that time), or one *Radio Fun*, mint condition, for an incomplete copy of *Illustrated Chips* and a cigarette card of Don Bradman.

The best time around our lamp-post was on autumn evenings, after the rain. You looked gloomily out of the window, tired of Meccano and Dinky toys and craving human company. You'd see the gas-jet flicker and go on magically, by itself; its bouncing reflection would light up the puddles and tell you that the rain had stopped.

Out of the shadows would stroll some boy from up the street, looking about him, eager for companionship.

You'd watch him loafing around under the lamp-post and pray that he wouldn't go indoors again before you'd struggled into your raincoat. You'd hurry out and hang about with him, abstractedly discussing sex or football or floating a matchbox down the gutter, but all the time keeping a sharp look-out on the doors for signs of life.

Soon other figures would emerge from the shadows, and soon after that the whole street would be alive with boys: diving through the wet privet hedges, swinging like Tarzan from the iron bar of the lamp-post, whooping and whistling and yodelling, running in and out of that friendly pool of light.

As I said, our lamp-post has disappeared now. The concrete column that replaced it is far more serviceable and it probably holds a silver medal from the Road Safety Council. But there were no children playing beneath it when I passed. Where were they, I wonder? Watching television, or doing homework, or joining in constructive games in an adventure playground?

Has the magic gone out of childhood – or is it just that my generation were lucky possessors of a magic lamp?

GRANDAD'S LAST POST

My old grandad would have got hot and bothered over the postal strike. He liked getting letters and he liked sending letters, although he could neither read nor write.

He was over ninety years old and he lived alone in a little mining village in Derbyshire. His married daughter, my mother, lived in Leeds.

She couldn't get down to see him all that often and it was pointless writing because there was no one to read her letters to him, and he wouldn't have cared to show them to anyone who wasn't family.

So they worked out between them a unique way of keeping in touch.

Every Monday morning my mother used to sit down at the kitchen table with the Stephen's ink-bottle and the Basildon Bond. As if it were the most important job in the world she would carefully address an envelope to herself.

Then she would stamp it, fold it in two and place it inside another envelope which she addressed to Grandad.

She caught the first post every week.

His Majesty's mails being a bit more reliable in those days, the envelope always reached Grandad on the Tuesday.

The postwoman once told my mother he so much looked forward to receiving it that he would often walk to the end of the lane and wait for her coming.

He would open his letter on the spot, take out its enclosure and study it for several moments, as if it contained some message that only he could understand.

Then he would walk across to the village post office and dispatch his stamped addressed envelope back to Leeds.

It always arrived by the first post on Wednesday and, in this way, my mother knew that he was safe and well. She never bothered to open the envelope, for of course it contained nothing.

This ritual went on for several years.

Sometime after Grandad's ninety-fifth birthday, my mother noticed one Wednesday morning that the postman had walked past the gate. She ran after him to see if he had forgotten her but no – there was no letter from Grandad that week.

She put on her coat, took the next train to Chesterfield, caught the little bus to the village where he'd lived, and buried him.

FATHER'S DAY

Any attempted voyage round my father would at once founder in the shallows, for he died when I was three or four, and was not recollected much thereafter, except in respect of his cavalier failure to sign the war pension papers (he was wounded at Mons, and I thought his campaign star was the Victoria Cross) that would have made bringing up five kids that little bit easier.

He was a bankrupt costermonger – an early victim of technology in the shape of a yellow fruit-and-veg lorry which snatched such desultory trade as he had built up with his horse and cart. He would never have mechanised: a Foden lorry couldn't find its own way home from the pub. But to the end he had grandiose dreams that his luck would change. The wildest of these ambitions was to have his own stall in Leeds market, where he would be known as the Cucumber King. 'When my ship comes in ...' he was fond of saying.

I have only two real memories. One is of him standing magisterially astride the fireplace, like God in a brown suit. My sister had been pestering him for her Saturday penny. He dug deep into his pocket and threw a cascade of glittering coins across the room

– pennies, threepenny bits, sixpences, shillings, florins; even a half crown or two rolled heavily under the leatherette settee. It was like a cornucopia uptipped. The family scrambled for it and recovered more money than we had ever held in our hands before. I thought it a wonderful, wild, mad, extravagant, larger-than-life gesture, and it didn't matter at all that the treasure trove was at once impounded as being rightfully the housekeeping money. It was not until I had reached the maturity of about six or seven that I guessed, from guarded remarks, that he must have drunk a lot.

The other memory is of being plucked out of bed in the middle of the night (five in the morning, adult time), swaddled in a potato-sack and jogged through the sweating cobbled streets on the back of his cart, whither he had deposited me like a box of apples in the belief that I would sleep. He did not wear the cloth cap of his calling and dew shone on his thick mane of grey hair, creating a nimbus effect.

Presently we drove into Aladdin's cave. All was light and brilliant and shining and noise and the smell of oranges. We were, I was to learn – though whether I comprehended it there and then I don't recall – at the wholesale end of Leeds covered market, where he went to replenish his supplies.

I have revisited the place hundreds and hundreds of times since then but whenever I think of it I see in my mind's eye what I saw then – a shimmering crazy-mirror montage of burnished scales, brass weights, marble slabs, naptha lamps, mountains of cabbages, horses' breath, billy-cans, iron-clad wheels, squashed blood oranges, and big men in smudged white overalls with pencil-stubs behind their ears. I was in a grotto, the personal guest of a wizard.

I rode home on top of a sack of brussels sprouts, nibbling a doorstep of bread and dripping so thick I never finished it. All I can remember after that is the brown suit without him in it, after he had gone to hospital and died. My mother went through the pockets and found a halfpenny – his entire estate, not counting the fruit crates in the stable which became bedside tables after the bailiffs took away the furniture. His last words had been: 'My ship's come in.'

2

ADVICE TO A MOLLUSC

THE CONSUMER COWBOY . . .

THE CONSUMER COWBOY ...

That distinguished social historian Dr Rhodes Boyson deduces that the present wave of muggings and other such unpleasantnesses is all down to the Sixties. The Beatles era, he believes, has much to answer for.

It is with a shock that I realise that when the Beatles were singing 'Love Me Do', Dr Boyson was still in his thirties. Trying to visualise the bewhiskered pedant as a young man is like imagining Noah as an apprentice boatbuilder. But that is neither here nor there.

Personally, I recollect the Sixties not with distaste at their permissiveness, but with amazement at their energy. For a while, Britain was a young country and cock of the walk in all sorts of directions. And I wonder how all that fizz came to fizzle out.

But there are so many ways of squinting into the kaleidoscope of the past that sticking labels on decades is always a futile game. Which will not, however, deter me from prematurely musing today on what kind of labels are likely to be stuck on the Eighties.

Although we are barely into them there are already discernible patterns taking shape in the kaleidoscope: the unrest, the violence, the vandalism, the anarchy, the spectre of unemployment, the spectre of Dr Rhodes Boyson. This is not going to go down as the Age of Sweet Reason, that's for sure.

We have an embarrassing and confusing choice of horrible images to sum up the Eighties. Yet when I try to project myself into the future, the better to look back on the present, it is an insignificant and obscure little illustration of our times that comes to mind.

I am thinking of a court report concerning a man of previous good character who made a bungling attempt to hijack his firm's wages in order to pay for £4500-worth of double glazing.

I cling to that item (well, drowning men clutch at straws, don't they?) as a key to what the Eighties are up to.

The prospect of an honest man making a hash of stealing to foot the bill for something he doesn't need, and for which he is plainly paying through the nose, says all sorts of things about the cowboy society we are now living in. To get this combination of ingredients together you have to have your feet very firmly in an age where the botched job, the rip-off, the con and the easy touch are an established and indeed an essential element of the economy.

The cowboy, of course, has been with us since the war when he used to be called the spiv. But it is only lately that it has become possible to identify, as a recognisable type, the cowboy consumer, who is an eager customer (often with ready money) for the services the cowboy provides.

I was going to say that the cowboy consumer is what we used to call the sucker, but that isn't strictly true. What we have here is the paradox of the city-wise sucker, where hustlers themselves are hustled, everyone makes a bob, and everyone is happy.

The cowboy consumer lives the lifestyle of one who has spiritually emigrated to Australia. While economically he belongs to the suburban middle class, he has recycled its values to suit his own needs. He has more affinity with Bondi Beach than with Bromley.

The cowboy consumer, who does a lot of overtime, is a big earner and a big spender. There are siz-packs and frozen pizzas in the fridge and a stack of soft-porn video tapes in the bookshelves. With his double glazing, his cash-down loft conversion, his d-i-y shower unit, his hi-fi, his CB radio and other gadgetry that may or may not have fallen off the back of a Cortina, he is the cowboy's best customer – or punter, to use the trade jargon.

While not averse to the kind of transaction where questions are not asked, and while regarding VAT as a personal affront, the cowboy consumer will happily put wads of fivers in the hands of absolutely legitimate businesses, though of the kind that tend to keep illegal shopping hours. The perfect sitting duck for the home computer and telecommunications boom, he responds to the soft sell when buying his hardware and to the hard sell when buying his software.

The Beatles, whose emergence in the Sixties was to cause Dr Boyson so much sorrow, had a song called 'Paperback Writer'. To catch the essence of the cowboy consumer they would have to compose Paperback Reader. His policy is buy it (preferably at a knockdown price), gulp it down, chuck it away.

As a phenomenon of our times, he may or may not have the built-in obsolescence of the stuff he invests in. I suspect not. But certainly for the present, if you look around at who is selling and who is buying, in other words at where the action is, it cannot be doubted that like it or lump it, this is the age of cowboy consumerism we are living in.

... AND THE COWBOY TENDENCY

Quite as alarming as those elements infiltrating the Labour Party – even more alarming, if you ask me – are those elements *not* infiltrating the Labour Party.

I mean the swelling ranks of working men and women whom Labour leaders still confidently talk about as 'our people' – but who are their people no longer.

If, indeed, they ever were: for there are many young first-time voters who haven't lived long enough to become disenchanted by Labour. They were never enchanted in the first place.

For the rest, there is an evergrowing number of voters (or non-voters) who also never saw Labour in its great crusading days. To have voted in the 1945 or 1950 elections you would have to be over 50. Anyone below middle age would be quite justified in regarding Labour merely as a party of management rather than the party on the dashing white charger.

A relative handful – particularly the young, and more particularly the young with a bit of higher education – have taken one look at the Labour Party, fallen about laughing, and joined the Far Left. Those in their thirties and over, who have not experienced the polytechnic crash-course in militant socialism, have more likely not joined anything.

Many of the people in this group would be what they themselves would call non-political and the politicians would call apathetic. At election time they give their vote to the party that has the most attractive window display. When they get the goods home, of course, they are often unpleasantly surprised – but let's not bother with that just now.

The substantial and increasing minority that make up the rest of this group are not so much non-political as anti-political, often violently so.

They will set themselves against a government – any government – not because they want to see the other lot in power, but because they want their own short-term goals to be realised, at any price. They will strike – with or without their unions' blessing – whatever the effect on their fellow-workers in other industries, let alone the public at large. They remain unmoved by pleas of hardship, unimpressed by dire predictions of what is to become of us all. In many cases, they are concerned with screwing as much as they can out of dying crafts before the death takes place. They are, in short, looking after No. 1. They are a very powerful force. They are the Cowboy Tendency.

Now before you glance at the top of this page to check that this isn't the *Daily Mail* you are reading by mistake, give me another moment. If it *were* the *Daily Mail*, it would be trying to persuade you that every disruption in our industries or institutions, every flying picket, every ugly incident at the factory gates, every patient turned away from hospital, is entirely motivated, indeed entirely organised, by the militant Left. My case is if that were so we should have little to worry about, since the militant Left can be identified and contained. But I doubt that the Special Branch keep files on the Cowboy Tendency.

What made the Cowboy Tendency so bloody-minded? I think the answer is to be found in the recent welter of reports suggesting that all efforts to make Britain an equal society have failed. In one of these, a major study of social mobility, Dr John Goldthorpe (writing, says the *Daily Mail*, 'from a Left-wing class-orientated point of view that will infuriate those who see the world differently') argues that increased industrial unrest is a natural consequence of this failure, and that more and more workers will fight for a better deal to the point that they present 'a potentially serious threat' to society.

I don't suggest that members of the Cowboy Tendency sit around brooding about the public schools or *The Times* serving smoked trout to upwardly-mobile traitors. But they do observe that this is definitely not a country where life is going to be appreciably more attractive for their children. And while this deficiency may inspire them more towards part-time mini-cab driving than to Marxism, they are no less angry than the student slogan-chanters.

Labour may have cause to be worried by the Militant Tendency's entryism programme. It should be at least equally worried by the Cowboy Tendency's stuff-youism programme, which had already helped to lose it one election and may well lose it the next.

LIFE IN THE SEVENTIES

Strobe-light London snapshots:

A Me-generation disco narcissist practising the Time Warp while trying on a woolly hat in front of a Top Shop mirror.

Audio typists wearing high-protein fun jewellery (a hamburger, a half-eaten doughnut) in the queue for a health-bar grated-cheese salad.

Fantasists and role-players: an undiscovered Lorraine Chase wafting down from Leyton on the 38 bus, an Islington Green Comprehensive Boomtown Rat, an A-level Woody Allen wondering neurotically whether the hour of the Polytechnic Footlights will ever come, an identikit Bogie (*Casablanca* vintage) sipping iced tea through a straw at Peppermint Park. A veteran of the army surplus stores, who has never been further east than Southend, sporting a stencilled map of 'Nam' on his flak jacket and the legend: I KNOW I'LL GO TO HEAVEN CAUSE I'VE SERVED MY TIME IN HELL.

White girls with designer-labels on their blue-denim bums, looking from behind like black girls.

Sprigs of royalty – mainline and branch – as handsome as Kennedys.

Rich kids reading *Ritz*.

Poor kids whose Jagger lips move as they read the flyposter advertising Friday night's gig.

Rich kids pretending to be poor kids, reading *Sniffin' Glue*.

A mobile tramp, his bundles in plastic carrier bags stacked in a Tesco check-out trolley, researching the dustbins around the corner from Joe Allen's restaurant.

70s people, hereinafter known as 70spersons (joke: the decade's most overworked one) tended to live in, or work in, or be looking for a pad in, or use the lunchtime pub-theatres, art cinemas, ethnic restaurants, folk-clubs, wine bars, real-ale houses, delicatessens and 32-flavour ice-cream parlours of, or be familiar – either as client or counsellor – with the run-down social services of, or sign petitions against the pulling down of a Victorian tram-shed in, or be a friend of someone who was trying to save the adventure playgrounds of, or at least know how to take a short cut home through the back doubles of, or otherwise have some affinity with that half-hopeless, other-half-hopeful, gerrybuilt, bulldozed, concrete-and-any-old-iron, overplanned, under-valued urban wilderness that came to be known, in the jargon of the 70s, as the inner city.

It was what was left of Camelot after Merlin had gone down for seven years on charges of conspiring to bribe the borough council.

70spersons were the ones who had looked around, picked up the pieces, lowered their sights, salvaged what they could, learnt to adjust. They were survivors: not in the of-the-fittest sense but in the sense of being resourceful refugees. They had shrugged off the cornucopian promises and photogravure dreams of the 60s and were starting again. In black and white.

Or, as they put it to each other, they were getting it together.

Like the inner city itself, 70spersons had a scrag-end and a topside. They were corrugated-iron or chromium, basement or studio, Hackney or Barnsbury, down or upmarket. But a visitor from Mars or a time-traveller from Surbiton would have difficulty in telling them apart.

They had identical phone-in accents, grew identical mature-student beards or frizzed their hair in the same golliwog perms, wore the same type of sneakers and the same, or same-looking, denim shreds and patches. (Two 70spersons at a bus stop, one reading about the prospects of *The Times* in the *Guardian*, the other reading the obituary of *Reveille* in the *Daily Star*, and one of them on her way to lunch in Covent Garden with her art director while the other is on his way to the Supplementary Benefits Office, could otherwise be taken for brother and sister, or at least fellow-students of the same breezeblock university. Not only unisex but uniclass.) And they were living, though at different levels, on the same ecological slagheap of squandered resources.

An off-duty punk rocker wearing a save-the-whale T-shirt and Levis. But with green hair.

Street theatre in the rain: mime artistes with runny make-up, as if they've been crying, sheltering in the Jobcentre doorway.

A scarlet placard nailed to the only tree in the housing complex: DUMPING IS AN OFFENCE. THIS AREA IS UNDER SURVEILLANCE. A woman drags a charred mattress out of a ventilation shaft and dumps it under the tree, which itself is already scorched.

Vandalised graffito: a football enthusiast (SHED RULES OK) uses the tab of a soft-drinks can to score viciously through KEEP INCEST IN THE FAMILY in a tube-station lift.

A townscape that looks like a vast but deserted National Car Park, bisected by cobbled roads that need weeding. A jogger in a blue tracksuit is running on the spot at the crumbling kerbside while a funeral procession cruises at fifteen miles an hour past him and towards the flat horizon.

Only convert was the mantra of the spaced-out 70s.

There was a population shift, as noticeable as a small earthquake and a possible infringement of the Town and Country Planning Acts which served as a liquid cosh for restless prisoners or the municipal archipelagos.

From the three-dimensional glass-and-pebbledash blueprints they'd been brought up in, those 70spersons who were able to began to drift, as if by Ur-instinct, to whatever was left of the long-dead streets and buildings they had perhaps been born in but could not possibly recall, and whose unexpected corners, un-scheduled alleyways and anomalous iron lamp-posts and other eccentric street furniture could only have been a folk-memory. Committing the once unthinkable transgression of *change of use*, they proceeded to adapt whatever they could find to their own needs.

Thus it was that 70spersons ate their dietburgers in converted coal-cellars, drank their white wine spritzers in converted banana warehouses, ran their poetry workshops from converted chapels and their minority rights advisory centres from every converted nook and cranny, and watched fringe theatre in the con-verted morgues of abandoned hospitals. They campaigned from converted storerooms for grants to save recreational centres converted from old market halls; those with job-satisfaction xeroxed creativity in Edwardian office suites wrenched from the jaws of the bulldozer, or sold macrobiotic foods from Welsh dairies which the council had meant to flatten until the money ran out, or ran mobile playgroups from converted double-decker buses.

Small was beautiful, but old and small was more beautiful still. 70spersons mourned the passing of the corner shop, found a corner shop going relatively cheap, got an improvement grant to convert it into a house and lived in it.

They were not only making the best of what the planners (having meticulously planned it) called 'urban blight', they were reacting – sometimes angrily – against the cruddiness of the tower blocks, against the destructiveness of comprehensive development, against the soullessness of the light industry battery-farms on the greenfields factory estates, against the clinical, corporate, day-care-hostel-annexe school of architecture that, when the caring society was still a growth market in a hurry, had taken design standards back to the utility level of the postwar prefabs.

(Where 70spersons were unable to adapt – through lack of resources, deficiency of education or simple absence of what those who had it called upward mobility – the reaction was no less decisive. The concrete canyons became an aerosol-sprayed Pompeii, the graffiti insinuating itself like lava over every flat surface and devolving, as it spread, from crude yet recognisable words and letters of the Roman alphabet to clusters of mysterious and alarming hieroglyphics that looked like the secret language of a secret cult.)

70spersons, rejecting the gimcrackery of the high street chain-stores where Festival of Britain 'contemp'ry' was still on its last splay legs, filled their converted houses with secondhand furniture or, at worst, 20s and 30s repro – the once-despised plastics having been discovered to be the ideal material for cheapo replicas of art deco and all that jazz. Only their giant beanbags, their Manhattan-skyline window blinds and their elaborate lighting arrangements – the domestic sculpture of the 70s – were bang up-to-date new. Their knick-knacks and bits and pieces and many of their clothes came from inner-city souks such as the Portobello Road. Here, squatting like peasants with raffia mats spread out before them, they sold one another jewellery or candles which they had made themselves, usually from reclaimed materials.

70spersons passed on the word that they were into recycling.

They had been into recycling long before the Yom Kippur War that had sparked off the energy crisis, which when it came only confirmed their forebodings of a consumer-goods apocalypse. The North Sea oil bubble and its spurious promise of untold wealth did not fool them for a second, they didn't even bother to check the dipstick. Born into what a media-guru of the mid-60s, now passé, had dubbed the global village, they had a satellite's-eye-view of events – a perspective fanning out so far beyond their own environment that it made the dwindling band of short-back-and-sides Europatriots look positively parochial. The 70spersons looked across from their own mean streets to the slumlands of the Third World and knew that the packaging-industry affluence they'd known as children belonged as much to the Arcadian past as the Edwardian gentleman who had once, long, long ago, told their parents that they had never had it so good.

A skater on silent wheels, carrying a black executive briefcase, glides effortlessly past a traffic jam in the Aldwych and into Bush House.

An African in robes is carrying on his shoulder about £200-worth of portable stereo cassette player/radio with digital tape counter, sleep timer and dual coaxial speakers. He is listening to 'Afternoon Theatre', which can be heard within a radius of 100 yards.

Only where technology touched their lives were 70spersons reckless and extravagant. Knowing only a push-button world where the transistor was no less of an everyday object than the electric light bulb, they neither marvelled at technology nor feared it. They simply used it, like tap water.

When politicians and trade union leaders – alerted by a Prime Minister who had seen a television programme on the topic – began to sound alarms about the widespread effects of the silicon chip including the threat to conventional skills, 70spersons merely glanced at their digital watches, adjusted the low mass woofer and cone tweeters on their music centres, and worked out how many hours casual labouring it would take to pay for a video recorder.

The politicians, getting no feedback from their input (they had picked up a technological term or two themselves in middle age), were baffled by the 70spersons' cool, and called it complacency. It was not the first time that such a misunderstanding had arisen.

70spersons coming up to thirty when the decade drew to a close would have been three years old when Queen Elizabeth acceded to the throne, five when Kingsley Amis published *Lucky Jim*, seven when the first nuclear power station was built, eight when Russia launched Sputnik I, fourteen when John F. Kennedy was assassinated at Dallas. They grew up with immigration and ITV. They do not remember Jarrow.

They were the first complete generation of a melting-pot Britain that had changed out of all recognition since the flag-waving 50s. Sociologically monitored from the cradle, comprehensively educated (or not, as some would argue), polytechnically trained – if only in the jaw-breaking, ongoing-situation jargon of the software sciences – they were programmed, or perhaps they programmed themselves, for a new Britain so remote from the old one that to some they seemed like a generation of moonwalkers.

They had little in common with the conservative working class or conventional middle class that had spawned them – their 'sub-culture' as they patronisingly dubbed it. They were in a class of their own: the polyocracy. They dressed their own way, created their own values, spoke their own language ('That's *right*' – 'That's weird' – 'That's really weird'), did their own thing. They were mobile, flexible: couldn't see why anyone should want to do the same job for life, live in the same house for life, stay in the same country for life.

Politicians of vision, prophesying that the day would come when we would have to invent a new concept of work, didn't know that the patent had already been filed. 70spersons cheerfully took on the dirty work their parents had left to immigrants, or they did three months' 'unsocial hours' on the buses and a stint in the biscuit factory before taking off on a Laker to New York. (The politicians misunderstood the Laker revolution, too. They thought it was about flying.)

The unemployment statistics, broken down by age, sex, colour, trade and geographical location, were no hang-up for 70s people. You worked when you wanted to, at what you could get. Or you drew your benefits and worked the system. And you moonlighted: got some wheels and minicabbed, cash only. (The pejorative phrase 'social scroungers' has always been something of a puzzle to 70spersons, who were encouraged from infancy to look on public money as a kind of bran-tub.)

Only in their own polytechnic professions – teaching, the social services, local government – did 70spersons look for old-fashioned job security. They took every public-spending cut as a personal affront, which in a sense it was: like every young generation there has ever been, 70spersons were keenly disliked by those who were no longer young (such as the angry old men of the 50s). When they took to the battlements in the wave of public-service strikes that crumbled the Labour government, it was their weirdo clothes, weirdo beards, strange manner of speech and irreverence towards their elders and betters that most got up other people's nostrils.

When given the opportunity at the polls, many of the old duly voted against the young.

Hand-in-hand him'n'her couples browsing in a Charing Cross Road sex aids shop, handling and discussing the products as they would in Foyle's a few doors away.

A child of nursery-rhyme age being held up to a telephone, so that it can lisp an Elvis Presley song, in full, to LBC's 'Jellybone' programme.

A plain-clothes policeman wearing an ear-ring, an astrological pendant, psychedelic top and blue velvet strides.

Two single-parents, their offspring carried in baby-slings, standing in the post office queue, breastfeeding as they chat. A flustered old age pensioner sticks a TV licence stamp on her granddaughter's birthday card and becomes very upset.

As for their own politics, 70spersons tended to be left of left of centre, though fewer of them were card-carrying Marxists or banner-carrying Trots than was popularly supposed. Generally, mainline politics were a turn-off: it was not that they were disenchanted by the major parties, they had never been enchanted. Labour, with its politburo of grey men in blue suits propped up by a shrinking minority of grey men in blue overalls, was a joke. The Tories were a bunch of shits. The Ecology Party might be an ongoing relevance but when it came to their own preoccupations – consumerism, sex discrimination, non-smoking, minority rights, seals, abortion, wholefoods, motorways, nukes, plus whatever might be the fashionable conspiracy theory of the moment – 70spersons went for direct action.

Like crossbred amoebas they divided and redivided continually as they splintered into pressure groups, the pressure groups themselves sometimes dividing as they fell out among themselves.

70spersons became fanatical, sometimes even violent, when pursuing lost causes, humour was never their strongest point and the reputation that many of them had for being a pain in the arse was often well earned. They did, however, have a strong sense of justice and a lot of compassion, though mostly for themselves.

It was to themselves, to one another, that 70spersons responded – *related*, to use the key word. None of them came forward, as in the 50s and 60s, to explain their generation to the outer world: they would have called that exploitation. Reputations were made, but only among themselves. Their culture was private. Their instinct was to scale down, keep it small. They mistrusted the big time, the big stars. When the record industry thought that with punk rock they could clean up the sub-literate market as had never been done since the days of Harmsworth's *Tit-Bits*, it was on the 70spersons' contempt for instant fame that their hopes foundered.

With their almost paranoiac fear of being ripped-off – either financially, politically, communally or culturally – 70spersons looked on the world with a kind of naïve cynicism. The 50s face was angry, the 60s face well-fed, the 70s face was foxy. Perhaps it was the right expression: there was a lot to be wary about.

The hard times ahead will not be too hard for the 70spersons, because they don't expect very much. Clutching their stand-by tickets to the 80s they are prepared to travel coach, provided that not too many others are going first-class.

Mufflered pickets roasting chestnuts on the brazier they have set up outside their workplace, fanning the flames with a placard: 'SOCIAL WORKERS HAVE TO EAT TOO.'

A young man dressed as for guerrilla action in Southern Africa but with an off-public school accent, fingering a set of tiny silver spoons in an antiques boutique and asking: 'Do you take Access?'

ADVICE TO A MOLLUSC

The latest news from Mars is not, as some of us hoped, that it is populated by little green men with TV aerials sprouting from their heads.

All the same, the intelligence to hand is quite intriguing. The hot tip from the red planet is that up there on the other side of the stars, life as we know it is only just on the verge of beginning.

In other words, if the scientists are right (and when did you ever know a scientist to be wrong?) Mars as of 2 August 1973 is in pretty much the same shape as the Earth was 2,000,000,000 years ago.

You will recall, if you cast your mind back, that although nothing very much was going on at that time, big things were in the offing. So they are on Mars.

An ice cap on that silent planet is going to start shifting and creaking and soon, say in about 500,000,000 years, a new life-cycle will be under starter's orders.

When all that remains of the last man on Earth is a flake of white dust in the desert of Kent, the first primeval mollusc will crawl out of some fetid Martian swamp.

It will look around and consider its needs, and after a suitable pause for thought (call it a couple of million years, to be on the safe side) it will begin to develop into something more ambitious than a snail.

It will grow legs, ears, a nose and other appurtenances – all in easy stages. It will find new and amusing ways of reproducing itself. As the centuries roll on and constellations die and the Moon is swallowed up by a black hole in the heavens, Martian brontosauri will stalk the crimson plateaux in the flapping shadows of Martian pterodactyls.

Species after species will originate, evolve, die out, emerge, adapt, combine, coalesce, mutate, engender, propagate, diminish and multiply until at last, when the Earth is but a floating cinder in the sky, some hairy member of the mammalian order of primates will discover that it can stand on its hind legs.

A millennium will pass and then, in a clumsy, arthritic manner, it will close the beginnings of a fist around some object such as a piece of flint.

Another millennium will pass and it will reach out, tentatively, and pluck an apple from a tree. Martian Man will have taken his first giant step.

Towards what?

Towards the bow and arrow, the sling, the blowpipe, the spear, the lance, the sword, the cannon, the musket, the rifle, the hand grenade, the machine gun, the field gun, the anti-tank gun, the anti-aircraft gun, the incendiary bomb, the rocket, the napalm bomb, the atom bomb, the inter-continental ballistic missile, the anti-personnel device, the Molotov cocktail – and the hydrogen bomb.

Towards a six-day war and a seven-year war and a thirty-year war and a hundred-year war, and a thousand civil wars, and an opium war, and a punitive expedition, and a peasants' revolt, and a people's rebellion, and a preventive war, and a massacre of the innocents.

Towards the motor-car, the aeroplane, the tanker, and the juggernaut. Towards the steam train (late), the diesel train (de-layed) and the electric train (cancelled). Towards the tram-car in all its versions, and the trolley-bus. Towards the long queue for the non-arrival of the double-decker bus.

Towards a plundering of the mountains and a befouling of the seas, a squandering of minerals and a polluting of the rivers. Towards industrial waste, oil slicks, smog, slag heaps, DDT, strontium 90, carbon monoxide and effluent of potash.

Towards thalidomide and other discoveries.

Towards nerve-gas.

Towards thrombosis, syphilis and hatters' madness.

Towards slum houses and slum schools, inadequate pensions, old women eating cardboard, low wages, high prices, great profits and silly taxes. Towards computers, motorways and pneumatic drills.

Towards greed and vanity and lust; towards murder, rape, arson, vandalism, and robbery with violence. Towards the bank-ruptcy of architects, the follies of politicians, the peccadilloes of disc jockeys and the major misdemeanours of presidents.

Towards inquisition and torture. Towards treachery and be-trayal. Towards hanging from a cross on a green hill.

My advice to the Martian mollusc: stay in that swamp.

GOING THROUGH THE MOTIONS

And another thing. Conference declares its full support for the
Labour Party in its titanic struggle to sink the Labour Party.

It congratulates all those at constituency level who are working
assiduously and tirelessly to remain in opposition, sometimes at
great personal sacrifice of their sitting member.

Conference reiterates its determination not to be led mindlessly
by the nose into a hollow election victory by so-called moderates
slavering for the fruits of office.

Conference remains convinced, on the other hand, that despite
Tory-biased distortion by the gutter meejah, Labour's message to
the ordinary working people has come over loud and clear from its
calm and considered deliberations at Blackpool.

Conference is therefore utterly confident of a Labour landslide
with an overall majority in any future election of, oh, call it no
more than four hundred seats to be on the safe side.

While heeding the warning of chairperson Eric Heffer that 'we
must not become complacent – we have a long way to go,'
Conference cannot help thinking that chairperson Heffer is a bit
of an old gloomy-chops and that winning the next election, once
the cowardly Thatcher dare expose herself to the wrath of
3,000,000 unemployed embittered by the plight of working miners,
should be a doddle.

Recognising wholeheartedly that Neil Kinnock is the present
leader of the Labour Party under the unsatisfactory procedure
whereby the job has not gone to an activist from Liverpool in a
bomber jacket, Conference nevertheless urges that Arthur
Scargill should play an active, continuous and decisive part in
putting Labour's message across if an overall majority of six
hundred over the clapped-out Tories and pathetic rump of the
Alliance is to be in the bag.

Believing that the next election will be fought exclusively on
the single issue of pit closures and the attendant police violence
which has sickened the nation, Conference recommends that all
Labour's party political broadcasts for the foreseeable future
should be left in the capable and expressive hands of Arthur.

Conference fervently reckons that no one better than Arthur, backed up by his own private supply of statistics, can convince the electorate that just as there are no uneconomic pits, only those deliberately starved of investment, so there are no hopeless constituencies for Labour, only those cruelly deprived of Labour votes.

Conference calls upon all those who did not vote Labour last time to make good this provocative and unacceptable deprivation by voting Labour the next time.

Conference welcomes the active support given to the Labour movement by those victims of the Thatcher police junta branded by the unthinking Tory robot meejah as yobboes. For too long yobboes have been without a voice except on the football terraces and on the walls of public urinals. Now the unheeded yobbo minority group has freedom of expression within the broad church of Labour, always provided that it does not nick the lead off the roof.

Conference condemns the intransigence of its own so-called wishy-washy moderates in withholding their full and fervent support from the yobbo tendency out of a mistaken and elitist belief in their own intellectual superiority. It reminds the faint-hearted and the toffee-nosed that the Tolpuddle Martyrs were as thick as two short planks.

Conference utterly rejects the nit-picking and insulting argument that a gullible electorate will be in any way swayed against Labour by Conference's contemptuous rejection of the over-simplified and undemocratic principle of one member, one vote.

If the party cannot see that letting all local party members have a say in the re-selection of their MPs would be a real threat to Labour's democratic principles and a blow to Labour activists who are working night and day to undermine their MPs, then Conference simply gives up.

But the ordinary people of Britain are not to be fooled by the trashy meejah newspapers which they throw away each day by the tens of millions. The ordinary people of Britain will look long and hard at all that has been said and done in Blackpool this week, and their response will be: 'Yes, those are the people we can trust.'

THE LUCKY DOG

Mythology, like history, has a habit of repeating itself. Old wives' tales remain in a state of perpetual renewal like favourite library books.

For example, each succeeding generation since the invention of the motor car has produced a grandmother who has the misfortune to die while driving with her family through some remote foreign region.

They put her in a boot, as is the way of the bereaved with dead grandmothers when there is no undertaker to hand. Whereupon the car is stolen ...

Nearly everyone in the land knows someone who knows someone to whom the above anecdote actually happened. Which brings me to my text for today. Nearly everyone also knows someone who knows someone – unless, by a seven-to-one chance, they happen to be that someone themselves – who is out of a job.

Myths about the unemployed do not turn up with the same regularity as myths about dead grandmothers, since there have been periods – though my younger readers will not remember them – when everyone had a job. But there is a rich vein of them nonetheless.

They revolve around the proposition that the reason the unemployed don't have jobs is because they don't want to work. In Brighton last week you could hear Tory ladies asserting to one another: 'They don't want to work, that's the truth of it,' with the regularity and predictability of parrots trained to repeat the rubric: 'Have a nut.'

Then would come all the stories which I can remember, without exception, from the Thirties. How a certain boss offered jobs to a mob of right-to-work demonstrators, whereupon, to a man, they turned tail and fled. How most of the unemployed are not really unemployed at all but are moonlighting as window cleaners and taxi-drivers. The same taxis, presumably, in which, like their grandfathers before them, the jobless turn up to collect their dole money ...

I even heard one lady assert – no, I tell a lie, it was a friend of a friend who heard her, actually, but I have read much the same suggestion in the *Sunday Telegraph* – that there was nothing to stop the unemployed from getting positions as domestic servants. Politicians used to say exactly that fifty years ago. The prospect of a Britain teeming with three million butlers, pantry-maids and under-gardeners is an awesome and spectactular one: 'Upstairs, Downstairs' crossed with *Gone With The Wind*.

As for the realities as against the legends of being out of work, I want to tell you of a little street scene I chanced to come across the other day while taking a constitutional in order to fortify myself for Mrs Thatcher's rhetorical burblings about how rhetoric won't cure unemployment.

Strolling along a busy shopping thoroughfare I became aware of a pleasant-looking, neatly-dressed young man, his face alive with excitement, threading his way at great risk to life and limb through heavy traffic and waving his arms at the girl friend he had espied on my side of the road.

'Hey! Wait! Listen!' he was calling as he caught up with her. 'I've got a job!'

The girl seized him by the elbows and they did a little jig of pure pleasure. 'Fantastic! When do you start?'

'Monday! Terrific, isn't it?'

'Marvellous! You lucky dog!'

That's all there is to the story. And so they prattled on, the girl's reciprocal excitement perhaps tinged with envy. And as they moved out of earshot I realised that he had not yet told her what the job was. To have got one was all.

Just a little snapshot of life in Mrs Thatcher's Britain where the abiding achievement of her Government after three and a half years, and the promise they bring to the future, is that young people dance in the street and count themselves lucky when at last they land a job.

Any job.

THESE BRUTISH ISLES

Nearly one week on, there is still no other topic of conversation. But perhaps by now we can put the night they murdered soccer into grisly perspective as but one more step, though admittedly a giant one, in the brutalisation of Britain.

It is a process that has been going on for a decade or so now, and you do not need to go anywhere near a football match to see how, like spilled acid, it has been gradually corroding our national fabric.

As I write I can barely hear myself think for the sound of the tapedeck blaring from a parked car two streets away. Its owner probably doesn't class himself as a hooligan, probably has no idea how much anger and distress he causes wherever his travelling Tannoy system takes him. He has been brutalised. He belongs to a brute culture, a tin-ear society where such things as consideration, common courtesy, common decency are as exotically foreign as kiwi fruit.

So what has that to do with the EuroCup slaughter, which, while it has been blamed on a whole cornucopia of causes ranging from the National Front to the victims themselves, has yet to be laid at the door of drivers who play their radios too loud?

The soccer thugs (your old-fashioned soccer louts sound like Little Lord Fauntleroys by comparison) who are responsible for the deaths belong to that same brute culture.

They did not set out to kill thirty-eight people, any more than the man with the motorised megaphone two streets away set out to drive everyone mad. They set out for what in their brutish lights was a bit of fun – a giggle, as they would say, though the brutish British seen having a giggle are as mirthless a crew as cadavers in a mortuary.

They wielded iron bars because that is the way one wages battle or 'has a go' in the ever widening circles they move in. They have been brutalised. Thus it may be said, while excusing or exonerating none of them, that their victims were in truth the victims of the brutalisation of Britain.

This brutalisation, arising not only from the well-known social causes of deprivation and decay but from the general coarsening of standards induced by hard-sell consumerism, is all around us.

Almost every facet of life has been brutalised in some way, to a lesser or greater degree. Television, the great brutaliser, has itself been brutalised by sick video films, radio by the ghetto blaster. Noise in ear-blasting general is the brutalisation of street life.

A uniform of vest, jeans and tattoos is the brutalisation of once-liberating casual wear. Junk food is the brutalisation of appetite. The electronic fruit machine and canned pub music are the brutalisation of social drinking.

Bigotry is the brutalisation of politics. The hard-nosed Municipal Left is the brutalisation of local government. Picket mobs are the brutalisation of trade unionism.

The tower block is the brutalisation of architecture – whose practitioners, indeed, proudly coined the term 'brutalism' for their concrete wilderness. Graffiti is the brutalisation of the once-homely neighbourhood. Vandalism is the brutalisation of high spirits. Litter is the brutalisation of prosperity.

Pornography is the brutalisation of sex. Computerised games are the brutalisation of pleasure. The thick-as-a-brick airport novel is the brutalisation of literature. The *Sun* is the brutalisation of journalism.

Over-sized under-equipped schools – especially those with militant or politically-motivated teachers – are the brutalisation of education.

Jargon, sloganising and feminist word-neutering are the brutalisation of language. The threatening rattle of plastic collection buckets is the brutalisation of charity. Truncheon-wielding riot police are the brutalisation of law and order.

The poverty trap is the brutalisation of the family. Unemployment is the brutalisation of the spirit. Thatcherism is the brutalisation of life itself.

And something is to be done about the brutalisation of Britain, is it. By – according to one suggestion – issuing all soccer fans with membership cards without which they would be denied admission.

To what? The human race?

LIFE IN THE JUNK AGE

In New York, a punk rock 'star' on a murder charge slashes his wrists with a broken light bulb and a razor blade. In London, a fourteen-year-old girl has a social contract to stay out all night.

In Toronto, a judge hears of the 'despair' of a millionaire pop-idol who became a heroin addict. In Berkshire, an unmarried mother sets herself on fire with paraffin.

Anyone who knows how to read the straws in the wind can tell that the Permissive Age is reaching the end of its tether.

One day someone is going to look back on the cinder-shell of the Seventies and remember it as the era that tried to throw itself out of an eighth-floor window.

In the floodlit nightmare we are sleepwalking through, the dancing shadows grow more grotesque by the minute. We will wake up soon – and only then will we see what it all meant.

Fame, we will realise, came too cheaply. All you had to do to be famous was to turn yourself into a stick of human bubble-gum. Well-packaged, easy to digest – and disposable. You were favourite until the flavour wore off and then someone blew you up and you went pop.

That thing of shreds and patches called human dignity died some time in the Seventies. The really tragic point about that little girl who plays truant to earn £50 a week to pay for her mini-cabs home from the all-night clubs is not that she is a spoiled brat or that the social workers are buffoons, but that she has no dignity. Probably doesn't know what we're talking about.

Football hooligans, so we're told, lack a sense of identity, and vandals lack a sense of values. But what both lack most is dignity – which is self-respect plus a few more ingredients such as an inner peace of mind arising from a belief that tomorrow may be better.

To have self-respect, you must be respected by others and there is no evidence that the Seventies gave a monkey's toss for any single individual, young or old. All the social engineering by the Brunels of health, housing, education and welfare was no more than an ego-boosting adventure in crowd control.

We will see, when we wake up, that we were living through an Ice Age, when there was a lot of noise but nothing happened, when all endeavour came to a stop, when brand-new machines were kept well-oiled and idle, when jobs were manufactured and products were not, when politics ceased to be the art of the possible and became the art of survival, when Governments tinkered with the system like a mechanic under the bonnet of a clapped-out car, and when ideas were so few in the air that any crackpot theory zooming in over the horizon was greeted with the rapture of the inhabitants of Noah's ark welcoming home the dove with the olive branch.

The answer to it all is not to flog every teenager who moves or make life sentences mandatory or patrol the streets with guard-dogs or send the immigrants packing or treble the police force or censor all television or introduce a curfew or castrate the rapists or any of the other remedies that are usually packaged under the heading of 'a return to common sense.'

Nor is it to pine for the golden days when fourteen-year-old girls (some of them) wore grammar-school blazers and pigtails and did their homework over a beaker of Ovaltine. Nor is it, like Paul Johnson – the man who met himself coming back on the road to Damascus – to remember, with great wistfulness, when sixteen-year-old boys (one or two of them) listened to Beethoven instead of the Boomtown Rats.

We have tried looking back. We have frittered away the Seventies looking back. We have used up so much of the past that even the year 1969 is now garlanded with the pathetic tinsel of nostalgia.

When we wake up, we have to look forward. And someone among us, with rather less sleep in his eyes than the rest of us, will have to do the thinking.

Who it will be, I have no idea. But there have been, from time to time, important statements that have changed the direction of this country. The Beveridge Report was one such statement. The Labour Party Manifesto of 1945 was another. Anthony Crosland's book *The Future of Socialism* was a third.

At present, a Green Paper on the question of phasing out road tax is just about all that comes to mind as a statement for the Eighties. But there must be someone with the vision to see that the Junk Age we are sleep-walking through is as transient, and as illusory, as the Jazz Age. And who, when we awake, can lead us out of it?

3

IN PRAISE OF
MOOCHING

LOVESOME LITTER-LOUTS

LOVESOME LITTER-LOUTS

Now, so I usually learn from reliable sources, is the time to mulch those rose bushes, sow those hardy annuals, apply that fertiliser, spray those apple trees, and prune those forsythias.

Or if the thought of all that physical labour makes you ill, now is the time to loll in a deckchair and read that gardening magazine. Which – not being much given to mulching – is what I have been doing this Easter weekend.

Come these sunny days of Spring, when my green-fingered friends are bedding out their variegated nepeta like men possessed and sowing their stump-rooted carrot as if there were no tomorrow, I always make a point of browsing through a gardening mag. It helps me keep in touch with Mother Nature.

As always, I stand appalled (or rather loll appalled) at the plagues and pestilences that the malevolent old bag visits upon all who are foolhardy enough to tangle with her. Scab, weed, lichen, slugs, cutworm and bacterial canker are, it would seem, as inevitable a feature of the gardener's daily round as applying John Innes compost to the black currants, or whatever the black currants' dish of the day may be. As for the common woodlouse, it is apparently as common as the common cold, if not commoner.

Amateur Gardening even has a feature called Pests Of The Month, in which it alerts its readers to watch out for blackfly, apple capsid, gooseberry mildew, and unnamed fungal nuisances. And that's only for April. God knows what May holds in store. Probably the spring-onion equivalent of the Black Death.

It is not only obvious enemies of the peace such as the First Battalion of the Greenfly Regiment that are at the root (not to mention the branches and most of the leaves) of the trouble. It would seem that along the perilous one-way primrose path to the compost heap, you cannot trust anybody.

A reader of *Amateur Gardening*, for instance, complains about violets. Now you and I – or I alone, if you insist on brandishing that pruning fork – have hitherto regarded violets as blemishless. They may do a bit of shrinking in their spare time, but that's as far as their riotous living goes. Or so we thought.

Not a bit of it. It is now revealed that violets are barely one petal removed from a gang of soccer hooligans. 'A few years ago,' one of their victims writes bitterly, 'some violets appeared in my garden. They were quite pretty, but they have now become a nuisance and are even spreading into the lawn. How can I get rid of them?'

The way to show unwelcome violets the door, I learn from the answer to this anguished correspondent, is to treat the little swine to a draught of Tumbleweed – kidding them, I should imagine, that it is vodka and tonic, or lemonade for the non-drinkers among them. But giving violets the elbow is not the theme of this column.

What the theme of this column is, now that I have got round to it, is the paradoxical obsession with neatness that all gardeners seem to have.

I say paradoxically because while hell-bent on apple-pie order in their lawns and flower beds to the extent that no violet's life is safe and the weeds might just as well make a block booking with the undertaker and be done with it, gardeners are themselves the messiest creatures on earth, bar perhaps the slovenly blackbird that regularly turns my Earl's Court acres into a passing replica of a Wigan pit-heap in its search for worms.

Observe the work pattern of your common or garden gardener. He is up with the lark mowing the lawn and he continues to mow the lawn long after the lark has had its Ovaltine and is tucked up for the night. He then waters the lawn, weeds the lawn, feeds the lawn, and trims its edges with nail scissors. By the time he has done pampering, the lawn looks as if it has just come out of Vidal Sassoon's. It is a lawn you could eat your dinner off.

Having torn out the last lone lurking mini-clump of clover by its offending roots, the gardener carries it fastidiously to the bin and goes indoors. Leaving what objects scattered on or around his pristine lawn?

A fifty-foot winding trail of hosepipe, the grass-cuttings box from the lawn mower, an oil can, a pair of rubber gloves, a rusty old rake, a hoe, a stack of plastic flower pots, a broken polythene cloche, a half-full sack of turf-conditioner, a roll of wire netting and a pair of wellies.

The gardener gazes proudly out of the french windows at his pest-exterminated garden and he does not see any of this junk. He simply edits it out of his vision. He therefore does not tumble to the blazingly obvious fact that of all the garden pests on which he relentlessly and unremittingly wages war, he himself is the biggest garden pest of all. He is human lichen.

No garden is complete without a toad, wrote Charles Dudley Warner (of whom you have never heard.) He was famous for nothing except one sentence: 'Everybody talks about the weather, but nobody does anything about it.' He might have added that no garden is complete without an upturned wheelbarrow.

A lovesome thing, God wot? God not!

IN PRAISE OF MOOCHING

Among the ragbag of just-fancy-that facts thrown up by the annual Social Trends statistics is that watching TV and going for walks are our most popular leisure activities.

If slumping in front of the late-night snooker over a glass of wine can be counted as watching television, and if pottering about the streets can be construed as walking, then I am certainly of that half-soporific, half-energetic, Jekyll and Hyde majority.

I am not too sure about the walking part of the combination, though. Walking suggests striding out across the heather with stick and knapsack, pipe puffing fitfully and obedient dog at heels.

Not my style – and there is little heather in the Royal Borough of Earl's Court, except that sold in sprigs by gypsies.

I was, it is true, once the walking reporter of the *Yorkshire Evening Post* when I tramped every dale in the paper's circulation area, as well as walking every Yorkshire river from source to mouth for some purpose which now eludes me, given that one river bank looks much like another.

It is a long time now since I hung up my dubbined boots and nowadays I do not so much walk as mooch – which, however, I do in considerable quantity. I have mislaid the trusty pedometer about which I once wrote here, but I should be surprised if my A-registration suede shoes – one owner only, mark – have clocked up less than 1500 miles in a year.

Let me define what mooching is by first describing what it isn't. There is nothing brisk or purposeful about it. The moocher does not set out to get from A to B – unless he is going via X, Y and Z.

Mooching is not a form of exercise – indeed, it may even be detrimental to the health since the moocher's characteristic habit of staring at his feet while on the mooch could cause curvature of the spine as well as head injuries consistent with having walked into a lamp-post.

Mooching is essentially an urban activity, involving as it does a good deal of stopping by the wayside to take in the passing show. There are, my more rustic readers may argue, interesting things to be seen in the country – berries, leaves and so forth – which may cause the rambler to pull up short and exclaim: 'Hello! What an interesting berry or leaf!' But that is no mooch he is on, it is a nature walk. We could get all that at school.

Mooching is about staring in shop windows, studying menus outside restaurants, watching traffic wardens going in for the slow-motion record for writing out a ticket, and tickling cats under the chin. It is about reading bus destination indicators and wondering idly why the hell anyone would want to go from Hounslow to Richmond or for that matter from Richmond to Hounslow.

It is about ambling around corners to see where they lead – and ambling sheepishly back again upon finding that they lead into a cul-de-sac.

It is about dropping into second-hand bookshops, impulse-buying a pullover at Marks and Sparks, and impulse-consuming a bag of crisps and a pint at the Dog and Duck. It can take up to anything from half an hour to the whole day, and there is nothing in the rules against coming home by taxi if mooched to exhaustion or taking home a stuffed parrot from a far-flung junk shop.

I personally favour what might be called the staircase mode of mooching – that is, taking the first right then the first left alternately as a city-bred crab might when out for its constitutional. It is as agreeable a way of getting from Earl's Court to the depths of Putney as I can think of (perhaps that's how they work out those obscure bus routes?)

But – probably a throwback to those river-walking days – I also like mooching along things – railway cuttings, park perimeters, cemetery walkways. Show me a canal towpath and I will show you a moocher's paradise.

Once, starting off from Islington, I mooched so far along the Grand Union Canal that people encountered on the way started to have northern accents. Actually, I turned out to be in Paddington – but the lock-keeper and his mate came from Lancashire.

And on that note, I shall mooch off.

IF I HAD A MOVING PICTURE OF YOU

I once saw a man making a home movie of a man making a home movie. I wish I'd had my cine-camera.

The man making the film that the other man was making a film of – we'll call it Movie A, to make things simpler – was, while heavily under the influence of Fellini, obtaining footage of a child walking into the sea. The man making the film of the film that the first man was making – Movie B, or A½ if you prefer it – was not at all satisfied with what he was getting in the can. He thought the man making movie A didn't look enough like a film director and was urging him to sit in a canvas chair and square his fingers like a viewfinder. Meanwhile our star was obediently sloshing on towards the horizon and was up to its armpits in sea. A dramatic and tearful rescue was effected by the tot's mother – a piece of cinema vérité entirely missed by the two squabbling directors.

Home movies have certainly come a long way since those early, flickering studies of father pretending to be asleep while the kids bury him in sand. I believe we have television to thank – not its influence, but its existence. No longer are audiences content to squash up on the leatherette settees of suburban lounges with the smell of burning tin in their nostrils while a string of animated lantern slides captioned '*Our Holidays*' is projected from the dining hatch. Nowadays, if it is to get anywhere in the Jictar ratings, your home movie must be a cleverly-scripted, brilliantly-lit, skilfully-edited cross-fertilisation of the best of Alan Whicker and the worst of 'It's A Knock-out', with appropriate incidental music, a droll voice-over and zoom shots in plenty.

While, due to jealousy among rival cinéastes, my own home movies have yet to win an Oscar – my *Incident on Brighton Beach* was narrowly pipped at the post by J. Cakebread's *High Noon, Torremolinos* – I do feel qualified to advise budding Eisensteins and Hitchcocks among *High Life* readers. My three-volume authoritative work, *The Golden Years Of Home Movies*, is not yet off the presses, but here are a few wrinkles to be going on with.

1. Titles. The convention of scratching these with a pin on the actual celluloid had a certain naïve charm in the era of L. Peabody's *Janet's First Birthday* but it is now old hat. So are 'handheld' titles (so called because they are scrawled on a bit of paper and held up in front of the camera – a device also pioneered by Peabody in his earlier *Janet Begins to Crawl*). Nowadays titles must either be superimposed on a long shot of some palm trees in silhouette, or they must be tastefully inscribed on cards. Young children, by the way, with their tendency to embellish all their work with pictures of duckies, do not make the best graphic artists for this branch of cinematography: hence the disastrous failure of *Janet's Christmas Party*.

2. Plot. D. Sibson got away with a breathtakingly simple plot in his *Picnic in Epping Forest*. A family sit down to a picnic and the son, attempting to swat a wasp, swats his father by mistake. That is all. The joke, of course, is that we never see the wasp. Indeed, neither do we see the family, since Sibson was greatly influenced by the 'available light' school at that time and shot his entire opus in deep shadow.

But that was thirty years ago. Sibson's latest epic, *Picnic in Windsor Safari Park*, shows how the plot-line in home movies has strengthened and developed since those pioneer days. A family sit down to a picnic and the son, attempting to swat a wasp, swats his father by mistake. The father, attempting to take his revenge, accidentally knocks his daughter into a fruit tart. The daughter, retaliating, throws a blancmange which hits her mother. Meanwhile, thanks to clever cross-cutting, Sibson has established an escaped baboon on a foraging expedition . . . It would be unfair to give away the punch-line but all who have seen this cunningly-constructed film pronounce it a laugh a minute and certainly much funnier than L. Peabody's heavily derivative *Janet Comes A Cropper*.

3. Acting. In the earliest home movies – R. Hutchinson's *Two Weeks in Majorca* is a typical example – the players were encouraged either to wave at the camera or to pull silly faces at it. This school of acting was effectively demolished by N. Tompkins in his brilliantly original *Baby's Bathtime*, in which neither the baby nor its mother appear to be conscious of the camera's

presence. Even when, in a deft comedy sequence, the mother (superbly played by Mrs N. Tompkins) falls into the bath and the baby (N. Tompkins Jr.) gurgles with pleasure, the camera is the invisible witness rather than (see Peabody's clumsy *Janet's Bathtime*) the intruder. The style pioneered by Tompkins is now 'The Method' of home movies.

4. Directing. It is no longer good enough for the director simply to aim his camera at the action and hope for the best, as D. Benson did to admittedly superb effect in *Grandfather's Snooze*. The modern home-movie maker would start this shot on the back of the deckchair, panning slowly round to reveal grandfather asleep with the panama hat over his eyes. The fly that settles on his nose could have been more wittily established in a separate take, and the dénouement, where the tide comes in and grandfather wakes up to find himself ankle-deep in water, would have been far more effective if Benson had been able to zoom back into long shot. S. Enright's *Grandfather gets his Feet Wet*, while greatly influenced by Benson, shows what can be done with a versatile lens.

5. Editing. In the formative years, cutting was what the home-movie-maker did with a pair of scissors when he had reached the end of his exposed film. S. Peabody's *Rover Looks for a Ball*, probably the most stupefyingly boring home movie ever made, is nevertheless worth its place in the archives because it was completed in a single twenty-seven minute take. The idea of cutting to the ball when Rover is looking for it, or switching off the cine-camera when Rover tires of the game and disappears off-screen to eat his dinner, never entered Peabody's mind.

In these sophisticated times, when there is a splicer in every dark-room, a home movie must be a montage — a veritable jigsaw of dozens or hundreds of connecting shots. Remaking his film today, Peabody would have established shots of dog and ball, cutting between the two as Rover got nearer or farther away. There would be a tracking shot of Rover disappearing into the house, followed by interspersed footage of the neglected ball and Rover wolfing his dinner. See R. Potter's *Our Holidays* (do not be put off by the unoriginal title). The inter-cutting between Mrs R. Potter going into the St Ives public toilets and the sign that says 'Gentlemen' is superb.

6. General. I have no space to deal with the more technical

aspects of home-movie making, such as how do you stop every-body squinting when you are shooting away from the sun and they are looking into it, so one last general hint must suffice. Hitchcock once told me that the essence of making films was that one of the actors glances off-screen and the audience say, 'Hello, what's this fellow looking at?' You then show them. Follow this golden rule — but remember, as T. Jackson did in his prize-winning *Pontin's Paradise*, that in home movies, the actors must do more than glance, they must point.

MY POOLS PARADISE

One reason why I should like to win a million pounds on the football pools is to enable me to make the following statement to interviewers:

'Yes, this will make a great difference to me. Yes, it will change my life utterly. Yes, I do already know what I intend to do with the money apart from buying Auntie Clara a bungalow and taking a short holiday in Cornwall.'

Another reason why I should like to win a million pounds on the football pools is to enable me to translate this positive thinking into action.

The first thing I should do would be to buy a newspaper. Not from the corner kiosk, to check that the reporters had quoted me correctly. From a business broker, or whoever deals with such matters. When I say I should buy a newspaper, I should become a newspaper owner.

I don't see myself in the Rupert Murdoch class, of course – not even the treble chance can buy that class of day-dream. This would be quite a modest affair. A small, thriving weekly such as you find in most country towns, with titles like the *Loose Chippings Advertiser*.

But those undynamic titles are deceptive. Most local rags have by now been jazzed-up into modern new-tech tabloids with bold black headlines worthy of Mr Murdoch at his Sunniest, and they look about as truly rural as a field of oil seed rape. My aim would be to nurse the *Loose Chippings Advertiser* back to its old soporific self.

I should start by restoring the original title – *The Loose*

Chippings, Higher Chippings and Lower Chippings Advertiser and Chronicle, with which is Incorporated the Market Chippings Weekly Intelligence and Agricultural Prices Review – at the same time releasing it from the confines of its little blue or red corner masthead to a stately gothic banner running across nine columns.

This act of liberation would mean abandoning the tabloid format and going back to the former page size, known in the trade as 'bedsheet'. Dust-wrappers would be thrown over the upstart web offset printing machinery, and we should revert to a steam flatbed press with the type set by gnarled hand. News would be banished from the front page in favour of a hectare of closely-printed small ads.

The staff would be bound to notice that something was afoot and so I should call them together to explain my policy.

'Henceforth,' I should say, 'bicycle clips will be worn by every reporter. I want every man-jack of you ready to cover a village whist drive at a moment's notice. I want to see more and longer coverage for jumble sales, amateur theatricals, prize marrows, and the doings of the Ladies' Guild, and less and shorter coverage for exhibitions of packaging machinery and plans for £3 million leisure complexes.

'I want fewer headlines on the lines of "Sharon (16) Bids Fair To Become Beauty Queen" and more on the lines of "Parish Church Choir Outing. Delightful Day Had By All. Picnic Venue Voted A Success." The TV page will be abolished. In its place I shall myself contribute "Notes From The Clocktower" under the sobriquet "Watchman". That is all. To your duties.'

The reclaimed *Advertiser* would be at once my business loss-leader and the restorer of my sanity. It would be to my roll-top desk in the turret overlooking a market square that I should repair to pen my thoughtful, soothing paragraphs on the brass-rubbing craze and such matters of the moment, after an abrasive week spent tilting at the windmills of commerce. For I should, of course, having bought my little newspaper empire for a song, have invested the bulk of my fortune in a thriving enterprise.

When I say thriving, I mean that I should have been the one to make it thrive. What I would have done would be to buy up, for another song – a mere ditty – a derelict bottling plant. Under conditions of great industrial secrecy I would then have set about launching my idea.

Everyone in the world has a money-spinning business idea, the same as everyone in the world has an idea for a TV sitcom series, a quiz game, a board game, and an airport novel. Mine is a pippin. It is based on the observation born of experience that you cannot get a soft drink – I exclude boring mineral waters – which properly quenches the thirst while not leaving a kind of sticky rim or residue about the mouth.

I have invented one. It consists simply of the juices of the melon – pure, refreshing, delicious, non-fattening, and kind on the teeth – which I should market under the name of Waterhouse's Melon Drink, in a distinctive yellow bottle. There would be watermelon flavour, honeydew flavour and up-market Ogen flavour, or, in the smaller cocktail-bar bottle, an amalgamation of the three.

'Hm,' I can hear my bank manager musing, in the event of my having to go to him for my capital (but I don't: remember, I have just won a million pounds!). 'I can readily see that this is a brilliant, innovative, money-spinning notion and that Waterhouse's Melon Drink is likely to become a dominant force in the soft drinks market, but is not extracting melon juice a wasteful process, considering what you have to spend on importing bulky melons? What are you going to do with all the skins, pulp and pips which are deadweight on your costs?'

I have thought of that. I am going to feed them to pigs. Waterhouse's Melon-fed Bacon Rashers, and Waterhouse's distinctively-flavoured pork pies – Melon Mowbray, we might probably call them – would quickly acquire a reputation. Farmer Honeydew, a cartoon figure, would advertise them on TV. Deals would be done with supermarkets. Tie-ups would be arranged with sportsmen who would train on Waterhouse's Melon Drink and endorse Melon Mowbray, the lighter pork pie. Meanwhile, my subsidiary line – haven't I mentioned that? – apple crisps (they're like potato crisps, but less savoury) – would be taking off. The residual apple cores from this offshoot business, also fed to pigs, would yield Waterhouse's Apple-sauce Pork. And that would only be the beginning. Melon-flavoured apple crisps would be in the pipeline ...

Eventually, opting for the quiet life, I should sell out to one of the big food corporations, taking a large clutch of their shares and a few millions in cash. With the few millions in cash, just as a hobby, I should start my own football pool, the coupons being run off on the abandoned web offset press of the *Loose Chippings Advertiser* – which, I should not be surprised to find as I continued to write those trenchant notes on brass-rubbings, would by now be such a favourite with the public that I should be encouraged to start a chain of old-fashioned country weeklies all over Britain, later diversifying into the world's first old-fashioned cable TV station, where the announcers would have to wear evening dress.

But back to my football pool. It would be like any other football pool, with prizes up to a million pounds or so, except that it would have one extra rule of entry. Printed in clear type on each coupon would be a condition as follows:

'I understand that in the event of my winning beyond my wildest dreams, any statement to the effect that it will not change my life and that I do not know what to do with the money apart from buying Auntie Clara a bungalow and taking a short holiday in Cornwall, will invalidate my million pounds immediately.'

DICING THE NIGHT AWAY

The world will little note, nor long remember (the quote is from the Bonus Gettysburg Card in my yet-to-be perfected exciting game for all the family, Lincoln!, copyright in all countries, video rights reserved) how I came within an ace – oh, all right, then, a jack – of becoming a board game zillionaire like those legendary chaps who developed Monopoly from a square of linoleum.

It's true, though. My game was called General Election, the object of which was to corner the most Parliamentary seats by means of dice, cards, spinning arrows, luck, skill and low cunning. I had it professionally designed and sent it to Waddington's, who are to board game inventors what the double six is to board game players.

To my utter astonishment and unconfined joy, instead of my unsolicited box of tricks slithering back to square one like a losing counter in a game of snakes and ladders, an important-looking letter from Waddington's landed on my doormat.

While not enclosing the hoped-for cheque for a million pounds in advance of royalties (go back three squares and wait till you throw a six), it did contain the next-best thing – the news that Waddington's then managing director, no less, liked my board game and was arranging to have it played by his panel of experts in – appropriately enough – the boardroom. (Advance three squares and have another turn.)

There was then an interminable wait (it was an interminable game). Finally the verdict was delivered. Nice try and all that, but General Election took too long to play. About fifteen hours, to be more precise: the merest smidgeon of time when compared with how long it takes to fight a real general election, but seemingly interminable if played around the dining table when the Conservative Party has run out of cigarettes, Labour is missing a good programme on telly, and it is long past the Liberal Party's bedtime.

So there it was: the die was cast. Or rather, the die was not cast – I put it back in the game of Ludo from which I had borrowed it, packed General Election away in the cistern cupboard, and resigned myself to becoming a zillionaire some other way.

It rankles, however, to this day. What's so unmarketable about a fifteen-hour board game, I should like to know? Some years ago, when I shared an office with my fellow-scribbler and fellow-board-game fanatic Willis Hall, we perfected a version of Monopoly which went on not for fifteen hours but for fifteen weeks.

Having spotted the essential flaw in two-handed Monopoly, which is that, while the winner wants to go on playing, the loser would rather switch to Cluedo (this must be why Monopoly sells a mere half million sets a year), we evolved a variation by which neither of us could lose. This entailed, by a system of dice-controlled bank loans, takeover bids and share deals, forming ourselves into one enormous property conglomerate which controlled every house, hotel and utility on the board – truly, by the time we were finished, Monopoly really was the name of the game.

The trouble was, we never *were* finished. The game went on and on and on, and while we were growing richer on paper – our Old Kent Road properties alone carried a valuation equivalent to Mayfair in the conventional game – we were becoming poorer and poorer in person. For while it is all very well whiling away the long winter evenings with a nice board game, whiling away the long winter mornings and the long winter afternoons is a sure way to bankruptcy. (Now *there's* a good idea for a board game. You start with a million pounds each and the first one to squander it all is the winner.) So we weaned ourselves onto Scrabble, which is shorter – especially if one player throws the game out of the window in pique because his opponent won't let him have the American spelling of *ax*. But it was no good. There was only one way to cure ourselves of going down to the office every morning and playing board games all day, and that was to give up the office. Now I sit at home and play Solitaire.

I have been hooked on board games since before I could read (indeed, it was thanks to a game called Mr Mouse that I learned to count, so insistent were my opponents that I was not allowed to move six places after throwing a two). Starting with the simplest variations of the Snakes and Ladders formula, where the object is merely to get from one end of the board to the other, I quickly moved on to the more sophisticated games like Totopoly, where the object is to move back the other players' pieces when they're not looking. Soon I was the Sherlock Holmes of Cluedo, the Charles Clore of Monopoly, the General Montgomery of L'Attaque and the Stirling Moss of Motoring.

Though most of these games specify that any number can play, the ideal number is four, and after my first hundred or so marathon sessions with dice and cup, I began to learn how these four are typically and temperamentally made up.

First there is the instigator, the enthusiast – the one who desperately wants to play, the one who would rather play Peter Rabbit or Go! than watch the cartoons on television, read his nice new book, or anything he likes so long as he stops his pestering. He is usually the owner of the game, having been given it for his birthday.

Then there is the reluctant player – the one who does not wish to play, who would much rather be doing a crossword or staring at the wallpaper. This is usually the instigator's father, who now wishes he had given the lad a pair of roller skates.

The third player is the blackmailer – usually the instigator's brother. He is quite keen to play really, but disguises the fact and will only join in after protracted negotiations whereby the instigator gives him a boiled sweet, a six-place start and a solemn undertaking that after three games of Peter Rabbit he will take on the blackmailer at draughts.

The fourth player is the novice – frequently the instigator's little sister. Almost as enthusiastic as the instigator himself, she is hampered only by not knowing the rules, which have to be explained to her at every throw. Being possessed of an attention-span of about five seconds, the novice furthermore has to be reminded at regular intervals that it is her turn.

Even adult games like Diplomacy, played by adult people, seem to attract these four disparate elements. Certainly in all the four-handed games I have ever played, there has always been one player who would rather be doing something else, one who is only playing since it will put him in a strong bargaining position when it comes to suggesting a hand of bridge, and one who has to have it constantly pointed out to him that when he is instructed to go to jail, to go directly to jail, not to pass Go and not to collect £200, he does not have the option of paying a small fine. The fourth member of the quartet, the enthusiastic instigator, is ... guess who?

I don't know how many board games are on the market at any given time, but I think I must have played just about every one ever devised – except one. This was a shiny, wonderful Steeple-chase game given to the children next door by a rich uncle when I was a boy. Daily I used to hang around their doorstep hoping to be invited in to play. Alas, the game was so expensive, with so many exquisitely-made fragile pieces, that they were not even allowed to play it themselves. The most that was permitted was for the game to be laid out on the kitchen table, under adult supervision, for them to look at but not to touch. After a wistful five minutes of this they would then come round to my house for a game of Mr Mouse – at which, to this day, I remain the world's greatest living expert.

'YOU CALL THIS WORK?'

A complete stranger wrote to me a while ago asking whether, as a personal favour and in a good cause, I would come round next week and mow his lawn for nothing.

Actually that's not strictly true. What he really wanted of me was to 'dash off' a 1000-word contribution to the charity publication he was bringing out. Oh, and he was sorry about the short notice but everything was a bit disorganised ...

I explained as kindly as possible that he was asking for three or four hours' solid work –or seven or eight hours if I was not on 'dashing off' form that day – which I could fit in only by letting down one of my regular customers. I offered, instead, to let him reprint one of my slightly-used articles.

The response was a miffed silence. It is plain that in that quarter I am now regarded as a cynical brute who, when kindly invited by someone he doesn't know to come round and mow his lawn, sarcastically offers the loan of his lawnmower.

Another request that reached me recently was from a man of the cloth who thought I would be delighted to hear that for some years he had been entertaining village concerts and other functions with readings from a collection of my newspaper columns. As he had by now run out of suitable material, would I dig out some more of my stuff and run if off on the photocopier for him?

I wrote back, not so kindly this time, explaining that using my work without my permission, however readily it might have been given, was on a par with strolling into my house, sitting down at my table and scoffing my breakfast. I received a wrathful reply on the theme of my lack of Christian charity and enclosing a grubby, scornful fiver. This I lobbed back with the comment that he who steals my purse steals trash, but he that filches from me my good name is in breach of the Copyright Act 1956.

But it is not the man in the street's ignorance of the copyright laws that leads to these little unpleasantnesses, of which every writer can quote dozens of examples. It is the man in the street's unswerving belief that writing is not real work, not a proper job, that a morning's agonised pecking at the typewriter keys is 'dashed off', that a full-time writer's life is one long holiday.

One reason why the impression is so widespread is that it is at heart shared by writers themselves –probably the reason many of them enter this overcrowded field in the first place. I have myself lived off my pen for thirty-five years now, but I have never quite been able to convince myself that it is a seemly and permanent way of earning my keep – that there is any connection between the article I am composing at this minute and the electricity bill waiting to be paid. There is still a lurking feeling that this writing lark is a luxury, a hobby, for which any financial reward comes as a bonus, like winning the Spot The Ball contest in the paper.

Occasionally – when, for example, my head is swimming from having just finished 'dashing off' the first rough draft of a novel – an experience not unlike digging a small quarry – I do manage to persuade myself, with no small measure of self-pity, that pen-manship is not, after all, only one off from conmanship.

Yet even when hardworking journeymen writers such as myself go all earnest and straight-faced about what professional crafts-men we all are – just like any grocer, as Arnold Bennett used to say – there is the residual fear, sometimes amounting to a dormant terror, that we are fooling nobody but ourselves.

A craftsman, a proper craftsman, is one who applies his tools to a block of wood and transforms it into something. An author has the tools but he doesn't have the block of wood. Even when he's writing factually rather than fictionally – a biography of Nelson, say, or an article on DIY double-glazing – he is obliged to work with raw materials that do not have any tangible existence at all until they drop into his head out of the sky. Should the golden words not meet their delivery date, there is no warehouse mana-ger to whom he can complain.

There must be safer, more reliable, if not easier ways of keeping the mortgage company happy. No wonder so many in this bizarre trade suffer from that dreaded psychosomatic occupational disease called Writer's Block – the chief symptom of which is the sensation of someone having performed a secret pre-frontal leucotomy operation on the sufferer's head, depriving him forever of the ability to put together an opening sentence.

It is a terrible condition, leading to drunkenness – if the victim has got an advance from his publishers – and muscular twitchings upon encountering editors, landlords and the like. The writer fortunate enough not to fall prey to this literary equivalent of phossy-jaw or hatters' madness may yet find himself a victim of Writer's Block Hypochondria – the reluctance to start work for fear of discovering that one has been smitten by Writer's Block. This may account for a common professional tendency towards procrastination – or 'I can only work to a deadline,' as it is known in the trade.

WB hypochondriacs know as part of their folklore the story of the hack starving in his garret when a lush American magazine comes to his rescue. All he has to do is write a short piece on a subject he knows inside-out, and he gets a thousand dollars. This has to be by the end of August. The deadline comes and goes and he hasn't delivered. He gets a stay of execution until the end of September ... October ... November ... Still no article. Finally the exasperated editor sends a cable: 'MUST HAVE ARTICLE AT ONCE OR DEAL OFF. ARE YOU GOING TO WRITE IT OR NOT?' Our starving hero responds promptly: 'COMMENCING ARTICLE AS SOON AS I HAVE CLEANED MY TENNIS SHOES.'

What the afflicted professional scribbler tends to forget as he stares gloomily at the ceiling, waiting for words to fall off it, is that he has already jumped most of the hurdles. It is far, far harder to establish oneself as a writer than to keep going as one.

Many of my fellow-craftsmen would beg leave to doubt this, pointing out that it doesn't get any easier. True enough: like acting and playing the saxophone, it's one of those callings where the more you know the more you can see how much you have to learn. But if you were to tell me that of the next hundred-plus articles and stories I write, less than half a dozen will ever see publication, and that my earnings from writing this year will amount to no more than two pounds, next year to nothing at all, and the year after to twelve pounds, I think I should probably take up selling used cars instead. Yet that was my track record for my first three years in this writing game.

It's in these early years that the will-be writers leave the would-be writers behind – and it's sheer slog that does it. The initial flair or knack has to be there, of course, but thereafter the secret is in a line from Judy Garland's *Born In A Trunk* – 'I practised when the others had all gone.'

Once he has got his foot in the door, the writer's success or otherwise depends entirely on the talent, industry and professionalism he brings to the job.

Talent can't be learned but it can be nurtured and cultivated from whatever is there – when you read the apparently effortless output of some of our more polished prosifiers, you are looking at the literary equivalent of a hot-house grape.

Industry, so far as the writer is concerned, is being so hooked on not working for a living that he is prepared to put in a seven-day, sixty-hour week at it.

Professionalism is largely a matter of not delivering a piano when the client needs a wardrobe (ask any editor of any non-fiction magazine how many unsolicited short stories he gets a week).

There is one other element: luck. Every writer needs it. The mother of the celebrated American dramatist Moss Hart was once congratulated on her son's good luck in having three Broadway hits running simultaneously. 'You're right,' Mrs Hart agreed. 'And you know, the funny thing is, the harder he works, the luckier he gets.'

SUNDAY PAPERS

If I were an artist aspiring to the Royal Academy Summer Exhibition, I would choose the Sunday papers as my subject.

Perhaps a George Belcher-type charcoal of Pa snoozing on a horsehair sofa with the *News of the World* draped over his face. Or a Carel Weight-ish study of a suburban shopping-parade newsagent's with its battery of placards: INSIDE THE HOUSE OF SHAME, MAYFAIR'S VICE QUEENS, TOWN HALL SNOOPERS – and the hint of a good old English murder somewhere in the leafy background. Maybe a Lowry: Peel Park awash with tabloids. Hockney: colour supps on the patio. Stanley Spencer: 'Christ Reading the *Sunday Telegraph*.'

It's an institution we're talking about, of course, and a peculiarly British one. Other countries have a Sunday Press but they do not have Sunday papers in our sense – not even the Americans, whose cholesterol-high Sabbath diet of classified ads, arts reviews, real estate sections, sports sections, funnies and gravure poolside-living magazines is but a bulkier version of what is served to them all through the week.

No American, furthermore, would ever buy more than one Sunday edition, even if the choice was there: apart from the haulage problems involved in conveying his own weight in reading-matter from the news-stand to the trunk of his Chevrolet, there are just not enough hours in the day to merit the expenditure of that extra thirty or forty cents. Here, on the other hand, the essence of Sunday papers is that they are consumed in quantity.

Look at the phenomenon again with the artist's eye: where the daily paper, propped up against the coffee pot, is undoubtedly singular, the Sundays, strewn across the eiderdown, are uncontrovertibly plural. Umbrella, briefcase, buttonhole, and a neatly-folded copy of *The Times* or *Telegraph* (but not both) are the stereotype accoutrements of the working day. On Sundays the props are cravat, pipe, dog, pint – and an armful of newsprint.

The daily paper records the passing show but the Sunday papers *belong* to the passing show, like deckchairs by the Serpentine or the afternoon queue for Odeons 1, 2 and 3. 'Just popping out for the papers' is as much a part of Sunday as roast beef or taking flowers to the cemetery. Reading the papers, swapping the papers ('After you with that rag'), littering the floor with the papers, are not so much Sunday activities as a Sunday tradition, a feast as immoveable as Christmas.

All human life is there? All English life, anyway. In that most English of English plays, *Look Back In Anger*, practically half of the first act is taken up by the familiar, desultory scrutiny of the Sunday papers. What better way of exploring our national character? Jimmy Porter's epithet, 'the posh papers,' for instance, says more about our class structure than the entire twelve volumes of *A Dance to the Music of Time*.

I was hooked on Sunday papers long before I could read. Their opulent, substantial whiteness was in generous contrast to the utilitarian buff of the northern Posts and Echoes and Arguses which were the only other newspapers I ever saw. A tactile experience, that. I found their Gothic titles fascinating, and spent hours tracing the *People's* Germanic serifs on lard-paper.

As I became more or less literate, I looked forward to the *People* and the *Empire News* as other boys looked forward to bank holidays. They had the same element of escape. Their wired photographs of airships and actresses, their special commissioners' scoops, the spendthrift opulence of their giant X-word prizes and insurance schemes, all carried the sophisticated touch of the metropolis – or at least of Manchester, a far-off city across the Pennines of which I knew nothing. The *People* was delivered in the orthodox way through the letter-box, but the *Empire News* arrived unaccountably in the house very late on Saturday night, to the accompaniment of singing; and all through the long day of rest its creased pages retained the raffish odour of the saloon bar.

Orwell's decline of the English murder had not yet set in. ('It is Sunday afternoon, preferably before the war . . . You put your feet up on the sofa, settle your spectacles on your nose, and open the *News of the World* . . .') Suburban Pooters at the end of their tether still bought unprecedented supplies of weedkiller and developed an interest in rockeries; there were strangulations in the bluebell woods; children sang street songs about Dr Buck Ruxton ('Bloodstains on the stairs . . .') and there was still a sporting chance that any portmanteau abandoned at Victoria would contain, not a bomb, but a human leg. As Orwell wrote in another context (*Boys' Weeklies*), 'Everything is safe, solid and unquestionable. Everything will be the same for ever, and ever.' Hannen Swaffer warned against Herr Hitler and England slept – on a horsehair sofa, with the Sunday paper draped over its face.

The war-time Sunday papers are less vivid in my memory – either because the society they had so accurately reflected was in the melting-pot or because those with the knack of performing this narcissistic feat were mainly in uniform. I remember that they were disappointingly thin and carried a disproportionate number of articles by retired military men, illustrated with baffling diagrams of pincer-movements. I believe the exposure technique (We Name The Guilty Men) was beginning to come into its own, although the guilty men named would have been spivs, drones, restaurant guzzlers, black marketeers and column dodgers rather than the homosexual headmasters, evil doctors, pimps, drug-pedlars and dog-dopers of the years of recovery.

The early days of peace are clearer: Forever Amber and C. A. Lejeune; Ivor Brown and Midnight Orgies In The Mansion House Of A Leading Industrialist; top-brass memoirs and A Lorry Ride To Shame; The Poisoner Who Paid With Her Life For One Small Slip and Cyril Connolly. It wasn't all dried eggs in the age of austerity. But we were reaching the end of a road – a long path of destiny that had led, almost unbroken, through generations of tranquil Sundays from Jack the Ripper to the Cleft Chin Murder.

Times change, people change; *The Sunday Times* changed, the *People* changed. We altered our habits, customs, aspirations, expectations; grammar schools closed; Asians took over the corner Post Office; and the Sunday papers altered with us, not so much reporting upon as reacting to every subtle shift of temperament. Not only did we lose the Empire, we lost the *Empire News*. The *Observer* came back from Suez with the haunted, bewildered expression of a young infantryman who has been over the top at Passchendaele.

Porn kings, sex clinic doctors, blue movie barons and importers of illegal immigrants joined the fluctuating cast of Sunday paper villains. Where is the *Sunday Graphic* that boasted of being 'clean and clever' during its genteel lifetime? Didn't it gas itself, in an upstairs bedroom in Betjeman's Leamington Spa?

There was a time, not long ago, when the *News of the World* sported a masthead like a cross between a Coronation beaker and a sailor's tattoo acquired on a three-day jag down Cable Street. They should have slapped a preservation order on that masthead. Too late now. It was demolished and rebuilt to a more functional design that mirrors our concrete wilderness of car parks and Poulson shopping malls. Only the occasional headline – AFTER THE NAAFI DANCE and NUDE HAD CORNFLAKE BOX ON HEAD – reminds us that there is some corner of this European field that will be for ever England. CHICKEN SEXER WITH TWO FALSE LEGS ACCUSED OF BIGAMY ... and is there honey still for tea?

The Cudlippian *Sunday Pic*, of course, became the *Sunday Mirror*. That was in the heady, mutinous era of 'That Was The Week That Was' and Willis Hall and I wrote a sketch about the transformation called 'Come Home *Sunday Pic*':

' ... *A desperate mother, I make this appeal to the old* Sunday Pic. *Come home now and I will sell you my son Kevin, aged five, for fifty pounds. I will authorise any series you like on the subject of Guilty Mothers. As I make this dramatic appeal my children are peering out of the window looking in vain for the* Sunday Pic, *which I dare not tell them will never come. They are not old enough to understand why it has changed its sex ...*'

How it all dates us – like a fading short-back-and-sides snapshot. There are few Guilty Mothers in the *Sunday Mirror* nowadays, although there may be a Secret Ordeal or two; and the paper does not often urge errant priests to go and unfrock themselves. Religious Sects That Are Nothing More Than A Cloak For Sin no doubt still exist, but they seem more in keeping with belted mackintoshes and ties tucked into the trousers than with the T-shirts and denim you will find on the *Sunday Mirror*'s fashion pages. We have moved on apace, or at any rate moved, and the Sunday papers have followed. The *People*, which in its broadsheet form never quite lost its typographical resemblance to Gamages, became the tabloid *Sunday People* and is now as much a feature of the Seventies as the Chinese takeaway. The *Observer* began to recover from shell-shock. *The Sunday Times* expanded into a kind of journalistic exhibition centre with pavilions for all tastes. Meanwhile the staid *Sunday Telegraph* (the *Sabbath Telegraph*, shouldn't it be called?) had arrived on the scene, to fill a void that did not seem to exist – a black hole in the Sunday constellation. Only the colour supplements stayed still, marooned for ever in the never-had-it-so-good oasis of Macmillan affluence.

Every country has its ritual on Sundays. In Italy, men gather in arcades and at street junctions to wave their arms about and discuss politics. In France, they proceed purposefully across the town carrying citrus-flavoured gâteaux in delicate white cartons. In America, they travel tremendous distances to eat ice-cream. In England, they buy Sunday papers.

In any large city, quite unexpected locations such as the doorways of shoe-shops, the steps of the civic centre or the expensive frontage of the Electricity Board showrooms are commandeered by the news-vendor, whose wares are spread out before him, like rugs in a Marrakesh bazaar. His demeanour is relaxed: unlike his daily counterpart, he doesn't have the anxiety of catching the last wave of commuters before the noon racing sheets render his ephemeral stock obsolescent. The news-bills with which he tempts the passer-by have the timelessness of Sunday itself: HAVE WE LIVED BEFORE? and THE PLEASURES OF LIFE. The transactions come in waves: pre-Mass, post-Mass, pub opening time, pub closing time; we go on buying Sunday papers, on the basis that just one more can't do us any harm, until quite late in the afternoon. The compulsion punctuates the business of the day like the monk's bell.

On this sub-fiesta level, the Sunday papers are one of the few remaining excitements of street life since the demise of the hurdy-gurdy and the German band. And I don't know whether any circulation manager has ever thought of this, but they are probably responding to some deep anti-Puritan urge to go out and buy something when all the shops are closed. Question: if we could buy books, tights, records and tins of grapefruit segments on the Lord's Day, would we buy more newspapers because of our greater mobility in shopping areas, or fewer because consumer choice was widened? Something for those trenchant tabloid leader-writers to ponder when next exploring the lunacies of the Shops Acts.

But such sociological doodlings do not explain what Sunday papers are *for*, what they are in aid of, what need they fulfil. The daily paper, it's easy to see, is among life's necessities: as well as mitigating the agonies of commuter travel and providing certain services such as the closing prices and the card for Kempton Park, it is a compact dock brief on all the topics that will be debated in office or factory during the day. Its strip cartoons, word-games, astrology columns and so on are often a small shared pleasure among work-friends; its features and regular corners provide a filler for the odd moments when there is nothing much else to do.

Few of these uses seem to apply to the Sunday. It is read largely at home, where there are many other distractions. Practically the only utilitarian service it offers is the television programme – an invitation to put the review sections aside, if ever there were one. So no one *has* to read the Sunday paper; but the need seems to be there.

Well, no one has to go to the theatre either, but you will get queues in Shaftesbury Avenue. And the appeal, of course, is the same: the Sundays satisfy our appetite for drama. We may have travelled far from the 'orrible murders of Lloyd's *Weekly News*, but we still need our fix. Sunday, still, is the day of revelation.

Nor does the drama have to be lurid: it can have the pleasing shape of a well-made play. Perhaps that's why I like to breakfast with the *Sunday Express*: it has the tea-tray appeal of a matinée. It has a beginning, a middle and an end – it gives the impression of being edited by Terence Rattigan.

The *Sunday Express*, more than any other paper, favours the narrative form. Here, for example, is the beginning of a page lead news story: 'The family driving daily across town in the new blue

Mini were a familiar sight. Usually at the wheel was Mrs June Fanning, 26. But often her Irish-born husband Anthony took his turn ...' The travel column: 'Moonlight silvered the minaret of the Soleiman mosque. The scent of exquisite spices and perfumes filled the warm air ...' A medical feature on lumbago: 'Duncan Cook was loath to get up. He had had a busy week at the office and had worked late hours at home in order to catch up.'

The *Express* should put on a touring production for Britons abroad who miss their English Sunday. You have only to pick it up and you can hear the drone of the lawn-mower and the slap of wash-leather on Cortina 2000 wafting in through the french windows.

Having devoured the front pages with their promise of impending storms, forthcoming clashes and expected scandals (Sunday news, you may have noticed, often veers towards the prophetic) I tend thereafter to treat all the papers as one paper – a super-*Sunday Times* with more supplements than were ever dreamed of in Gray's Inn Road. Eating, drinking, snoozing and waking up, going for a walk and coming back, switching on the telly and switching off, I pick and choose my way through acres of newsprint: from the *Sunday Mirror*'s down-to-earth but always witty, radical leader to the sophistication and common sense (how does she make them mix, like oil and vinegar?) of Katharine Whitehorn; from the urbane Alan Watkins to the knowledgeable and infuriating Woodrow Wyatt; from this or that pop star or footballer talking as he has never talked before to How The Arabs Sold Sterling Short; from the *Sunday People*'s EXCLUSIVE investigations and its refreshing glimpses of provincial Britain (too Londonish by half, most of our Sunday Press) to *The Sunday Times*'s reconstruction of some encounter in the corridors of power which quite often tells us more about that encounter than we actually need to know.

And, discarding page after page so that the carpet takes on the appearance of a print-orchard in blossom time, I renew my weekly grudges: smug Elkan Allan, silly Anne Edwards, snide Clive James, and the unspeakable Gambols ('George, you've torn your pyjama trousers.' 'Not to worry.' 'But suppose the house caught fire – what would the neighbours say?' Boom boom).

Indigestion sets in at last. The crosswords half-done, the travel coupons clipped, the magazines skimmed through, and the

Business News can be put aside for tomorrow ... or never. The HOW and the WHY of the posh papers' inquiring news pages recede into a cheap-wine mist. HOW Mr Healey ... WHY Dr Kissinger ... Does it matter, in the twilight of a perfect Sunday? It was nice while it lasted, like a very long buffet lunch in the garden lasting well into the evening, but we're sated now. Curtain. Sunday's passing show is over. All human life ... .

CHAMPAGNE CHARLIE

I have always regarded champagne as – well, the champagne of alcoholic drinks.

Non-alcoholic ones too, come to that: given that I were permitted to salvage either a case of champagne or a crate of my favourite sparkling mineral water when shipwrecked, I know what I should be brushing my teeth with during my desert island vigil.

I have drunk champagne (or rather, I should say, sipped champagne – for no matter how quickly one guzzles it, such is its pervasively civilising influence that one always retains the illusion of having dealt with it in a properly deferential manner, of savouring, not swigging) at every conceivable hour of the day and on every possible occasion – not excluding the odd funeral where the familiar and welcome popping of corks has been accompanied by a murmured chorus of 'It's what old Harry would have wanted'.

Like everyone else, I would guess, I developed my champagne legs at weddings. In marquees, village halls and the upper rooms of superior pubs, my earliest reactions to the earthly equivalent of nectar were also the same as everyone else's – that it was nothing like what it was cracked up to be, and that the bubbles got up one's nose. What, we wondered, was all the fuss about?

I was, of course, far too young to be let anywhere near the stuff – most first encounters with champagne are at an age when the only comparisons possible are between liver salts or Tizer. Furthermore, despite all its celebratory connotations, weddings are not really conducive to the full and proper enjoyment of such a momentous new taste experience. Weddings tend to be in the hands of caterers who serve it lukewarm, and in dish-shaped glasses that look as if they are needed back in the kitchen for serving the trifle in – an impression strengthened by the fact that it is extraordinarily difficult to get them replenished. Champagne, as we all know, should ideally be served properly chilled, in thin tulip glasses – and often.

My trade as a scribbler expanded my acquaintance with the Widow, as I was now, in the sophistication of youth, beginning knowingly to call it (Charlie, Champers, shampoo, bubbly and fizz were euphemisms yet to infiltrate my provincial Smart Set). It was served at all the best press receptions where, if you took up a strategic position by the end of the buffet where the drinks waitresses replenished their trays, you could quietly and steadily continue to exchange your empty glass for a full one without so much as a ten second pause to wonder where your next mouthful was coming from.

By then I had acquired the taste, and it was clear to me that, as soon as I had acquired the income to satisfy it, I should embark on the reckless, profligate course of buying champagne for myself (and others: for of all libations it is the one that most needs to be taken in company).

As things turned out, it was to be many weddings, christenings, receptions, parties and other red-letter days later, and if not a river then a substantial bubbling brook of largely other people's champagne was to pass down my gullet, before I acquired the habit to go with the acquired taste and the acquired income. Bar the odd tankard consumed at race meetings, and the odd round bought at Yates's Wine Lodge, Blackpool – where I was early introduced to the egalitarian delights of draught champagne and chip sandwiches – I found it difficult to dissociate champagne from special occasions.

There had to be some pretext for serving it, some sound potential reason (a birthday coming up, the approach of New Year, an impending anniversary) even for having a few bottles of it at hand. (Of the ten million bottles drunk each year in Britain, I wonder just how many have had to put up a fight with our native puritanism?)

There are only so many feast days in the social calendar – and thanks to one or two judicious buys they had begun to be outnumbered by the bottles of champagne in my cellar. Thus I entered a kind of transitional period, halfway between prudery and permissiveness, where I would all but invent occasions to provide the excuse for another cork to hit the ceiling. I won't say I went as far as a certain Fleet Street landlady, renowned for her conviviality, who would accept any justification offered for a party, from Anzac Day to the anniversary of the invention of the wellington boot. In retrospect, though, I can see that it was stretching credibility almost to its limits to make a special celebration out of – for example – the end of the school holidays, an obscure by-election, or putting a losing bet on the Grand National.

But a *raison d'être*, however flimsy, had to be found. Drinking champagne for the hell of it would have been as unthinkable as eating Christmas pudding in November.

I cannot remember on what particular bygone bright morning I impetuously said – or someone impetuously said – 'It's such a beautiful day – why don't we open a bottle of champagne?' But said it was, and opened the bottle was, and it was like drinking the sunlight. Now that truly was a champagne red-letter day – a breakthrough – and, ever since, I have called for champagne wherever and whenever the mood has taken me.

Not any old mood, mark you. Champagne, at least for me, does little to raise flagging spirits – the bubbles have to be already there before the bottle is even opened. In other words, euphoria has to be in the air. So to some extent, I suppose, there is still that lurking requirement for it to be a special occasion of sorts.

As to what I might be feeling euphoric about, however, here there is scope in plenty. Sometimes I could be feeling good because I have just finished a particular piece of work. Sometimes I could be feeling irresponsible because I have yet to start a particular piece of work. Sometimes I may drink champagne because I'm feeling flush – at others, because I've just paid my tax bill and can't possibly afford such extravagance. Lunch in agreeable company is always a good excuse for a bottle – as is an unexpected encounter with an old friend, when champagne takes on the character of liquid serendipity.

Though you certainly wouldn't find me sticking to orange juice at one, I am not really keen on big champagne parties these days. Small companies are best for champagne drinking – ideally four, and preferably in a garden or on a balcony. In a comfortable hotel suite, an even more ideal number is two, when a bottle waiting in its bucket of ice will give the lie to the theory that it is better to travel hopefully than to arrive.

I do not, as a rule, like to mix champagne with things (black velvet, to my mind, ruins two classic drinks), though I have been known to accept a Buck's Fizz at breakfast. I do not like to see champagne thrown at the bows of ships, or sprayed over the heads of sportsmen.

It is made to be drunk – as, I suppose, are those of us who drink it.

4

WHINE BY THE GLASS

THE POT-BELLIED GOLDEN SUMMER STARTS

THE POT-BELLIED GOLDEN SUMMER STARTS

A question that used to be widely (if idly) debated, as one drizzling wet-blanket summer followed another, was what effect a good long spell of Mediterranean weather would have on our misery-guts national character.

I seem to remember a general assumption that we would improve no end. Just give us a reasonable excess of Riviera-type sunshine and we would come over all Continental in the nicest possible way.

We would loll about under café umbrellas like the French, snooze all afternoon like the Italians, dance in the streets like the Spanish, and carry on during the torrid evenings as if auditioning for a foreign film.

There was no mention of our adopting any of their more disagreeable traits like a tendency to throw paving stones to make a political point. All would be sweetness and light, c'est la vie and mañana.

Well, if one swallow doesn't make a summer I suppose one summer doesn't make a Sorrento, so it may be early in the day to judge what a hot spell really does to our character. But my interim verdict, while we await the official findings which will take not less than ten thousand years to arrive at and then only if the weather holds out, is that Continental we ain't.

All the evidence so far is that the British, when perpetually exposed to sunshine, begin to resemble not so much the best kind of European as the worst kind of Australian.

There has been something aggressively pot-bellied about Britain this long golden summer.

The image that will swim into my mind, if during our next twenty-five-year cold snap I am asked what it was really like in that fabulous scorcher of '83, will be not of long cool drinks at café tables or of bronzed topless belles on beaches, but of hordes of tattooed, medallion-swinging, bare-chested video-arcade cowboys swaggering around with a can of warm fizz clenched in one fist and a crumbling chapati in the other.

If there is a civilising ingredient in prolonged sunshine it must have been filtered out to suit our northern clime. The higher the temperature has risen the grosser we have become – noisier, nastier, coarser, dirtier, fatter and uglier.

I don't say that the rays of the sun in themselves generate these unlovely qualities – a kind of spontaneous combustion of bovver – but they do seem to accelerate a national tendency towards loutishness that was already there – if only by bringing outdoors all the oafs who normally skulk indoors.

Perhaps my most unfavourite observation of this memorable summer has been of the high incidence of railway passengers clad only in trousers, training shoes and vests. I am by no means sartorially choosy but I find it incomprehensible that a man can undertake a hundred-mile rail journey in his vest without a nagging feeling that he has forgotten something. (He does not forget, however, to leave the carriage looking like a sump-pit.)

Still, who am I to grumble? September's here already, and we must be nearing the end of the sparkling summer wine. Let's enjoy it while we can, drink up, and chuck the bottle into the next-door garden.

Thoughts of the Great Unwritten

The generality of readers being reluctant to accept that the essence of fiction is that it is made up, novelists are constantly being asked on whom this or that character is based.

In my own case, because most of my novels are effectively in the first person, even when written in the third, in that everything is seen through the eyes of the hero, I'm more usually asked if my characters are based upon myself. Little ice does it cut when I protest that if they were, I should be locked up in Broadmoor by now.

I have to admit, however, that there is one facet of Edgar Samuel Bapty, the irascible hero of my new novel *Thinks*, that has been lifted straight from the private life of his creator. Bapty writes letters to *The Times* in his head. So do I. So, I shouldn't be in the least surprised to hear, do you.

Only a fraction of letters to *The Times* gets printed: that's common knowledge. What is probably not so generally realized is that only a fraction of that fraction ever gets written.

You see otherwise normal and respectable persons sitting in railway carriages with their lips moving convulsively. They are writing letters to *The Times*. Soberly-dressed pedestrians are to be observed bobbing their heads and twitching their arms like marionettes, only one removed from those unfortunates who stand in the middle of the road directing traffic. Do not be alarmed. They are only writing to *The Times*.

It is not that they do not happen to have writing materials to hand. Even as you read these words, there are thousands scanning the page opposite over the breakfast egg who will be reaching mentally for their pens to draft a scathing reply to this or that letter. They could just as well reach physically for their pens and pop it in the post on the way to the office, but that is not their way: the embossed notepaper of the Old Rectory, in their case, will remain forever virgin of that declamatory 'Sir!' They belong to the silent army of cerebral correspondents to *The Times*.

The letter that never is comes, from my observation, in two forms. The first encapsulates the 'I've a damn good mind to write to *The Times* about it!' *Punch* cartoon colonel who lurks inside us all, trying to get out. Something vexes us – a sloppily dressed railway guard, a shop assistant who can't add up, a public clock yet to catch up with British Summer Time – and we channel our indignation into a sardonic letter to the Editor concocted on the hoof. Usually it tails off around the second paragraph, the desire to express oneself in pungent phrases dying as annoyance fades. It would have to have been an irritation of epic proportions to sustain us through a blistering hundred words or so to 'I am, Sir, yours etc etc'.

The second form is the letter that never is at its purest. It too is never finished, but only in the sense that the job of painting the Forth Bridge is never finished. It is revised and reworked all through the day, often over several days, sometimes over the course of weeks, months or even years. It concerns, as likely as not, a particular bee in the bonnet (I have one on decimal currency which I have been drafting since 1970).

But the subject is neither here nor there: it is the object that matters, and the object is to get the thing right, to hone and polish until it becomes the perfect letter to *The Times*, as much an example of the epistolary form as Lord Chesterfield's letters to his son.

Unlike the indignant fragment ('Sir: If this indeed is the age of the train ...') induced by some passing irritation, the Mark II letter is seriously meant to be set down and submitted for publication. But the intention is always thwarted in the search for perfection.

I remember, in the course of some education controversy or other, coming across a letter to *The Times* from Kingsley Amis, one of those fellows who actually writes things down instead of sitting around thinking about them. His retort was to the effect that what he'd really said was 'More *will* mean worse', which was not to be taken as meaning the same as 'More means worse'. I was on the tube at the time. Fellow passengers began to edge away as, with the aid of gesticulating fingers, I set out to prove that Amis didn't understand his own aphorism. Unfortunately, by the time I'd marshalled my argument and reduced it to a glittering aphorism of my own, a week and a half had passed and I had missed the boat.

That, perhaps, is subconsciously the idea. Just as it is sometimes better to travel hopefully than to arrive, for some temperaments it is better to think about writing to *The Times* than actually to do it. Procrastination it may be, but look what we save on postage.

THE COMPUTER'S NOT KIDDING

The Sizewell nuclear power station inquiry has started and threatens to run and run even longer than the Stansted airport inquiry, which is to these public hearings what *The Mousetrap* is to the theatre.

The main debate will centre on whether Britain's first pressurised water reactor – PWR, to the trade – is most likely to put Sizewell on the map or to remove Sizewell entirely from the map, in the kind of accident that nearly reduced Three Mile Island to Two Mile Island.

There will be other considerations such as cost, currently put at £1147 million – one of those eye-glazing figures you only have to look at to know that it is sure to end up nearer £7411 million. The end-product, runs the case for the defence, will be cheap electricity. You know – like the North Sea was going to yield cheap gas.

Then of course there is the environment. It would be surprising if the PWR did not upset a bird's nest or two. You will remember how prominently the survival of the Brent Goose figured in the Maplin Sands inquiry. I gather that there is now more or less a plague of Brent geese, but that is by the way.

One objection I would have thought worth a whirl is that when the wretched thing breaks down, as it is sure to, it is going to be hell's own job – and a costly one at that, adding an unexpected nought or two to the estimate just quoted – to put it right again.

I know nothing whatever about how these nuclear contrivances work, and I am none the wiser for studying one of those cross-section diagrams such as you used to get in the pages of the *Eagle*. What I do know is that work is what they frequently don't. They are plagued with snags which keep armies of maintenance men in full employment.

But that is the way of modern machinery, particularly the kind of modern machinery which (it says in the glossy brochure) is hellbent on transforming our lives.

'Teething troubles' is the technical expression. But the teeth are only half the trouble. When one of the old donkey engines had teething troubles – or conked out, as they used to say – the charge-hand got it going again by substituting his braces for the broken fan-belt.

Perhaps *The Times* newspaper was harking wistfully back to that makeshift era when it headlined this week's RAF court-martial, 'MISSILE FIRED AT JAGUAR HAD NO SAFETY-PINS'. Be that as it may: when you get teething troubles in these white-hot technological days, everything has to come to a stop while you send for the dentist.

Take the office copying machine, the smartest device ever invented for making copies of recipes torn out of women's magazines. Every time you want to use it, it has a sign round its neck saying, 'Out of order'.

Unlike the old wind-up duplicator which was maintained by a spotty junior, no one knows how to mend this sullen infernal machine when it rumbles and blinks like a dyspeptic owl. And the service mechanic doesn't respond to the call on this answering machine.

There is a kind of supersonic Sod's Law relating to high-tech gadgetry, to wit: that not only will anything go wrong that can go wrong, but that it will go wrong in such a highly spectacular fashion that it will make your head spin.

When a computer fails, it isn't kidding. And as if refusing to do its own job weren't enough, it refuses to disgorge the means of doing the work by hand until the man with the oil-can turns up. It keeps your livelihood locked up in its innards like a train stuck in a tunnel.

A computer on the blink is, to its nearest and dearest, the next worst thing to the world coming to an end. And talking of the world coming to an end, we seem to have come a long way from the nuclear power station at Sizewell – and the further the better, some would say.

Actually, the only point I set out to make was that while I am not a nuclear or pressurised water Luddite, I would like to know what happened to that excellent idea for getting electricity from windmills.

LISTEN TO THE BANNED

The book-banners are at it again. A Mrs Gillian Klein, employed by the Inner London Education Authority and described as a 'library specialist', has drawn up a black-list of volumes which she feels are 'potentially damaging to young minds'.

They include the immortal Dr Dolittle books, some of the works of Enid Blyton, a short story by Walter de la Mare, the Beauty and the Beast fairy tale (Mrs Klein reportedly feels that the colour of the beast should be green rather than brown) and other favourites that have brought delight to generations of children.

Some craven headmasters have promptly removed the offending titles from their school libraries. Others, I hope and trust, will have advised the lady to go and pay a visit to a taxidermist, with their compliments.

Defending this latest witch-hunt (Enid Blyton must be the most consistently persecuted author since John Wilkes, and her persecutors are always those who are supposed to be disseminating reading matter rather than suppressing it – the librarians), Mrs Klein says exactly what someone of her turn of mind would be expected to say: 'This is not a witch-hunt.'

She then adds: 'I have great reverence for the heritage of literature. But there are some books, even classics, which do not always have a positive attitude to race.'

There are indeed. I would even go further than Mrs Klein and amend her preposterous statement to read: 'There are some books, *especially* classics, which do not always have a positive attitude to race.' And the reason I make this amendment is that it is not the function of literature to have a 'positive attitude' as understood by this zealot, and that any literature which did not have such an attitude would go in great danger of being mistaken for blancmange.

Mrs Klein falls, or rather dives head-first, into the trap that lies in wait for all who set out to learn everything about literature except how it's done: the belief that it is the duty of every writer to be nobler than his readers, and that it is the function of all writing to improve the human condition, like *Paradise Lost* or Kellogg's Bran Flakes.

It is not. Many of our most justly celebrated authors have been – or, in the case of those who have not yet drunk themselves to death, still are – buffoons, criminals, perverts, liars, and/or cheats, with disgusting personal habits and absurd, irrational prejudices against practically every form of life higher than the sponge. Yet to read them is to enter a garden of enchantment.

Nor did they, or do they, or should they, give a fig about revealing their bigotry in print. Indeed, some of the finest works in English literature have bristled with prejudice, and not only are they none the worse for it but they are manifestly the better for it.

To take a typical high-class author absolutely at random, namely myself, I have in some half a dozen novels discriminated most monstrously and unfairly against, among others, the following categories:

Schoolteachers, policemen, social workers, working-class parents, factory girls, suburban typists, Sloane Rangers, undertakers, landladies, fat black women, 'characters', antique dealers, publicans and club-owners, town councillors, bureaucrats, clerks, estate agents, caretakers, prostitutes, professional Yorkshiremen, freemasons, traffic engineers, architects and actresses.

And that's only in the opening chapters. Yet when this Waterhouse publishes his next novel later this month (advt.) they will have to build rush barriers outside Foyle's and Hatchard's.

The Mrs Kleins of this world, who steep themselves in literature as a pickled herring is steeped in brine, quite wrongly believe that book-reading is a traumatic experience like having your head set on fire. In fact for most people, including most children if they have not been put off books for life by all these local literary prodnoses, it is but one of many incidental pleasures such as eating pudding.

Millions of adults read Agatha Christie (an appallingly slipshod scribbler in my view, but that is nothing to do with the case) without even noticing, let alone being offended by or influenced by, the fact that she was an obnoxious snob. Millions of children read Enid Blyton (an even more rubbishy writer, but that is equally neither here nor there) without registering that such titles as *Here Comes Golly* are not perhaps 'positive' in their approach to how life ought to be lived outside hard, or even soft, covers.

Story-tellers were operating in the market-place long before all the social workers and all the inspectors and all the community relations advisers came along. They will still be here to tell the tale long after the fad for obsessive nannying has blown over.

JUMP OFF DOTTED LINE

One of the greatest benefits bestowed upon mankind by modern technology is the sharp drop in the percentage of bank-holiday picnics ruined because some oaf has forgotten the corkscrew and/or the tin-opener.

You will remember the scene in *Three Men In A Boat* where they try to open a tin of pineapple without the necessary implement:

'... Harris tried to open the tin with a pocket-knife, and broke the knife and cut himself badly; and George tried a pair of scissors, and the scissors flew up and nearly put his eye out. While they were dressing their wounds, I tried to make a hole in the thing with the spiky end of the hitcher, and the hitcher slipped and jerked me out between the boat and the bank into two feet of muddy water, and the tin rolled over, uninjured, and broke a teacup ...'

Nowadays, with the supermarkets crammed with foil-wrapped instant goodies, only a masochist on a fruit-free diet would add to the picnic hamper a sawn-up pineapple that has been soldered into a tinplate container as unassailable as the hull of a submarine. Whatever has to be opened can be opened merely by pulling a tag or tearing along the dotted line.

Or can it?

Have you ever found the perfect wasp-free picnic spot, arranged the folding camp-stools, unpacked the paper plates and the Thermos flask, secured the chequered tablecloth with a stone on each corner – then tried to open a vacuum-sealed piece of cheese?

The manufacturers of this sweating carbolic-textured practical joke tell you on the packet what to do with the thing. (How you dearly wish you could tell *them* what to do with it.) They urge you simply to find the seam in the plastic and pull it apart.

Ho ho.

Jerome K. Jerome and his pals finished up beating that tin of pineapple into a shape so hideous that they took fright and heaved it into the river. If they had had a vacuum-sealed wedge of Cheddar to contend with, they would have done things so terrible to it that it would have given them nightmares.

On reflection, the packets and packages that infest our lives have got no simpler to open than they were two hundred years ago when it required half an hour's work with a mallet and chisel to get at the contents of a can of bully-beef. As for the instructions, they are harder to understand than they have ever been. At one time they said simply 'Tear flap to open.' Now they say, 'To open, press on this edge, slide finger under flap and move to left and right.'

How the hell can you move to left and right when you've got your finger stuck in a packet of cornflakes, that's what I want to know? And when you *have* moved to left and right, what have you got? A squashed cornflakes packet, that's what.

It seems to me that those instructions would be far less ambiguous if they told you what the result of following them is actually likely to be, rather than what the packaging industry hopes it will be. Having roved an eye over my own stock of impenetrable household goods, I have taken the liberty of correcting some of this optimistic small print:

To spill milk all over kitchen table, fold right back then draw wings forward to form spout.

Pull ring to spatter ceiling with fizzy drink.

To pour ten fluid ounces of tomato sauce down sink, hold neck of bottle under cold running water and unscrew cap clockwise.

Press here to get thumb jammed in perforated section of soap-powder carton marked 'Press here.'

Insert coin under rim and twist to get bent coin.

Lift ring to pierce finger. Pull up to flavour sardines in olive oil with human blood.

Snip corner to get small triangle of cellophane stuck to scissors.

To break finger-nail, slide finger backwards and forwards under flap.

Pull tab of padded envelope to cover carpet with what looks like most of a shredded mattress.

To get screwdriver jammed in corned-beef tin, punch small hole in top of can then wind off top with key provided.

Pull red tag to get thin strip of plastic with red tag attached.

Detach cardboard backing from plastic protective covering to lose tiny nails without which enclosed picture-hooks are useless.

Tear here to obtain torn piece of wrapper.

A READ IS A READ IS A ...

A row has broken out in the cloistered world of the public libraries. And by row I mean literally a noise, clamour or commotion as defined by that pit-prop of the reference shelves, *The Shorter Oxford Dictionary*.

The sound that offends the bye-laws on silence and the non-commitment of nuisances is the bleep and burp of Space Invaders machines, those electronic Goths and Vandals which in their relentless march through our civilisation have now infiltrated the central library of the ancient diocese of Guildford.

Nor is that all. (Well, it wouldn't be, would it?) The county librarian, John Saunders, who as you gather is a bit of an innovator, has further scandalised parents and teachers by scrapping the children's section of the library.

His view is that modern ten- to twelve-year-olds are inhibited about using the children's section and that they should have wider access to the shelves. He believes furthermore that while children's requirements are changing, many of their parents still regard libraries as institutions which should be immune to change.

Many librarians feel as Mr Saunders does (although many do not) and they are supported by progressive educators, councillors, social workers, and other municipal oddballs who call the public libraries all sorts of nasty names like elitist, la-de-da and fuddy-duddy, and demand change.

This change usually consists of making the libraries look as little like libraries as possible, for fear that children who don't like reading will not have their stomachs churned by the sight of a book.

Swimming-baths without water will be the next logical step, I suppose. Meanwhile some public libraries feature more technological hardware than the average nuclear submarine, and it will not be long before library assistants glide to the Return Fiction shelves and back on fluorescent roller-skates, to the sound of piped music.

I will tell you where I stand on this controversy. I am so deeply conservative about what a public library should look like (the reading-room of a gentleman's club), what it should sound like (a cathedral on early-closing day), and even what it should smell like (Mansion polish) that if my attitude on this were projected into general life, I would be somewhat to the right of the National Front.

A public library should be a place where people go in pursuit of reading matter. It should not be a leisure centre where they go to play games, or a 'communications' centre where they go to press buttons. A library should consist not of 'materials' – i.e., video-tapes, micro-film, language laboratories, etc – but of books. If it does not consist of books then it is not a library.

It is no use telling me that times have changed and that there are now more sophisticated means of storing knowledge. It is not the function of a library to supplement its stock of books with so-called visual aids any more than it is its function to provide practical teaching aids so that if you were studying, say, carpentry, there would be a corner of the library where you could saw bits of wood in half.

What is more – and this is why any librarian introducing Space Invaders machines should be burned in effigy – children should be brought up to respect their public library, not to regard it as an adjunct of the Golden Nugget amusement arcade. Indeed, I would go so far as to say they should not only respect it, they should live in terror of it.

Mr Saunders speaks of youngsters being 'inhibited' about using the children's library. He does not know the meaning of the word. When I was a kid, our local branch librarian had us so inhibited that we used to stand outside cowering with fear for five minutes before we dared go in.

Before you were allowed past the counter – the equivalent, to us, of the frontier post in the Berlin Wall – your hands were inspected on both sides for signs of germ-carrying dirt. If you had not scrubbed them raw you were sent home.

Then the books you were returning were minutely examined as if you were suspected of being a diminutive drugs-runner. Any traces of jam, cocoa or pork-dripping and you got a monumental dressing-down.

The rules specified no talking, no coughing, no squeaky boots, no sweet-eating, no loitering and no giggling – and we loved the place.

You could not keep us out of it. I got through five books a week and would have devoured more but for the prevailing notion (which seems to be back in favour) that too much reading is bad for you.

We knew, and it was a source of great security in our lives, that library is a library is a library as a rose is a rose is a rose or a dog is a dog is a dog. The librarian who tinkers with this profound truth does so at his peril.

MOONLIGHT SERENADE

Of the very many odd things that have happened to our economy in recent years, not the least curious is that, on paper, we now appear to be regularly spending more than we are earning.

The main reason for this apparent phenomenon is probably that Government statistics are nearly always wrong. But the fact that many people are not entirely honest with the Inland Revenue, while others prefer to do their shopping direct from the back of a lorry, has also got something to do with it.

So, without doubt, has the astonishing rise of moonlighting. When the entire nation is having its roof repaired or its kitchen modernised on the understanding that payment is to be made in used fivers and no questions asked, there is bound to be some discrepancy when all the figures are added up.

I don't think anyone officially knows how much moonlighting is going on. If someone has two jobs, and the pay for the second of those jobs goes straight into his back pocket, he is unlikely to volunteer much information to the man who knocks on the door and says he is carrying out a Government survey on tax fiddles.

From my own observation, I would say it is very widespread indeed. I have just counted on my fingers the number of people I know who are having repairs or renovations done at the moment. The total is nine. Of those, only two will ever see anything that remotely looks like an invoice.

You will not hear anyone in authority say a good word for moonlighting. It is supposed to be greedy (taking work from the unemployed), dishonest (evading tax), dangerous (practising a trade without proper qualifications) and generally anti-social. Even those who defend it don't approve of it – they reckon it is a necessary evil thrown up by punitive taxation and the pay freeze.

For myself, I believe that as often as not the moonlighter is a useful and indeed an essential member of our society.

There is a strong case for regarding moonlighting as one of the honoured professions, with possibly a Duke of Edinburgh's Award for the Best Moonlighter of the Month.

Let me take one example from that mini-survey of my friends. This man is a second-hand dealer who needs a van to ply his trade. One day the van refused to move. He took his troubles to a garage where, having laughed in his face, they quoted a price that seemed to include the date and then told him the job couldn't be done in under ten days.

Like most of us, he knew someone who knew someone who regularly did such work for what is euphemistically called 'a drink.' This chap was a car mechanic who came round in his own time, worked till ten in the evening, and got the van on the road.

Undoubtedly a crime was committed here. A transaction took place of which the taxman knew nothing. These two scoundrels ought to be in jail.

But look at it on the positive side. One: my dealer friend got the job done at a low price which keeps down his overheads, thus enabling him to do his bit in the fight against inflation. Two: he got his van speedily back in service, thus enabling him to carry on trading and add to the gross national product. Three: a certain amount of money has been put in circulation which would otherwise be under the mattress, thus adding a small fillip to the economy.

Setting such gains against losses to the Inland Revenue, I would say the nation comes out of it with a profit. But really, that doesn't matter a damn one way or the other.

These chaps weren't short-circuiting the system just to cheat the taxman. They formed their illicit contract because they belong to a great conspiracy, a vast secret society of people who have grown impatient of a country operating at half-speed. The members of this society do not believe in overtime bans or demarcation disputes, or in excuses about waiting for spares or having three men off ill. They believe in work being done by those who want to do it.

Moonlighting flourishes because free enterprise has gone underground. I doubt that a few bob off income tax will flush it out again. The real incentive for working hard in the open (daylighting, should it be called?) is public approval – and hard work is more and more being regarded as an eccentric and possibly subversive activity.

The way we are going, such crusts as this country actually earns will be provided by moonlighters, while others bask in the sun.

MA BELL AND BUZBY

If there is one artifact which reflects the quintessential rattiness of British street life, it is the public telephone.

I am not talking about vandalism, though God knows it is difficult enough to find a phone-box that doesn't look as if it has been in a pub brawl and lost.

I am talking about those instruments which (after their buzzing, crackling, pip-pipping fashion) actually work. They bring me out in a deep depression.

The British public telephone, no matter how streamlined, up to date and push-button its designers have tried to make it, is to telecommunications what a collapsed cheese soufflé is to haute cuisine. It exudes failure.

I was in one of our most modern post offices the other day, the one off Trafalgar Square. The scratched and battered public phones, housed in an underground passage, somehow contrive to look as if they would be happier being used for emergency-only calls in an eczema hospital.

The above thoughts, and others too blistering to set in print without a fire extinguisher at the ready, came to me as I read a report in this week's *Economist* about the state of our telephone service. It begins: 'Britain can forget about having a telephone system as good as America's Bell for a long time,' and ends, 'At the current rate of capital investment, even second best will look too ambitious for Britain in a few years' time.'

These are the upbeat bits. The rest is too melancholy to quote. In any case, why draw on the *Economist*'s precious store of pessimism when we have gloom of a better quality right here at hand? I too take the view that we are doomed to an inferior telephone service, but I would strike out that phrase 'for a long time' and substitute 'until the cows come home.'

Every country, I believe, gets the kind of telephone system it deserves – and we have got one that perfectly suits our low expectations as a nation.

By and large, the British use the phone-box to convey news about something going wrong – they are stuck at Victoria because their train has been cancelled, they are stuck at Heathrow because their luggage has been lost, they are stuck outside Birmingham because their clutch has gone and the breakdown van hasn't turned up.

It is appropriate that the mechanical disseminator of all these mournful tidings should itself be seedy, incompetent and unreliable.

The Americans, on the other hand, having extremely high expectations, enjoy a telephone system which reflects their ex-uberant lifestyle. Stand beside an American at a gas-station pay phone and you will find that he is telephoning *constructively*. He is not ringing to say he will be late home because his fan-belt has snapped and all the mechanics are off with bad backs. He is booking a theatre ticket or ordering some groceries or picking up his messages from the answering service or giving his sister in Albuquerque the name of a good divorce lawyer.

When we English marvel at the sophistication of Ma Bell, as the Americans affectionately call their telephone system, we always assume it's because they have a superior supply of expensive gadgetry. Not so. It's the superior *demand* for expensive gadgetry that makes their system the best in the world.

They have three-way phones because a lot of them want to talk to two people at once. They have phone-booths at every street corner because, to an American, not being near a telephone is like not being near oxygen.

If we lived in a country where it was possible to ring the local delicatessen and ask them to send round a cup of coffee and a pastrami sandwich on rye; or to ring a theatre booking office and get an answer; or to ring a railway station and not get the engaged signal; or to ring a department store and be treated like a prospective customer instead of a potential leper, then we too should have made so much use of the telephone service over the years that money for investment would be coming out of its earpieces.

We get a second-rate service because we're resigned to living like second-class citizens.

OUR MIXED PLASTIC BLESSINGS

To the accompaniment of a bare minimum of champagne-cork popping and not much dancing in the streets, an important anniversary is upon us. It is fifty years as ever was since plastic was invented.

I had better modify that statement at once, if not cancel it out altogether.

Such synthetically-produced items as composition billiard balls, celluloid collars and Bakelite light switches have, as all the molecular scientists among my readers will testify, been around for much longer. But the kind of plastic that nowadays confronts us at every turn came out of the test tube exactly half a century ago.

It was a devillish mixture of benzaldehyde and ethylene gas which when swished around for a bit and rolled through the mangle produced a substance called polythene. One small step for man but a giant leap for the manufacturers of washing-up bowls and airline cutlery.

After polythene came polystyrene and polyurethane and polyester and poly-this and poly-that until in the fullness of time it began to look as if the entire surface of the earth was covered with a thin and highly-coloured veneer of plastic.

Never has a blessing been so mixed.

It is the most wondrous and versatile of materials – yet with a fathomless capacity for ugliness.

It has lightened the domestic burden to a degree unsurpassed since the invention of running water, and with its wipe-clean shiny surfaces has diminished squalor – yet only to place shoddiness within the reach of all.

There are few artifacts so depressing as a plastic plate with a cigarette burn in it, so thoroughly slummish as a plastic stacking-chair with a jagged piece broken out of it, so grotesque as a bubble-warped plastic bucket that has been too near the fire.

Midas found that when granted the power to turn everything he touched into gold, there were certain inbuilt disadvantages to this slice of good luck. It is the same now that everything we touch is turned into plastic.

A plastic watering can is cheap to buy and light to handle, but it has all the charisma of half a brick – whereas the sound of tapwater gurgling into a zinc watering can with a copper nozzle, and the cool zincy smell of it, was one of the small delights of summer.

A plastic picnic box is handy and hygienic but cold chicken tastes better out of wickerwork.

A plastic moulded bath is good to look at and doesn't chip but its avocado-green elegance lacks the steamy enticement of the old-fashioned white-enamelled cast-iron tub with the two brass taps and the four claw feet.

But those are quibbles. The truly horrendous flaw in plastic is that its malleability and sheer availability came as soya-based manna from Heaven to anyone at all disposed towards the stamping out of good taste. It was like giving matches to a pyromaniac.

Brewers went through their pubs like deathwatch beetles, destroying everything that was made of wood and replacing it with plastic grained to look like wood. (Plastic has many of the qualities of the chameleon but when it tries to look like mahogany it succeeds only in looking like sucked toffee.)

Shopkeepers took down their painted signs and engraved glass fascias and put up garish plastic shop-fronts that usually had as much harmony with the buildings they adorned as a carhorn in a cathedral.

The interiors of hotels and public buildings began to look like airport lounges. (If plastic had not been invented, it would have to exist if only to make airport lounges look as ghastly as they do.)

Councils littered their streets with plastic litter bins and bottle banks and daubed the gutters with yellow lines of plastic paint.

Discarded polystyrene foam food containers became as common a sight as discarded cigarette packets. (They did in the Royal Borough of Earls Court, anyway.)

And every single householder in the country bought a bright blue plastic clothes basket and threw out their handsome old varnished wicker one (everyone except me, that is. I use it for storing old newspapers in).

Never mind. Like those early examples of the good uses to which synthesised materials may be put – the Pickwick, the Owl and the Waverley Pen – plastic with all its faults comes as a boon and a blessing to men.

But 'Happy birthday, plastic?' No, I can't quite bring myself to sing it.

WHINE BY THE GLASS

Surprisingly, for an administration which is opposed to nannying, the Government seems poised to meddle with the nation's drinking habits.

Because more and more people are drinking more and more booze, there are plans to put up the price of alcohol, control liquor advertising, and introduce a pub code whereby customers judged to be putting away too much will be refused service.

The result will be that more people will continue to drink more but they will have to pay a scandalous price for it, there won't be any more of those jolly beer commercials on the telly, and pub landlords will be even more obnoxious than they are now.

There will be another unpleasant side-effect. The whining anti-drink lobby, which is already well on the way to becoming as much of a pain in the neck as the whining anti-smoking lobby, will have become a power in the land.

You won't be able to walk five yards without being confronted by a poster warning you of the dangers of alcoholism (which, I should like to point out before the meaning of the word is irretrievably twisted, is defined by the dictionary as a disease condition due to the excessive use of alcoholic beverages. It is not, as the anti-drinkers seem to think, an umbrella synonym for all forms of over-indulgence).

There will be a proliferation of those bullying codes of conduct whereby the social half-nelson is applied to the parts the law cannot reach. Not only will the pubs have a code to discourage heavy drinking but the advertising profession will have a code, the television industry will have a code, factories will have a code, colleges will have a code. There will be so many codes that you will have to order your pint in Morse.

There will be, for all I know, alcohol-free sections in aeroplanes and cinemas where those who object to brandy fumes and the smell of stale real ale may suck their fruit gums in peace.

The worst aspect is that we can kiss goodbye to any hopes of relaxing our stupid and repressive drinking laws. Even though there is factual evidence that they actually *cause* drunkenness rather than prevent it, no one will ever persuade the anti-drink whiners that control is not a virtue in itself.

On second thoughts, perhaps that isn't the worst aspect after all. The worst aspect is that the anti-drink whiners are going to bombard me with long, patronising and boring letters.

I beg them to try to refrain. I know it's difficult, and I do appreciate that although they set out to write only short boring letters, some inner demon urges them on to write one more boring sentence and then another and another. They may think it harmless but I do warn them that there's no such thing as social boring. Boring, to grab but one statistic out of thin air, is now costing British industry £100 million a year in lost export orders, owing to commercial travellers telling long jokes to the Japs.

To return, however, to our main theme: yes, madam, I *have* seen at first-hand the misery that can be caused by heavy drinking. Probably more than you have.

Yes sir, I *have* studied the facts and figures. I accept that drink consumption has doubled in the last ten years. That is because this country has become a much nastier place in the last ten years. Where there is more drinking, there will be more drunks, more alcoholics, and more drink-related problems. If this country became a much more pleasant place in the next ten years, there would be consequently less drinking and consequently fewer drunks, fewer alcoholics and fewer drink-related problems. That is the magic of percentages.

One thing you may be sure of. Simplistic exercises in social engineering cannot cure heavy drinking, or alcohol abuse as it seems we must now call it. They are more likely to make it worse. Look at Sweden. Look at Russia. Look above all, at the United States. The more repressively the legislators tried to stop these countries drinking, the more pie-eyed they became.

Tighten the drink-driving laws, by all means. Impose heavier penalties for selling booze to schoolchildren, by all means. But there are some things the law cannot do, and shouldn't try to do. It cannot, for example, cure human weakness.

'Who do you blame?' the dying alcoholic was asked on this week's Panorama report on drink. 'Only meself,' he replied. I'll drink to that.

THE ABERRANT APOSTROPHE

Timed to coincide with its traditional May Day Rally, the AAAA (Association for the Abolition of the Aberrant Apostrophe) today issues a sensational report producing damning evidence of widespread infiltration of the apostrophe by Marxists.

The report was commissioned by the Association's life-president following an emergency resolution at last year's annual conference amending the AAAA's constitution to include among its aims the rehabilitation of the absent apostrophe.

The brief of the one-man sub-committee who compiled the document was to establish the link, if any, between the apostrophe's disappearance from words that demand one (Railwaymens Arms) and its appearance in words that don't (Railwaymens Arm's).

The report alleges that in pursuit of their avowed objective of an irreversible redistribution of wealth from the rich to the poor, extreme left-wing elements in this great movement of ours have stealthily set about an irreversible redistribution of the apostrophe.

Thus apostrophes believed to have once belonged to wealthy companies, stores and institutions such as Barclays Bank, the Childrens Bookshop and the Publishers Association are turning up in small shops and backstreet cafés where they are used to advertise tomato's, mushroom's, chip's and so on.

The audacious plot first came to light in the Royal Borough of Earl's Court, where a lynx-eyed AAAA member observed that while this wealthy borough is gradually losing its own official apostrophe, the more raffish streets of the neighbourhood are becoming so crammed with superfluous apostrophes as to resemble a spotted dick.

One day he noted that a street sign which had said 'Earl's Court' had been replaced by one reading 'Earls Court' without the apostrophe. The very next day a chalked sign appeared in the window of a small take-away snack bar: 'No Vat On Salad's.' A spokesman refused to say where he had got this aberrant apostrophe.

The report says: 'How the apostrophes are being switched, we have been unable to establish. Perhaps the operation is being carried out by marauding gangs of political fanatics – apostrophised Robin Hoods – at dead of night. Perhaps left-wing councils are secretly showering apostrophe grants on pressure groups representing small traders, while penalising the apostrophes of the rich with crippling rate demands.

'However this clandestine redistribution of apostrophes is being achieved, there can be no doubt that its effect on the community is disastrous. What we are witnessing is the political polarisation of the apostrophe.

'Because of the growing stigma attaching to the apostrophe, wealthy organisations and the so-called "sunrise" industries are now shaking-out and rationalising their apostrophes even when there are jobs for them to do, while smaller, hard-pressed businesses and the old "sunset" industries are burdening themselves with the upkeep of apostrophes they don't need.

'Apostrophically, Britain is becoming two nations – or two nation's, as one of them would say.'

A TROUBLE SHARED IS A TROUBLE HALVED

Correction: a trouble shared is a trouble doubled.

As the mathematicians would say, let x equal the trouble. Your spouse has found out x. Your house has developed a leaking x. Or the tax inspector claims you owe him £x, plus interest. You unburden your woes on a friend or advisor, whom we had better call y. We are asked to believe that $x + y = \frac{x}{2}$, which is absurd.

In the first place, it is not unheard of for x and y – that is, the shared trouble and person sharing it – to be one and the same. Thus, when you make what is theoretically the trouble-halving announcement: 'Darling, I think my spouse has found out about us,' the response is not: 'No – only *half* found out, now that you've told me.' It is 'Oh, my God!' That is because x is married too, and just as likely to be up to the ears in soup as you are.

What you have there is not trouble halving itself but trouble splitting itself, like some malevolent amoeba, into two equal parts – but of the same size and weight as the master copy. Others who fall into this category are the girl who has to see her boyfriend at once, on a matter she can't discuss over the phone, very urgently; the organiser of the winning pools syndicate to whom it falls to confess to his colleagues that he forgot to post his coupon; the herpes sufferer and Lady Macbeth.

Then there is the situation where the function of y, the trouble-sharer (who in this case does it for a living), is to point out that what you thought was merely x is in fact $2x$ or even x^2.

No motorist – and you may go back through the entire history of the internal combustion engine – has ever been told by the garage mechanic: 'This trouble is not as serious as you thought.' The hollow tooth, into which air is sharply inhaled, might have been specially designed by nature as a distress signal for use by garage mechanics – and roofing contractors, plumbers, electricians, watch and clock repairers – who have to break it to the wretched, innocent punter that the worst is yet to come.

Here we have the shared trouble swelling up like a carbuncle that started as a spot. And the more you share it – with the garage mechanic's foreman, say, or the man who makes out the estimate – the bigger it gets.

Not so much in this category as a mutation of it is the solicitor. Here x may indeed be halved, or even exorcised entirely (though not necessarily so) – only to be replaced by X, or more usually X! In other words, the worry over who is responsible for the crumbling party wall is finally lifted from your shoulders – while simultaneously an astronomical legal bill, which you can't pay, is placed upon them. Swopping one albatross for another is hardly a reduction of one's worry-load.

But so far we have only nibbled at the problem, or the half-problem, as some would prefer to call it. At the core of this fallacy about shared troubles is another proverb (coming next month), which is perhaps less fallacious – to the effect that a friend in need is a friend indeed.

Indeed? As listening post and sympathiser, like Sybil Fawlty on the blower ('I *know*! . . . I *know*! . . .'), very probably. As a baby-sitter, money-lender, hand-holder, car-pool-sharer, reference-giver, shopping-fetcher, recipe-provider and goldfish-minder, more than likely. But trouble-sharer?

Inside every friend there is a psychiatrist trying to get out. Only mention that you are in trouble, and without knowing quite how it happened you will find yourself metaphorically flat on your back on this unlicensed analyst's couch, telling more than you ever meant to. ('You see, what nobody else knows is the true extent of his drinking . . .') and generally carrying on as if a trouble were a nasty aberration to be confessed, like a sin.

Putting aside the awful possibility of one person's trouble being another person's gossip as something your best friend would never stoop to (otherwise you really would be in trouble), where do you stand when your course of self-imposed psychoanalysis is over? The next stage of the treatment will depend on the temperament and personality of the supposed trouble-sharer.

If the response is confined to 'Tut tut' or 'There there' or any other equivalent to the motor mechanic's hollow tooth-sucking (but without the bill), then you may count yourself lucky. You may not have diminished your trouble, but you have not increased it. You have merely unburdened yourself of it for an hour or so while you drink the wine bar dry or see off your best friend's best sherry; at the end of the therapeutic session you pack up your troubles in your old kit bag, as advised in the song, and stagger off no easier in your mind, no happier, no wiser, but at least no worse off than you were before.

It is the friend hell-bent on being shrewd that you have to watch out for. This class, unfortunately, includes most of the human race. Few are the mortals in whose book the testimonial, 'You gave me the best piece of advice I've ever had in my life' (or its corollary, 'I only wish I'd listened to you') is not the greatest accolade it is possible to receive; fewer still are the best friends who, when presented with trouble on a plate like a sucking pig with an apple in its mouth, will not strive to earn their laurels for hitherto unsuspected depths of sagacity.

'All right, you've asked me what I'd do so I'll tell you ...'
'You're not going to like me saying this one bit ...' 'Let's face it,
love, if you go on as you are, things can only get worse ...'
'You've got to think of yourself ...' 'All right, now listen to me.
The first thing we're going to do is make you up a bed here ...'
'I'm sorry, but I've got to tell you this for your own good ...'
There are as many constructive responses to trouble as there are
combinations on a fruit machine. Best friend pulls the lever – and
hopes for the jackpot.

Even if the advice is good, your trouble is still not halved,
because now you're allowing yourself to be cajoled and bullied
into putting yourself to the additional trouble of doing something
about it. If the advice is bad (and in my experience best friends
usually shine more as best friends than as marriage guidance
counsellors, careers officers, financial advisors, planning con-
sultants or Alcoholics Anonymous hotlines), then God only knows
the trouble you're in.

Finally, there is that special, saint-like, hairshirt-wearing breed
of furrow-browed friend – nearly everyone has got one – who
adopts other people's troubles, like kittens rescued from drowning, as her/his own. Not only is your trouble magnified by being
shared, but every stress symptom, every sleepless night, every
moan and groan, is vicariously duplicated by your personalised
agony auntie. If you could accurately quantify the total amount of
agonising here generated, you would probably find that in this
case a trouble shared is a trouble quadrupled.

Talking of proverbs, there is an old Yorkshire saying: never
trouble trouble, till trouble troubles thee. To which I would add
the rider: and when it does trouble thee, keep it to thyself.

Accounts Rendered

To talk of being partial to certain types of bill – except those for
£0,000.00 despatched by some demented computer; and even they
tend to irritate rather than delight – is like expressing a preference
for one form of toothache over another. Nonetheless, I have

always had a weakness for those ornate invoices sent out by Edwardian manufactories, wholesale warehouses and emporia.

They were an aesthetic experience. None of your tissue-thin oblong perforated slips in that golden age of billheads: they were printed on linen-finished paper and were about the size of a bed-sheet. They had to be, for a good two-thirds of the document was embellished with a splendid steel engraving of the model premises from which it emanated, together with the firm's name in extravagant lettering, its telegraphic address, its trademark like a sailor's tattoo, and a reproduction of the several gold medals its products had won at trade fairs in Leipzig.

In the top left hand corner, the expression 'D^r to' in an elaborate embossed scroll indicated the nature of the missive. The details of it were contained in whatever white space was left over. They were of a cryptic nature, usually running to little more than 'To Goods Supplied, £1 1s 0d nett'. At the bottom of the folio was another embossed italic rubric to the effect that errors and omissions were excepted, and some such printed pleasantry as 'Thanking you for your esteemed order'.

Such were the first, second, third, fourth and fifth applications. Now we come to the final notice. This was a replica of the above in all respects except that the bit in the white space now read: 'To Account Rendered, £1 1s 0d nett' and below it was rubber-stamped the peremptory warning: 'The Favour Of An Early Settlement Would Oblige'.

They are not writing them like that any more.

The last bill I had was from the Thames Water Authority. Instead of a tasteful engraving of Chelsea Reach or some such scene (one of the sketches from *Three Men in a Boat* would look quite fetching) it is peppered with fussy little thumbnail line drawings.

There is a picture of an envelope to indicate that payment may be made by post, a picture of a telephone against the information that enquiries may be made by phone, a picture of a cheque to indicate that they are not necessarily expecting me to settle with a bag of gold in a chamois-leather bag, and so on. Then there are pictures of a tap, a lavatory and what I think is a test tube, or it may be a tulip bulb, to illustrate the fact that I am paying for water supply, sewerage and environmental services.

The whole bill, in short, is designed to be understood by a

recipient so dim that his IQ must be altogether inconsistent with the earning power required to pay the preposterous amount demanded. The only thing obscure about it is the account itself. I am being charged at the rate of 3.200p for W and 2.600p for S/E. I have no idea what this means except that it comes to £51.13 for the half year. That bit, at least, is on a par with 'To Goods Supplied'.

It is clear that, where bills were once designed by graphic artists, they are now in the hands of consumer relations experts, or at least the ones from the public utilities are. There is a strong tendency to chummy, reassuring cosiness: 'How To Pay Your Bill', 'What To Do If You Think You Are Being Overcharged' and so on; the over-abundance of information being nullified by the fact of its being printed in indecipherable pale blue or Nile green.

Such bills also come damp with crocodile tears, or accompanied by the printed equivalent of an apologetic cough, to drive home the message, 'We are keenly aware that you are now paying more for your services than on your mortgage and your children's education, but unfortunately that is the way the cookie crumbles.' My rates bill, for instance, is always backed up with reams of explanatory leaflets and charts in several colours, demonstrating how my local council is cutting costs to the bare bones and how the antics of those spendthrifts in the county authority are completely out of its hands.

This disposition of bills to be wrapped up inside bundles of extraneous literature, so that they resemble small parcels, is another modern development. I do not suppose those handsome Edwardian invoices were accompanied by special offers of ivory-backed hairbrushes or electro-plated moustache tongs. Nowadays, however, it is rare for any bill to stand on its own feet. My monthly credit-card statement is customarily barnacled with so many glossy brochures for pigskin briefcases, holidays, Kruger-rands, charge accounts at Harrods and so forth that they will soon have to start sending it out in a Jiffy-bag. And that's on top of the advertising material plastering the statement itself: 'FEBRUARY 18TH IS GRANDMOTHER'S DAY. WHY NOT USE YOUR CARD TO BUY YOUR GRANNY AN ELEPHANT'S FOOT UMBRELLA STAND?'

I notice that none of this puffery ever accompanies final notices. Presumably they think that if you can't pay your phone bill you're a bad risk for a Mickey Mouse telephone extension. Or perhaps they're in such haste to send the final notice out (the ominous red letter demanding that I pay for my electricity before dreadful things are done to me quite frequently precedes the original bill itself) that they haven't time to stuff the envelope with junk mail.

What is the perfect bill? It depends which side of it you are on. From the point of view of the creditor, the perfect bill is the one that stupefies as it baffles as it enrages. The computer could have been invented for this very purpose. (Why is it that a computer can make a mistake in a billionth of a second, yet take six months to rectify it, sending out plea after plea of PLEASE PAY AMOUNT SHOWN. YOUR QUERY IS BEING DEALT WITH?)

But from the debtor's point of view there can be only one perfect bill. It is the search for such perfection that accounts for the entire credit industry.

Is there any credit-card holder who, upon signing for a restaurant meal or a few gallons of petrol, does not secretly hope that the charge slip will be lost? There is the clue. The perfect bill is the one that never arrives.

WHIZZERS AND CHIPS

The term whizz-kid had not been coined when, as a kid, I whizzed – or thought I did. Looking back, it is evident that I did not so much whizz as whirr, like a humming top – a resemblance strengthened by my aptitude for going round in circles.

By the age of twelve I had built up a profitable newspaper round, a nice little firewood business, a soapbox-on-wheels grocery delivery service for old ladies, the caddying concession with the only golfer in our street, and a contract from the corner sweetshop to trundle a bike-load of ice-cream from the Walls' depot every Saturday.

Some weeks I cleared a pound. But it was not whizzery. It was work. Character-building no doubt, but with all the millionaire potential of a stint on the treadmill.

The authentic, 22-carat whizz-kid in the neighbourhood was Bullock (real name changed to protect the group of companies of which he is doubtless now chairman).

Bullock, working for a rival newsagent, was my opposite number on the paper round. It was noticeable, however, that he was rarely to be found delivering newspapers. Bullock paid others to do that, being ever-ready to hand over his paper-sack, directly he was out of sight of his employer, to any urchin willing to do a shilling's work for sixpence. Some of the smaller ones even did the job for nothing, for the grown-up thrill of it. I would not have been in the least surprised to learn that one or two even paid him, like Tom Sawyer's friends clamouring to whitewash the fence.

Bullock did not fritter away the time thus saved on tree-climbing or games of marbles. He put it to good use in building up his window-cleaning round – already a substantial enterprise, for all that he had to restrict himself to bungalows and ground-floor flats on account of not possessing a ladder.

Here again, you did not often come across Bullock doing the donkey work himself personally. He had a tribe of sweated labourers to do that. Bullock's role was to drum up trade, collect the takings, and punch up rivals trying to infiltrate his territory.

Bullock did, in the fullness of time, become a professional window-cleaner, when no doubt to his disgust he was obliged for a while to sully his hands with the suds and chamois-leather. It was not long, however, before he had diversified, utilising his barrow to get rid of his clients' unwanted junk, as a favour to them. The last I heard of him he had his own scrapyard. He was not yet twenty.

Small beer, of course, compared with the whizz-kiddery you hear of these days. There are, I am told, young Rockefellers who would still be in knee pants if knee pants were still worn, making £50,000 a year out of writing computer games.

One young shaver in Lancashire has a chauffeur-driven Rolls Royce. He doesn't really approve of the ostentation of having his own chauffeur, but he isn't old enough to drive.

The principle, though, remains the same. A whizz-kid is an irrepressible force meeting an irresistible opportunity. When opportunity and opportunist are in perfect sync, like the winning symbols on a fruit machine, then the jackpot follows automatically.

Talent is not enough. Mozart was touring Europe at the age of six, but he was not a whizz-kid, which is why he died poor. Now if he'd had a six-year-old road manager, there really would have been a true whizz-kid in the Mozart camp.

By the time my own desultory efforts at whizzery had fizzled out, and I was obliged to put myself to the mortification of taking a job, the first pop stars of the pre-Beatles dynasty were beginning to appear on the scene. But they weren't whizz-kids either. The real whizz-kids were their equally youthful managers who perceived not only that their clients had tremendous selling potential, but what was far more to the point, that the new teenage audience had tremendous buying potential. You had to be young yourself to realise that the young now had money – and to know on what they were prepared to spend it.

The whizz-kids of the 80s, as we all well know, are totally computer-orientated, making their fortunes not only on incomprehensible, bloodthirsty games but on every kind of floppy disc activity. Being the first computer generation, they not only know as if by instinct how to operate the things (it has always seemed odd to me that what is first and foremost a communications system should have its instruction manuals printed in what appears to be technological Bulgarian) but they know to what use computer owners want to put them.

The boardroom decision-makers of Hirohito Software or the Grapefruit Corporation started out with the delusion that what the home computer buff mostly wants is a neat electronic system for filing his bank statements and insurance policies. It took Grapefruit and Hirohito's pint-sized young boffins to show them that what the home computer buff really needs is a game called Galaxy Terror which gives him a sporting chance of committing universal genocide.

Being well on the road to becoming millionaires before they need to shave every day is certainly a better prospect for the younger generation than working in the blacking factory or getting stuffed up chimneys, which is as far as their Victorian counterparts got with their junior entrepreneurism (though my friend Bullock, had he been around at that time, would have probably done a brisk trade selling his schoolmates to the sweep at three-pence a head). The pity is that of all the teenage opportunists we must be turning out each year, the opportunities are there for only a fraction of them.

I wonder how it would be if other industries, not only those in the business of producing discs either floppy or vinyl, were to try tapping the potential of the comprehensive schools, rather than the universities (where, anyway, the milk-round seems to have all but dried up), for their future high-fliers.

If I were a publisher about to launch a new comic, I wouldn't mind having a ten-year-old adviser to tell me that calling it *Our Children's Own Weekly* is perhaps rather a passé idea. Were I Rowntree-Mackintosh, I think I should regard a gobstopper consultant as an essential appointment. As a toy manufacturer, I should not dream of deciding whether to sink my hard-won capital into the new revolutionary Garden Slug Doll until it had been fondled by – or thrown out of her office window by – my Chief Dolly, Teddy and Golly Executive, and she had prepared a report on her toy typewriter.

It would all, I suppose, have to be subject to those tedious regulations originally framed to keep schoolchildren out of the coal-mines and now enlarged to keep them out of almost any form of profit-making activity without stringent supervision and strict limitation of their working hours.

Nobody would wish to shove them back into the factories, even if there were still factories to shove them into – but I do feel rather sorry for youngsters prevented by the Inspector from working in dad's shop (or dad's sweatshop) after school. It may stop them from getting rings around their eyes but it may also stop them from blossoming out as entrepreneurs in their own right.

Not that my friend Bullock would have put up with any of that nonsense about having to have qualifications before being allowed to learn the hard way that they probably won't get you very far. If he were starting all over again today as a schoolboy whizz-kid, you may be sure that being barely able to read or write would not have inhibited him from grabbing his share of the computer boom.

He would be out there with his barrow buying obsolete hardware for scrap.

INQUIRE WITHIN

Any non-textbook writer whose work is used in schools will recognize this as a typical letter:

'Dear Mr Waterhouse, Our class have been reading your novel *There Is a Happy Land* and we have to find out about its author and why this book came to be written. Could you please tell me about yourself? Have you written any other books, if so which? Why did this book come to be written? When did you write it? Are the people real? How did you get it published? ...'

Occasionally, if my thirteen-to-fourteen-year-old correspondent appears to have enjoyed the book, or even offers some trifling proof of actually having read a page or two, I might sit down and try to answer a letter of that kind in as much detail as I have time for. Otherwise it is the brief note explaining that I am very busy earning a living but would happily answer a questionnaire requiring brief answers. Back comes the questionnaire: Why did this book come to be written? When did you write it? How did you get it published?

Now I know little about how classrooms are run these days, but I imagine that children do not write and post these letters off their own bat without their teachers being involved somewhere along the line. Would a teacher have monitored the above letter, and if so, would it not have been within her brief to suggest some sharper questions? ('Are the people real?' is the only one out of the six likely to stimulate a reply worth reading.) And if she didn't monitor it, is she aware that a classroom of girls will soon be moving out of her care without knowing how to ask questions or acquire information?

My postal address will have presumably been furnished by the teacher herself, who got it from a reference book. Did she tell her class where this reference book might be consulted, so that they might research the basic facts ('Have you written any other books, if so which?') for themselves? If not, why does she keep this tool to herself? Are sources of information classified, to be consulted only by those with the proper professional qualification?

My earliest ambition was to become a composer of music. To this end I began to compile for myself a dictionary of musical terms, picked up from song books, sixpenny 'home pianoforte tutors' and suchlike. One day I showed this work in progress to a teacher, who congratulated me on my enterprise. He did not trouble to point out, however, that by going along to the reference library and consulting Grove's *Dictionary of Music* I could save myself a considerable amount of labour, as well as acquire a more accurate definition of *pizzicato*.

Was he anxious not to flatten me? Was he himself ignorant of Grove's? Or was he protecting his sources?

Schools have changed enormously since I was at one but it seems to me that in one respect they have remained the same. Children are not taught how to find things out. Nor, of course, is this deficiency confined to their inability to ask impatient authors the right sort of questions, or to their ignorance of the whereabouts (even the existence) of the nearest reference library, let alone the materials it houses. Children – I am talking in the wildest general terms – *do not know where anything is*. No one has told them about the Yellow Pages. No one has shown them how to use a street directory. They do not understand timetables – every bus station, during the football season, has its wandering tribe of youths drifting aimlessly from one bay to the next. Without the special ticket for the special train, and the cordon of officials and policemen to marshal them, they are lost.

This is beginning to sound like petulance. Very well: let me broaden my prospectus a little. The more complex our lives become (actually, I don't observe that my own life is becoming more complex, but the apparatus for running it certainly is), the greater the mass of data that must be kept on file. We don't have to know what this data is in detail, but we have to know where it is kept and how to get at it. Every citizen his own computer, with serviced memory bank. At the age of fifteen all children should be able to find the answers to these questions: What stamps would you need for a 1½oz airmail letter to Fiji? What is the address of the nearest NatWest Bank? Who is Lord Mayor of Birmingham? What number would you ring if your roof leaked? How would you get from here to Dieppe? And so on.

When I have pursued this theme with teacher friends they have usually, after giving me the inevitable apologia about how difficult it is to do anything outside the syllabus when O-level pressures are building up, gone on to protest that yes, they do perfectly understand the importance of equipping their students for Every-day Life and, indeed, to take last term alone, the class has paid fruitful visits to the town hall, the magistrates' court and the fire station.

But we are not, are we, talking about Everyday Life or that dumping-ground of all the virtues that used to be known, in my own schooldays, as Civics? We are talking about that dying art, initiative.

It is not a quality that is very much taught these days, because it is not a quality that is very much in demand. Certainly our old friend Everyday Life has little call for it: it is not only the holiday tour that is packaged these days.

And when we look at the kind of education society is going to need for the years ahead, then training in self-reliance (even the very phrase has an obsolescent, B-P at Mafeking ring about it) comes yet lower down the list. We are moving – or we have been told we are moving – into an era where more and more of us, perhaps most of us, will be working in the service industries, and only a small corps of technicians will be needed to help the microprocessor make things. When high employment depends on a very large number of people performing specialized tasks, in other words applying specialist knowledge, then personal initiative is economically unpopular. Why find out how to get from here to Dieppe when the travel agent will do it for you? Why keep a dog and bark yourself? Why learn to tell the time when you have a digital watch?

But it is not only the kind of education that society collectively needs that is important, otherwise everyone at Oxbridge would be wearing white overalls, but the kind of education that individuals need. Individuals have a need, a crying need in my view, to be less passive than they are becoming. Society has a vested interest in passivity: it is what makes the machine work smoothly. But I would rather that individuals were the grit in the machine than the cogs ... and I am not talking here about small acts of defiance against the computer (such as deliberately folding and spindling, whatever spindling may be, that which the printout decrees must not be folded or spindled), or painting the council-house door green contrary to regulations, but about not being totally reliant on whatever system has been provided, at whatever level of effi-ciency or non-efficiency that happens to be currently acceptable and economically viable. And come to think of it, society at large would be the benefactor after all, for where there are no regiments there can be no mutinies.

Teaching a child how to use *Whitaker's Almanack* is not, of itself, going to create a new breed or revive an old one. But those of us with access to a modern dictionary of quotations know what small steps for man lead to.

WHEN THE GADGETS HAVE TO STOP

I have just refused to give house-room to a self-employed time-switch. You have to make a stand somewhere. There are already time-switches in my house but they have regular jobs and I know what they are up to. One of them, with an intermittent zonking noise, controls the central heating. Another, when given the chance, operates the cooker. A third pads into the bathroom at dawn and puts on the immersion heater.

The freelance time-switch I have turned away from the door does not have its insurance card stamped by the North Eastern Gas Board, the LEB or any other organisation that will normally come and look at my household appliances when smoke starts coming out of them. This time-switch is responsible to nobody.

In appearance it is like one of those adaptors you take abroad to stop your hair rollers or electric razor blowing up when brought into contact with inferior foreign electricity. All you have to do with a cowboy time-switch is attach it to any plug in the house and at once it will start time-switching away like billy-o.

The versatile little chap can boil an electric kettle every hour on the hour, warm up the electric iron, switch on a fire (one bar or two – just state your preference), and, for all I know, put the dog out – all in your absence. It can, if you so desire it, make a quantity of toast while you are at the pictures.

I am sorry to be an old steam-age stick-in-the-mud, but I do not want plastic wiring devices pottering about my kitchen when I am not there, snooping into the breadbin and no doubt making themselves cups of coffee, scoffing the last of the Marie Louise biscuits and listening to the afternoon play on Radio 4.

I do not, if it comes to that, want a cooker that suddenly takes it into its head to give itself a good wash and brush-up at ten in the evening, when all normal cookers are asleep: but that is a battle I have fought and lost. I sometimes arrive home unexpectedly and find that cooker calmly basting a turkey for all the world as if it owns the place – and I swear it sniggers to itself when I tiptoe out of the kitchen.

I have so far stood firm, however, against having bedroom lights that flash on and off at regular intervals to let burglars know I'm on holiday. And I am standing firm against that roving time-switch – so if it is still hanging about on my doorstep, hoping to be let in, it can clear off.

I do not want you to think I am one of those anti-gadget people. My house is crammed with gadgets. I shave with a gadget, write with a gadget, drive a gadget to the office, ring up friends on a gadget, keep my milk and eggs in a gadget, watch Morecambe and Wise on a gadget; I command, in short, enough machinery to mount a small industrial exhibition. It is the machinery that tries to command *me* that causes trouble. Where gadgets and I part company is when they want to be boss.

Now at this point I can hear a plaintive time-switch in search of a home piping up through my letter-box: 'Please, mister, we can't do anything you don't make us do. If you don't want toast when you come back from the Odeon, you only have to say the word and I'll switch on your electric blanket instead.' A likely story. Let that time-switch across the threshold and it would have my toaster at it like a pop-up Pinocchio.

Take my television set – please. I have just said I watch Morecambe and Wise on a gadget. Correction: I watch Morecambe and Wise when the gadget allows me to. Now at one time, when I had one of those dear old-fashioned sets with a horizontal hold, a vertical hold and various other twiddling devices, the telly and I had a very clear understanding. If its picture went wobbly, it knew that it would get twiddled. If it went even wobblier, it knew that it would get kicked. A TV responds to treatment like that and no one was sadder than I when it finally blew up.

I got a replacement and what, to my horror, did I find? Or rather, not find? *No twiddling knobs.* What they have given me is one of those remote-control devices which you point at the set and then press a button. All very well for directing a child's electronic robot, I suppose, but not so hot at directing a television set. It can switch from ITV to BBC1 and from BBC1 to BBC2, it can make the colour brighter or unbrighter as the case may be, it can control the sound but it refuses to have anything to do with the picture when it wobbles. The loss of my twiddling rights does not only mean wobbling orgies. Worse still, this push-button thing is stone deaf. Now that the TV set calls the odds, *News at Ten* sounds like the night shift in a boiler factory and I'm powerless to intervene!

Emboldened by what it has been able to get away with so far, my TV is now trying to persuade me to take in one of its friends as a lodger. It keeps getting the rental firm which planted it on me to send me alluring brochures suggesting that I could transform my life by investing in a video recorder. You bet it would transform my life. I would only have to turn my back to ten minutes, and the pair of them would be making pornographic movies. With wobbling in all the right places.

If you are still not persuaded that these gadgets control their own destinies, I would like you to meet my cowardly thermometer. My heating system, as I have mentioned, is controlled by an intermittently-zonking time-switch. A close relative, for all I know, of the mendicant time-switch still mooning about outside: tipped it off, I shouldn't wonder, that I am a soft touch who will give passing time-switches a bed and a hot meal. Anyway: this zonking mechanism operates in tandem with the cowardly thermometer.

What happens is that the central heating goes on and off at specified pre-set times – *unless* it gets too hot, when it switches off at once in case the house catches fire. This is the duty of the cowardly thermometer. Being, however, a hysterical thermometer, it believes we are all in danger of roasting in our beds at a temperature of fifty-eight degrees. So I spend most of my life freezing.

As if stone-deaf push-button things, thermometers lacking in moral fibre and zonking time-switches were not enough, you will have read in the papers that before the decade is over our homes will be equipped with micro-chip consoles which we will only have to play like cinema organs to whistle up groceries, holiday arrangements, banking facilities and the like. When that happens, the machinery will truly have taken over and I propose to start life afresh in a remote country cottage powered only by burning logs.

In the meantime, if that itinerant time-switch doesn't move on instantly, I am going to get my Ansaphone to call the police.

MINE HOSTESS

Although I keep coming across the term 'brilliant hostess' in biographies, obituaries and society columns, I've never been sure what it means. How can you be brilliant at telling the cook there'll be sixteen for dinner tonight, or hiring a band and a marquee and inviting a thousand close friends round to your annual knees-up?

I have never personally witnessed this brilliance taking place. I have seen hostesses being competent, bitchy, drunk, mean, generous, hysterical, outrageous, but I have never seen them being brilliant. Perhaps I move in the wrong circles.

Does a brilliant hostess flit from group to group trilling epigrams? Does she do tricks? Can she balance a cocktail cherry on her nose, at the same time juggling with the cheese footballs?

Some brilliant hostesses are, or were back in those golden Cliveden days, brilliant *political* hostesses, influencing world events like billy-o. 'Neville, I don't think you've met Adolf Hitler. Adolf, this is Neville Chamberlain. Neville has been telling us all about his goldfish.'

Then we have hostesses so brilliant that mighty corporations have grown mightier as a direct result of their social HQ. The merger, so gossip has it, was sealed at a brilliant dinner party thrown by the brilliant Mrs Chequely-Stubbs. 'Talking of holidays – do have another choccy-mint – Alfred was saying earlier that the four of us ought to pop over to Bermuda next weekend. Bring a beach towel and your balance sheets.'

There are, however, brilliant theatrical hostesses, I know, because I have met them. A brilliant director spends three months getting it on the stage, a brilliant designer builds his set, a brilliant cast slogs its guts out, the whole thing is a brilliant success and then this brilliant hostess throws a first-night party and gets better reviews (in Jennifer's Diary) than the whole pack of them put together.

Brilliant literary hostesses collect fashionable authors as if they were commemorative pewter medallions. At the end of the day it is the authors who are remaindered, never the hostess, whose Wednesdays become legendary and get written about in Bloomsbury memoirs. Consider how many of the leading literary lights of the Twenties and Thirties were acclaimed for nothing more tangibly substantial than their anchovy canapés.

Before I get struck off the social register I should throw in the qualification that yes, I have often met brilliant women, and usually at parties. Sometimes they have turned out to be my hostess, so I suppose it could be quibbled that I am acquainted with brilliant hostesses in the sense that if I know a first-class violinist who happens to drive very well, then I am acquainted with a brilliant motorist. What I am trying to get at it that whatever these hostesses were brilliant at, it was not at getting the guests to mingle or telling the waitress not to give that lady with the cigarette-holder any more vodka. This is the kind of thing you pick up as you go along, or learn from magazine articles. You can become proficient at it but you cannot be brilliant at it, any more than you can be brilliant at repairing bicycle inner-tubes.

The real genius of most of the parties I have been to, it has always seemed to me, has been the catering firm that can judge to a fluid ounce how much gin, scotch, champagne and other libations 150 guests plus two dozen gatecrashers are likely to take on board. Compared with such a skill, the ability to remember the assembling freeloaders' names is as child's play. Yet women who would threaten you with a bunch of fives if you called them brilliant housewives will simper with pleasure if you call them brilliant hostesses. It is the last woman's-place role they still value as a social asset, the one Girl Guide's badge they still want.

Of course, plenty of women covet their cookery badge, too, but that's a unisex award. The party-throwers' chevron isn't. While a man may don his butcher's apron and acquire a reputation as a brilliant cook, you never hear of a man being a brilliant host.

Now why is this? Men do, after all, give parties. Some of them give memorable parties. But they do not make a career out of it. Otherwise they would list party-throwing among their accomplishments in *Who's Who*.

The fact is that parties given by men differ in one important respect from those given by women. Men give parties for their friends. Women give parties for themselves.

Male-gender hosts require nothing of their guests except that they turn up on the right evening, make themselves reasonably pleasant, don't break anything, and leave before five in the morning. Hostesses require that they arrive promptly, sober and well-attired and that thereafter – until departing within ten minutes of the time laid down on the invitation card – they obey a set of unwritten but rigid rules of protocol.

The one ritual the guests must observe above all others is that of repeatedly buttering up his hostess. He must do this for the first time the moment he crosses the threshold, when he extravagantly compliments his hostess upon her appearance. Thereafter, he must take every opportunity of making toadying remarks about the catering, the décor, the eminence of his fellow-guests and his hostess's cleverness in capturing them. He must perform a potted re-run of all these compliments upon his leave-taking, and summarise the choicest of them in writing in his bread-and-butter letter the next day.

The other important rule the fawning guest is expected to follow is that of instant obedience. He must mingle when his hostess tells him to mingle, start the queue for the buffet supper when she commands, fetch and carry, light cigarettes, find ash-trays, act as part-time cloakroom attendant and generally make himself useful. His reward – to be invited again. To another brilliant party.

It would be unfair to suggest that the brilliant hostess doesn't do any work herself. She has all that exhausting listening to do, to begin with, as her guests queue two-deep to tell her how ravishing she's looking. Then she has to keep an eye out for husbands talking to wives or old friends greeting one another, so that she can break them up and make them exchange small-talk with complete strangers. That's pretty tiring, too. And finally she has all that bossing around to do, as she orders one guest to be a darling and start a movement into the garden, another to phone for a cab for Mrs So-and-So; another to fetch her cigarette-holder.

At the end of it all, she probably collapses with a migraine, but it all seems worthwhile when she remembers how brilliant she was – or, if she cannot actually remember being brilliant at any given moment, how brilliant everyone said she was.

Why does she do it? For the same reason that the caterpillar turns into a butterfly, I suppose. But much as the butterfly is admired for its beauty as it dallies over a cocktail-hour nectar with its wide circle of escorts and hangers-on, no one, so far as I know, ever calls it brilliant.

HOW LONG, O LORD ...?

And God said unto Noah, Make thee an ark of gopher wood; rooms shalt thou make in the ark, and the length of the ark shall be 300 cubits.

And of every living thing of all flesh, two of every sort shalt thou bring into the ark, to keep them alive with thee.

And Noah said, Sign here, and leavest Thou a deposit.

And the Lord signed there, and left He a deposit.

And Noah was 600 years old when the flood of waters was upon the Earth.

And the Lord said unto Noah, Where is the ark, which I commanded thee to build?

And Noah said unto the Lord, Verily, I have had three carpenters off ill.

The gopher wood supplier hath let me down – yea, even though the gopher wood hath been on order for nigh upon twelve months. The damp-course specialist hath not turned up. What can I do, O lord?

And God said unto Noah, I want that ark finished even after seven days and seven nights.

And Noah said, It will be so.

And it was not so.

And the Lord said unto Noah, What seemeth to be the trouble this time?

And Noah said unto the Lord, Mine sub-contractor hath gone bankrupt. The pitch which Thou commandest me to put on the outside and on the inside of the ark hath not arrived. The plumber hath gone on strike.

Noah rent his garments and said, The glazier departeth on holiday to Majorca – yea, even though I offerest him double time. Shem, my son, who helpeth me on the ark side of the business, hath formed a pop group with his brothers Ham and Japheth. Lord, I am undone.

And God said in his wrath, Noah, do not thou mucketh Me about.

The end of all flesh is come before me; for the Earth is filled with violence through them; and behold, I will destroy them with the Earth. How can I destroy them with the Earth if thou art incapable of completing the job that thou was contracted to do?

And Noah said, Lo, the contract will be fulfilled.

And Lo, it was not fulfilled.

And Noah said unto the Lord, The gopher wood is definitely in the warehouse. Verily, and the gopher wood supplier waiteth only upon his servant to find the invoices before he delivereth the gopher wood unto me.

And the Lord grew angry and said, Scrubbeth thou round the gopher wood. What about the animals?

Of fowls after their kind, and of cattle after their kind, of every creeping thing of the Earth after his kind, two of every sort have I ordered to come unto thee, to keep them alive.

Where for example, are the giraffes?

And Noah said unto the Lord, They are expected today.

And the Lord said unto Noah, And where are the clean beasts, the male and the female; to keep their seed alive upon the face of all the Earth?

And Noah said, The van commeth on Tuesday; yea and yea, it will be so.

And the Lord said unto Noah, How about the unicorns?

And Noah wrung his hands and wept, saying, Lord, Lord, they are a discontinued line. Thou canst not get unicorns for love nor money.

And God said, Come thou, Noah, I have left with thee a deposit, and thou hast signed a contract.

Where are the monkeys, and the bears, and the hippopotami, and the elephants, and the zebras and the hartebeests, two of each kind; and of fowls also of the air by sevens, the male and the female?

And Noah said unto the Lord, They have been delivered unto the wrong address, but should arriveth on Friday; all save the fowls of the air by sevens, for it hath just been told unto me that fowls of the air are sold only in half-dozens.

And God said unto Noah, Thou hast not made an ark of gopher

wood, nor hast thou lined it with pitch within and without; and of every living thing of all flesh, two of every sort hast thou failed to bring into the ark. What sayest thou, Noah?

And Noah kissed the Earth and said, Lord, Lord, thou knowest in thy wisdom what it is like with delivery dates.

And the Lord in his wisdom said, Noah, my son, I knowest. Why else dost thou think I have caused a flood to descend upon the Earth?

BAH, HUMBUG

Another rousing victory for the fanatics of the no-smoking lobby, as a firm of stickjaw manufacturers gives this po-faced explanation of why its sweetie cigarettes are no longer red-tipped:

'We are changing the description of this product from cigarettes to candy sticks because of the general climate of opinion on smoking as a health hazard, and the product, therefore, is made without the red end.'

Stand by for future campaigns on the rampant sexism in jelly babies, the obesity factor in everlasting toffee, the threat to numeracy in the inaccurately-named hundreds and thousands, the dangers of alcoholism in wine gums, the cocaine-sniffing potentiality of sherbet dabs, the vivisection propaganda inherent in sugar mice, and the implied racialism in the colour of licorice boot-laces.

Humbug, I call it.

5

THAT PERFECT
SPHERICAL PUDDING

PASSING THE PARCEL

PASSING THE PARCEL

Christmas Eve seems as good a time as any to tell you about the most humiliating moment of my life.

There are those around me who regard me as the man who has everything. But this was the year I was the man who got nothing.

I was nine. The occasion was the most wonderful Christmas party I had ever been to, notwithstanding the distressing episode I am about to relate.

It was the most wonderful because it was the only one I had ever been invited to.

Parties did not grow on trees round our way. The year before, a boy called Jackie Arnold had given one but I wasn't asked. Thinking this an oversight, since he happened to be my best friend, I drew his attention to the omission.

'You can't come because my mother says you're too dirty,' confided Jackie. It seemed an eminently reasonable explanation and I readily accepted that one cannot expect to move about in society and boast a full engagement diary unless one washes one's neck.

I must have cleaned up my act a bit by the following year for I did receive a formal invitation to a reception given by no less a personage than the vicar, in his capacity as custodian of the Sunday School.

I accepted with alacrity.

It was quite a party. There were balloons by the ten. There were enough potted meat sandwiches to feed the five thousand. Jelly of all hues, including a violent purple that took my fancy, existed in such prodigious quantities that to this day I cannot look a purple jelly in the face without out-quivering it in my nausea.

But in particular there were parcels. There they were stacked up six deep under the Christmas tree – pink crepe-paper-covered parcels and blue crepe-papered-covered parcels, the size and shape of shoeboxes. I had never seen so many parcels. I tell you, it was like Mount Pleasant sorting office under that tree.

Tea was demolished, lemonade was swigged, and the walking wounded were escorted to the parish hall equivalent of the Roman vomitarium. Crackers were pulled. Hair was pulled, Games were played. Noses were bloodied. And then, the moment we had been waiting for.

Enter, stage right, Father Christmas.

Positioning himself by the parcel mountain, Santa proceeded to call out names in what seemed to me an uncanny imitation of the vicar's reedy voice. The guests trooped up in alphabetical order, to be handed either a pink parcel or a blue parcel according to sex.

As I have had occasion to note all through my life, it is a long wait to the W's. I squirmed with apprehension as I saw the Everest of parcels slowly diminishing to a mere parcel Alp – would there, I wondered anxiously, be any parcels left by the time it was my turn?

I worried the more so when I perceived that some lucky devils were receiving not one parcel but two. One young shaver even got away with three. I guessed that they must be the Sunday school teacher's pets. She was acting as Santa's assistant and probably tipping him the wink.

Despite this profligacy, there were still parcels a-plenty when my name was finally called. I positioned myself expectantly in front of Santa and simpered at the Sunday school teacher. Maybe, unknown to myself, I was one of her favourites too and would be the lucky recipient of two parcels?

I wasn't. One meagre blue crepe-paper-covered shoebox parcel was shoved into my hand and the Sunday school teacher hissed: 'What do you say to Santa?'

Aggrieved, I heard myself piping up, 'Could I have another one, please?'

Move over, Oliver Twist. There was an astounded gasp from the Sunday school teacher, an even more astounded gasp from Father Christmas, and a silence you could market to Trappist monks from the assembled rabble.

'This ungrateful boy,' announced Santa, now sounding more like Mr Bumble the beadle than the vicar, 'has asked for two presents! Have you,' he demanded of me rhetorically, 'a sister or brother at home too young, or too ill to come to the party?'

'No, he hasn't,' snapped the Sunday school teacher, snatching my parcel from me before I had a chance to smite my big sister down with measles, 'and just for that he gets no present.'

Blubbering, I was then banished, empty-handed. And I never

did learn what was in those enticing crepe-paper-covered parcels the size and shape of shoeboxes.

I hope it was shoes.

NEVER AT CHRISTMAS

Ah, yes, to be sure – the Christmas shopping. I thought you'd never ask.

Your wish is my command. I am here to serve. Pray tell me your needs in the way of fruit and nuts, dead birds, trees and vegetation, confectionery, pharmaceutical items, diaries and oven gloves, and I shall be on my merry way, scything through the festive hordes with the single-mindedness of a United States Marine capturing Tripoli.

I am not being sarcastic. Hand me the list.

I have not been drinking. The list, the list.

There is no catch.

Well, certainly nothing that your normal, sane, reasonable wife on the Clapham omnibus would regard as a catch, anyway.

The non-catch is that when I undertook to be on my merry way, I was not proposing to set off this very second.

No, nor first thing in the morning when the shops are quiet. That, as I have found to my cost, is a fallacy. The shops are never quiet. The shops resemble a bring-and-buy sale in Hell all through the Christmas period, with the possible exception – in this first year ever – of the one day I have in mind.

I will let you in on the secret. I have hit on the stunning wheeze of doing all the Christmas shopping in one fell swoop next Sunday.

Christmas Eve minus one, yes. Sunday as ever was.

No, I have no idea what you would get if you made one fell swoop on my jugular vein with a breadknife. Fifteen years, very probably. Think of it as fifteen Christmases with no one to do your shopping. Not that you'd have much call for a twelve-pound turkey in Holloway.

I am afraid you are behind the times. It is in fact now as easy to buy a twelve-pound turkey on Sunday as on any other day. Easier. The same goes for oven gloves, bath cubes, boxes of soap in the shape of lemons, and all the other garbage you ply your relatives with at Christmas.

Because of the abolition of the iniquitous Sunday trading laws which have hitherto made the doddle of Christmas shopping on the Sabbath an impossible dream – that's how come. Don't you ever read the papers?

Yes, I do read them too, and not the Hindustani ones either. I am fully aware that technically the abolition has yet to take place. But effectively, in that fewer and fewer shopkeepers are taking a blind bit of notice of them, the iniquitous Sunday trading laws of which we speak are a dead duck or a cooked goose.

How do you mean – but not a deceased twelve-pound turkey? Are you suggesting that having left this house on Sunday morning with your interminable Christmas list in my hand, I am likely to return minus the centrepiece of the entire bloody festivities, namely the bloody turkey?

By threatening that if I do, I will go out again quicker than I came in, you are unwittingly revealing your lack of faith in my ability to get all the Christmas shopping done between eleven and noon on Sunday morning.

Noon does happen to be the hour the boozers open, yes – the State not yet choosing to show the same relaxed attitude to the licensing laws as to the Sunday trading laws.

Why would I leave the twelve-pound turkey under a bar stool? According to you, twelve-pound turkeys are unobtainable on the Lord's Day. You cannot have it both ways.

I am not suggesting that Oxford Street this Sunday will resemble an Oriental souk, no. I am suggesting that certain stores will be open, certain others closed. Certain bath cube stores will be open, fear not. Certain turkey stores will be open. Certain oven gloves stores will be open.

Then we'll just have to wait and see whether I am reduced to restricting the Christmas shopping to what is on offer from a man selling novelties from a suitcase on the pavement, won't we? So long as he has twelve-pound turkeys for sale, no questions asked, I do not see how you will be in any way inconvenienced.

Yes, I suppose I could, rather than sit here arguing, nip up to Oxford Street this minute and find out exactly which shops will be open on Sunday.

Yes, I suppose I could, if you want to put it like that and you always do, get the Christmas shopping over with at the same time.

SHEPHERDS' WARNING

And there were in that country shepherds abiding in the field, keeping watch over their flock by night. And lo, the angel of the Lord came upon them, saying Fear not, for behold, I bring you good tidings of great joy.

And it came to pass, as the angels were gone away from them into heaven, the shepherds said one to another, Let us now go even unto Bethlehem.

And they rode out with great haste, until lo, they chanced upon an police road block, where an constable spake unto them, saying:

Lo, lo, lo, what is all this here? Hold your horses.

And the shepherds replied unto the constable, saying Asses, actually.

And the constable waxed exceeding angry, saying I do not want none of your lip. Who art thou and what art thou about?

And it came to pass, when they had told him who they were, the constable said If you are shepherds, where are your sheep?

Then did the shepherds tell the constable about the angel of the Lord who had come among them – and commanded them to go forth unto the city of David.

And having heard them, the constable said It is funny you should say that. I have just had three wise men along with the exact self-same story, but when subjected to a body search, lo, they were carrying certain substances.

Then chiselled he the names of the three shepherds upon his note-tablet, saying Verily, I have you lads banged to rights. You are part of this gold, frankincense and myrrh smuggling ring, are not you?

And the shepherds beat their breasts, wailing Verily, we are but poor shepherds who were minding their own business in yonder field when this zonking great angel came down and made us sore afraid.

And the constable asked How knowest thou it was an angel?

And the shepherds said He was flying.

And the constable commanded them Breathe thou into this bag.

And the shepherds protested unto the constable, saying We will swear it on a stack of scriptures. He had wings on.

Then did the constable say unto them Pulleth thou the other one, it hath bells on it.

And the shepherds asked Wherefore thinkest thou, then, that we are riding unto Bethlehem in the middle of the flaming night?

And the constable spake loudly, saying Wherefore thinkest I? Wherefore thinkest I? I will tell you wherefore I thinkest, sunshines. I thinkest that you are illegal pickets, and I am advising you to get back to that field and keep watch over your flock a bit sharpish, like good little shepherds.

But the shepherds stayed their ground, saying We are law-abiding citizens going about our lawful business. What authority hast though for turning us back?

And the constable regarded their asses, asking of the shepherds, Have these animals got MoT certificates?

And it came to pass that the shepherds produced their road-worthy scrolls for their asses, begging of the constable Now will you let us through to Bethlehem?

And the constable said I could always get you for obstruction, you know.

And the shepherds said It is thou who art obstructing. We are not pickets. We are not smugglers. We are not drunks. We are shepherds.

And the constable pushed back his helmet and scratched his head, saying Tell me again why you're so keen on getting to Bethlehem – for Verily, I am a bit hazy on the details.

And the shepherds told the constable that a sign had been given to them, that they would find a babe wrapped in swaddling clothes, lying in a manger.

And the constable said And you got all this from the angel, did you?

And the shepherds said Yea, Verily.

Then sighed the constable, saying, Lo, there are three born every minute. On your merry way, then, but when you get back to your field, do not come complaining to me that the sheep rustler you saw dangling from a tree with papyrus wings strapped to his back has had it away with your flock.

THE GIFT OF THE MAGI

Back in the year dot there was a master story-teller named O. Henry. The best story he ever wrote was 'The Gift of the Magi'.

It was about a poor young couple with no money to buy Christmas presents. All he possessed was his pocket watch. All she possessed was her fine head of golden hair.

The young man sold his watch to buy a comb for his wife's hair. The young wife sold her hair to buy a chain for her husband's watch. Thus both presents were useless, yet both their recipients had been blessed with a gift of the Magi.

I cannot hope to match that story but I do have a tale of sorts to tell. This one goes back only as far as the year dot and a dash, and while it too concerns a young couple, they were unmarried, being only around seven years old.

Nor was this young man penniless. Jack, as I shall call him, possessed great wealth in the form of a silver threepenny bit. Whether he had earned it, found it, saved it up, or acquired it by other means was unclear, and his mother did not enquire too closely. It was that kind of family.

She was very positive, however, about how the money should be spent. 'You can take yourself down to the shop and get a Christmas present for your dad,' she told Jack. 'It'll put his lordship in a good mood when he rolls back from the Mason's Arms.'

The rolling back of Jack's dad from the Mason's Arms regularly enlivened the neighbourhood. Sometimes it was so much enlivened that the police had to be called. There could be no shrewder investment of a silver threepenny bit.

'And if you spend it on yourself,' Jack's mother warned, 'you'll get a hammering.'

On the way Jack fell in with his friend Janet from next door. She too was going to the shop, but only to look in the window. There is no one so poor that someone else isn't poorer than Jack by threepence.

Yet magic things happen at Christmas time, and before Jack and Janet had reached the shop, the silver threepenny bit had changed hands. I would like to report that Jack had fallen victim to a rare attack of Christian charity, but it would not be true. Curiosity, not generosity, was the spur.

For several weeks there had been a rumour sweeping the district that girls were different in some physical essential from boys. Jack, a materialist rather than a theorist, put the suggestion to Janet that they should check the story themselves. Janet did not demur. The consultation took place behind the tin-roofed Baptist tabernacle next door to the shop. The consultation fee was threepence.

Jack planned to tell his mother he had been robbed by a gang of big boys. If he pulled out his loose tooth and smeared blood on his face there was an outside chance she might believe him.

After prolonged deliberation and much unsolicited advice from the silver threepenny bit's previous owner, Janet sank her earnings in three plumpo, pink, sugar pigs. One she ate on the spot, one she took home to her mother, who accused her of shoplifting and gave her a good hiding, and the third she gave to Jack.

Again I would like to say that the spirit of Christmas had been the motive but again it was not so. Janet was moved to hand over the sugar pig to Jack by a threat of physical violence.

Jack showed the sugar pig to his mother and told her it had cost threepence. If she suspected he had spent some of the money on himself she didn't let on. Presently, Jack's dad rolled back from the Mason's Arms in a mercurial mood wavering between ill-temper and oafish good humour. Jack gave him the sugar pig, now stickily embossed with fingerprints. 'He must have more money than sense, spending threepence on this,' grumbled Jack's dad. 'Anyway, he knows I don't like sweet stuff.'

'Get it down you and stop chuntering,' said Jack's mother. So he ate the sugar pig then dug two new pennies out of his waistcoat and gave them to Jack. 'Here – and don't spend them all at once.'

Jack ran to the shop and bought two more sugar pigs. He ate one on the way home and was about to start on the other when he came across Janet crying. And so he gave the second sugar pig to her.

For the third and last time I would like to say that here was an act of selfless generosity. And indeed, for once I cannot prove that it was not – although a likelier explanation would be that Jack was not all that struck on sugar pigs.

And that's all there is. As I say, it's not much of a story – certainly not a patch on O. Henry's. But rummage around in it and you'll find the gift of the Magi there somewhere, albeit a bit grubby.

MY GIDDY AUNT

Much ink – almost as much ink as drink – is consumed each Christmas on advice as to what we should take and what we should leave alone in the way of festive alcoholic beverages.

This year I am among the scribes to whom this annual task has fallen. Unfortunately, I am not much of an expert on which particular room-temperature Sauternes should be served with the roast goose. I shall confine myself, therefore, to a field in which I can claim to be more knowledgeable – the pitfalls attending Christmas drinking.

I give you my ABC of hazards to watch out for twixt cup and lip (not to mention after cup and lip have made contact).

Aunts, Giddy: Female relatives of a certain age who take only an annual glass of rhubarb wine should not be persuaded to drink champagne, port or any other intoxicant on the basis that it will do them good, that it is only once a year, that a thimbleful cannot harm them, etc. The cry 'Go on, be a devil!' ought particularly to be avoided. You have heard the expression 'Let sleeping dogs lie'? An alcohol-awakened aunt attempting the can-can is an awesome sight to behold. Besides, she might get the taste for it and squander your expectations of gin.

Bottle-openers, Missing: Unless you have a built-in bottle-opener in your kitchen or cocktail cabinet, you are going to discover one minute after the shops close on Christmas Eve that the bottle-opener has vanished. That's the new bottle-opener – the one you bought after last Christmas to replace the old bottle-opener which still hasn't turned up. Blame the borrowers and open a six-pack.

Corkscrews, Mislaid: I can tell you exactly where your corkscrew is – it's with the bottle-opener. Write it off and resort to ingenuity. Push the cork gently down into the bottle with your finger, wipe the wine off your best suit with a tea-towel, and decant.

Dogs, Hairs of the: (See also *Hangovers, Certainty of*) It is tempting, in a house that temporarily resembles the American bar of a cruise liner, to re-write the nautical almanac so that the sun is over the yardarm at about 9.30 a.m. Combined with this urge is a belief that tomato juice and Worcester sauce render vodka practically non-alcoholic. Resist it. If you feel awful now, when you didn't start drinking till almost noon yesterday, think how you're likely to feel tomorrow.

Eggnogs, Non-immunity of: (See *Dogs, Hairs of the*) Because these lethal concoctions contain a generous measure of what are usually breakfast ingredients, there is a school which holds that a shaker of them is a perfect way to start Boxing Day. The same school probably believes that because *crème de menthe* tastes of peppermint, it is good for brushing the teeth with. As noted above, the addition of health-giving materials does not make a drink any healthier.

Frappés, Dangers attending: If you intend to crush the ice with the coal hammer, like you did last year, you are once again going to finish up with a bruised thumb and some black ice.

Glass, Broken: It is inevitable that at least one glass will be broken over Christmas, so use that set of eleven surviving from last year, and leave the good stuff in the sideboard for a really special occasion – such as celebrating having broken the last of your eleven cheap glasses. The only other thing to remember about broken glasses is that, no matter how many pieces you pick up, there is always one more.

Hangovers, Certainty of: Popular belief (despite popular experience) has it that there is a hangover amnesty during Christmas. Not so. The liver knows no seasons. I will not waste your time by counselling you to avoid getting a hangover by drinking wisely and moderately. Wise, moderate drinkers do not get hangovers and so do not have to be warned. Unwise, immoderate drinkers need only be told that they have as much chance of finding a hangover cure as they have of curing the common cold.

Innovations, Avoidance of: An attempt will be made by someone or other over Christmas to introduce you to a new cocktail – the whisky Martini, say, or the Pink Pussycat's Whiskers. Refuse it – particularly if it is the perpetrator's own invention.

Jeroboams, Hidden capacity of: A bottle of champagne, once opened, contains less champagne than you thought. A Jeroboam, on the other hand, contains more than it can possibly hold – especially if your company is small. Either get one of those patent stoppers to keep the bubbles in or find some more guests and serve it with loaves and fishes.

Kirsch, Tendency to slosh: A general rule is not to encourage persons unused to drinking to prepare or serve drinks. A particular rule is never to allow them to pour kirsch over the fruit salad. By the time they have finished sloshing, you would be better advised to make your dessert of an orange and a bottle of methylated spirits.

Liqueurs, Exotic, Sampling by children of: If you insist on sicklying up your drinks cupboard with liqueurs based on cocoa, fruit, peppermint and similar sweetshop ingredients, and you have children, you may be sure that quantities of the former will end up inside the latter. Keep them locked up (the children, that is).

Mixers, Inadequate supply of: A common property of tonic water, ginger ale and other mixers is that you run out of them on Boxing Day. This rule does not apply to soda water, which runs out on Christmas Day. The only thing you can do is to ensure that you have an adequate supply, the same as you do every year.

Nine, Number, Fallacy concerning: The fallacy concerning the number nine is that not until you have had the quantity of drinks (ie, one over the eight) can you be considered intoxicated. In truth, it depends on the drinks. (See *Vodka Martinis, Caution regarding.*) The fallacy originates from the person inventing it being so smashed out of his skull that he couldn't count.

Off-licences, Uncertain hours of: Your local off-licence or wine shop keeps peculiar hours over the Christmas period. To be on the safe side, jot down the times on a piece of paper. After you have lost the piece of paper, see how much of the information you can remember. Go back to the shop to check that you are right in thinking it doesn't close till six. It will have closed at five.

Punches, Liberties taken with: Put a punch bowl on the sideboard and you are going to have half the family picking fruit out of it with their fingers and the other half adding half-eaten apples, slices of lemon from used gin-and-tonics, the remains of the baby's mashed banana and suchlike flotsam and jetsam. (Watch where the dog puts its bone.) If you don't want your punch bowl to resemble the bilges of a tramp steamer, put it in the fridge until it's needed.

Queen's broadcast, Strange accompaniment to: Not by so much as a disapproving glance does Her Majesty reveal, during her Christmas broadcast, her awareness that her subjects *en masse* are scoffing chocolate liqueurs by the crateful, with enough grenadine and *crème de cacao* to fill a swimming pool dribbling down fifty million chins. It is only a suggestion, but falling as it does between the post-punch port or brandy and the early evening sherry or gin, wouldn't this be a suitable period in which to go temporarily on the wagon?

Rouge, Vin, Acute shortage of: If, on the basis that most of your guests prefer white wine to red, you order your wines proportionately to their preferences, you are going to run out of red. If you order more red and less white, you are going to run out of white. The secret is to order too much of each, when you will run out of both.

Squalor, Matutinal: A room from which all glasses, empty bottle, corks, beer cans, ashtrays and pretzel-bowls have not been removed the night before is going to look and smell like a sump-pit the morning after. I know it's late but make the effort. If there is a jolly uncle (see *Uncles, Jolly, Piscine resemblance of*) under the table, sweep him up too.

Teenagers, Alcoholic capacity of: The teenager who assures you that he knows when he has had enough has almost certainly already had too much. It is in the nature of teenagers that they never know when they have had enough of anything. They will guzzle down any drink offered as if it were a can of fizz. Allocate them a strict ration and then switch them to fizz.

Uncles, Jolly, Piscine resemblance of: It is axiomatic that the more jolly uncles are assembled in one place, the quicker – by a factor you would not think mathematically possible – will that place's supply of booze diminish. Either stock up on booze or cut down on uncles.

Vodka Martinis, Caution regarding: Even during the festive season, it is highly reckless to knock back vodka Martinis as if there were no tomorrow. Half a dozen in one day and there will *be* no tomorrow.

Wassails, Deportment during: There is no medical evidence whatsoever to support the theory that God looks after drunks. A person who falls down the pub stairs after a skinful is just as likely to break his leg as a teetotaller. More likely, since the teetoaller wouldn't have been in the pub in the first place. Moral: stay on the ground floor.

Xmas, Abstinence during: There is no recorded example, either, of anyone ever having given up drink for Christmas. Lent yes, Christmas no. Don't try it: it will make you so unpopular that it could drive you to drink.

Yak, etc, The one about the: After a glass or two of season's cheer, persons who otherwise do not tell jokes the whole year round are likely to launch into the one about this yak, this Tibetan llama, and this insurance agent from Pontefract. The response to the accompanying invitation, 'Stop me if you've heard this,' should be 'Stop!'

Zizzes, Correct term for: The post-prandial nap is very often just a polite term for the alcoholic stupor. A quick zizz after lunch by all means, but better as a consequence of having over-eaten than of having over-supped. You have to wake up sooner or later and remember how you felt when you woke up this morning. Two hangovers on the same day would be overdoing it – even at Christmas.

A VERSE FOR ALL SEASONS

It is little known that, had Mr Sumpter liked my stuff, my literary career would have taken a vastly different turn and I should be a writer of Christmas card verse.

Mr Sumpter was the boss of a local printing works which did a line in greeting cards. Rumour reached me that he was paying all of five bob per stanza. I submitted a dozen. If half of them were accepted, so I marvelled to myself, I should have earned thirty shillings for a morning's work. That was as much as I was being paid for a whole week slaving over an office ledger. It was money for old rope.

I did not retain a copy for my archives and I can recall only one couplet:

> Christmas is the season we toast old friends anew,
> Christmas is the reason I send this card to you.

The inner rhyming scheme, I thought, was rather clever. Too clever for Mr Sumpter, alas – over his head, probably – for he sent my efforts back by return of post, with a printed note to the effect that he was overstocked with Christmas card verses and could not consider any more contributions in the foreseeable future.

Who, I wondered broodingly, had got in ahead of me and overstocked him, then? Who had cornered the season/reason meeting/greeting market? Was there a kind of Christmas card verse mafia or coterie, somewhat on the lines of the Bloomsbury Group, to which you had to belong to have any hope of publication?

I have since heard tell that Christmas card verses are mostly written by middle-aged ladies living with cats in suburban semis. An old wives' tale, I call that. The only Christmas card verse writer I have ever actually met was a hard-boiled, chain-smoking Fleet Street hack who had been landed with the chore by an aunt who owned a greetings card business. I expect she regarded him as the literary one of the family. In fact, all he used to do was to take a handful of existing verses and shuffle the lines round a bit, somewhat like that game where you have to place a number of words in a particular order to make a well-known phrase or saying. Thus he would ransack 'Though my dear we'll soon be meeting, I send to you this Christmas greeting' and 'May your house be filled with cheer, This merry Christmas and New Year' to produce 'Though we soon will meet my dear, a merry Christmas and New Year.' But the general run of Christmas card verses, it's my belief, are now composed by word processors. So perhaps it's as well that my material didn't appeal to Mr Sumpter. I should probably have been on the scrapheap by now, a victim of new technology.

Where I failed to crash into the Christmas card market, I can claim a modest success in the Christmas cracker field. Ever heard this one? 'See a pin and pick it up. All the day you'll have a pin.' That's mine. One of the golden moments of my career – equal, almost, to seeing my name in print for the first time – was unfolding a little pink slip of paper in a Christmas cracker (companion, I vividly recall, to a green plastic whistle and a blue paper hat) and finding my own joke on it. Printed in Taiwan.

There were only two snags. The first was that I hadn't been paid for it (it was worth half a crown in anyone's currency, I would have thought). It was a line I'd contributed to a David Frost show years ago and I suppose it must have been going the rounds of the Taiwan bars until someone picked it up at the Crackermakers' Arms. The second snag was that, as is often the case with Christmas cracker literature, it contained a number of misprints, so that it read: 'See a pan and pack it up. All the day you'll hove a pin,' which to my mind – mark you, as the original author I'm probably being hypocritical – rather takes the edge off it.

Despite my one contribution to the art-form, however, I do not think I would make a successful writer of Christmas cracker material. It is a very specialised metier, its surface simplicity concealing limitless depths of inscrutability. For instance, '*Q*: What piece of furniture is most shy? *A*: A clock, because it always has its hands in front of its face.' There is an air about that riddle of its having been translated from some obscure Slav language. It is intended to be funny, yet you cannot imagine anyone laughing at it. Or take the Christmas cracker motto: 'It takes thirteen muscles to frown but only one to smile.' That, I somehow feel, started its career in Chinese.

But who does write all those Christmas cracker mottoes, jokes and riddles? I find it difficult to imagine a Christmas cracker

editor wading through the morning's batch of unsolicited manu-
scripts and sending off rejection slips or encouraging letters: 'Dear
Sir, thank you for your riddle about the hen crossing the street. It
is unfortunately rather too similar to one we have already published, about a chicken crossing the road, but we are always on the
lookout for new material, and if you have any riddles with a non-
poultry theme we should be glad to consider them.'

Nor can I readily conjure up a freelance riddle writer at his
desk, murmuring to himself through a cloud of tobacco smoke:
'Why is a table-lamp like a pot of tea?', then getting writers'
block before he can think of the answer.

Most Christmas cracker literature, I wouldn't be surprised to
hear, has never been composed at all. Decomposed, yes. It is fossil
material, dredged up from the bowels of the earth by gnomes. '*Q:*
Why shouldn't a pig get sick? *A:* Because he will have to be killed
before he is cured.' That has surely been lying around for
thousands of years. It was probably a joke told by cavemen to
while away the long Stone Age.

Once brought to the surface, the jokes and riddles are at once
packed in hermetically-sealed crates and exported to Taiwan and
suchlike far-flung places, where they are set into type by com-
positors who do not speak any English. That, surely, is the only
way they manage to get into print. It is certainly why, at this
moment, I am staring, baffled, at a cracker riddle which reads: *Q:*
Two flie on a droo, which one angry? *A:* One wich flew of the
handle.'

THE GAMES PEOPLE PLAY

Although there are hundreds – there may be thousands – of
authorised Christmas games, I have rarely been to a party where
one was actually being played. I'm discounting the stickier end of
the market – where Pass-the-Parcel is still in vogue. Open any
Victorian family novel at random and, unless you happen to have
stumbled on the death-bed scene, you will find four generations
playing Sardines and Hunt-the-Slipper like mad. If it was so then,

it isn't so now. Has television killed off the art of Postman's Knock? We're told that the Royals play Charades down at Sandringham. I don't believe it. From the description given in *Cassell's Book of Indoor Amusements, Card Games and Fireside Fun* (1881) it is clear that no one has ever played Charades. There just isn't time. To spell out the example provided – the word 'go-bang', which I doubt even exists – it takes fifty-eight lines of closely printed and highly tedious dialogue. If the Royal family play anything at all in the Christmas hols, I bet it's the kind of game that ordinary mortals play. For the truth is that while we may have given Blindman's Buff and Pin-the-tail-on-the-Donkey the elbow, we do still play games at Christmas. It's just that you won't find any of them in your average compendium of indoor amusements and fireside fun. All of these games are traditional and they are played wherever families reunite to warm their hands by the blazing yule-log and watch the re-run of *She Wore A Yellow Ribbon*.

Guess Who's Missing For Dinner

This is a sure-fire ice-breaker for Christmas Eve, when all the guests have arrived except the inevitable black sheep. The first guest starts the ball rolling with: 'I saw him drunk in the Goat and Compasses.' The second guest continues: 'I saw him drunk in the Dog and Boot with a Christmas tree under his arm.' The third guest takes up the story: 'I saw him drunk in the Snivelling Coalman with a Christmas tree under his arm and a lampshade on his head.' The descriptions accumulate until the doorbell rings and the black sheep falls over the threshold with a Christmas tree under one arm, an unplucked goose under the other, a lamp-shade on his head, and three cronies singing 'Christians Awake'.

Bottoms Up

For this you will need an ordinary tumbler containing a trace of scotch-and-soda. Knocking this back ostentatiously, you have to make it plain to your host that you could do with another drink, without saying so in so many words. Much ingenuity can be exercised in this game: for instance, tapping your empty glass with a finger-nail so that it gives out a hollow ring, peering through it as if through a telescope, pretending that it is an eyebath, or balancing it on your forehead. This game causes much merriment among teetotallers.

Pass the Parcel

A miming game that should be played only by those with a real gift for facial contortions. It is played on Christmas morning, when all the guests pass parcels to one another. While unwrapping each parcel, the players must simulate, in rapid succession, expressions of anticipation, disappointment, bewilderment, recognition, incredulity, hate and gratitude. At the end of the mime, each player must repeat the catch-phrase: 'It's just what I wanted.' Lose a point if the reply is: 'I can always change it if you don't like it.'

Expectations

One of the women goes out of the room and the others have to guess if she's pregnant.

Tracking

One of the guests treads in a mince pie and then meanders through the house leaving a trail of flaky pastry and goo. The hostess picks up the spore and begins screaming abuse. This can be rather fun when the quarry turns out not to be her seven-year-old son but a rather distant-looking distant cousin.

Uncles

A guest is nominated by a child to be its uncle. He must then pass the following proficiency test: (1) read a story about a family of pigs, with squeaky voices, (2) make a model of a dwelling-house out of Lego bricks, (3) suffer the child to pull the hairs out of his nostrils, (4) assume a glazed smile when the child speaks of doing pop-pops, and (5) assemble a box-kite from instructions in the Korean language. It is then someone else's turn to be Uncle.

Snap

The equipment required is a large pack of Instamatic holiday snaps or, in the more sophisticated version, four or five hundred colour slides which have to be held up to the light. The owner of the photographs (known as the Tormentor) hands them *one by one* to his guest (known as the Victim) to the accompaniment of a

droning commentary: 'This is us feeding our faces in Tenerife.
Alfonso here, the waiter, was quite a character; apparently he was
sentenced to death under Franco and made his escape in a laundry
basket. A pity you can't see the sweets trolley, it was a wonder to
behold ...' The game goes on until the Victim snaps.

What's This Rubbish?
The father of the house enters an empty room and switches on the
TV to watch his favourite programme. All the guests must then
file in one at a time, asking: 'What's This Rubbish?' This sparks
off a noisy and animated debate about the low quality of television
programmes, culminating in Father rising with a sigh of exasperation and switching off the set. The players must then chant in
unison: 'Hey, we were watching that!'

When Are You Getting Married Then?
An unmarried daughter, visiting from her bed-sit in London, is
placed in the middle of the room, then everyone asks her if it isn't
time she was getting married. She has to think up ways of making
them shut up. This game is even more enjoyable if the chap she is
living with is among the guests.

What Time Is It, Santa Claus?
A variation of 'What Time Is It, Mr Wolf?', also played on
Christmas Eve. One of the children, having elected to stay awake
all night long, must call to any adult using the bathroom: 'What
time is it?' The child must be told that it is very late, and that Santa
Claus will not come until he has gone to sleep. This goes on until
an advanced hour, when one of the child's parents staggers to the
linen cupboard for the Christmas stockings. Upon being asked,
'What time is it?', the parent must reply: 'It's three o'clock in the
morning, and I've told Santa Claus to give all your new toys to the
poor children.' An old family favourite.

Got To Go Back Tomorrow
This is a game for Boxing Day, when Mother asks her grown-up
children if they can't stay on an extra day. In turn, they must offer
bizarre reasons why this is impossible, such as: 'I've got to go back
tomorrow because I promised to shampoo my half of the carpet' or
'I've got to go back tomorrow because I think I left the bathroom

window open.' The one who gets away with the thinnest or most outlandish excuse for escaping from the family octopus wins the game.

Home James

This is really another version of 'Got To Go Back Tomorrow' but in reverse: instead of persuading a reluctant guest to stay, the hosts are trying to persuade one to leave. The guest is known as the victim. The hosts must say things like: 'We'd love you to stay another day but the people next door want your bed back' or 'We'd love you to stay another day but we're emigrating to New Zealand in the morning.' The Victim has to think up convincing ways of staying put.

Who Did That?

A game for the kiddies. One of them has to pull the head off the baby's new teddy bear. The baby then has to scream, and all the adults rush into the room. Locating their own children, they must ask: 'Who Did That?' The children all put the blame on one another. The fun of the game is that no parent may directly accuse another parent's child. If this rule is rigidly adhered to, it usually ends with each child getting a smack from its own parent whether guilty or not.

Consequences

The baby eats its own weight in jelly. The consequence is that it is very ill.

All Change

The lights on the Christmas tree go out and someone has to unscrew all the little pear-shaped bulbs in turn to find out which is the dodgy one. You can make bets on this if you like.

Grandpa's Footsteps

Another game for Boxing Day, after the pubs close. The children wait until they see Grandpa reeling down the street and then they follow him, imitating his gait and in some cases falling over.

The Generation Game

For this you will need a sofa containing four or five teenagers. All the adults present make personal remarks about them, on the lines of: 'I see young Kevin's saving up his hair to stuff a cushion with' or 'If she put one more patch on those jeans they'd make a good eiderdown.' The teenagers leave the room one by one. The person who drives the last one out – probably with the remark, 'How they know whether to go to the Ladies' or the Gents' beats me' – is the winner.

Oranges and Lemons
Not the nursery favourite of the same name but a round for massed womenfolk. One asks her hostess what she paid for her Satsuma oranges and this is the cue for discussion, lasting two and a half hours, on the price of fruit. A good way of getting the men to do the washing-up.

THAT PERFECT SPHERICAL PUDDING

Plum duffs as round as footballs, shimmering jellies, mince pies by the hundredweight, fizzy pop, grapes, turkey, pigs with apples in their mouths; fat uncles with fat cigars, thin aunts doing the knees-up, tiny police inspectors in paper hats; Old Mother Riley pulling a cracker with George Formby, or Weary Willie and Tired Tim cracking a wishbone with a toff – I don't know where the hoi-polloi at the top of the street got *their* image of Christmas – Dickens or what – but I got mine from the pages of *Film Fun* and *Illustrated Chips* and the *Jester* and *Jingles* in those dear lost days of Bumper Xmas Numbers.

At home the Christmas pudding was implacably the shape of the white basin it has been cooked in, the uncles (thin) drank brown ale and fell asleep, there were no waits with lanterns but only my scruffy contemporaries who sang 'Good King Wenceslas looked out/Of his bedroom window' and kicked the door in. There was no snow and no Santa Claus; but for two new George the Fifth pennies, the Christmas box of an aunt (fat), you could toboggan down the hill with the Bruin Boys, or join in the party with Eddie Your Happy Editor who signed himself Yours Yulefully. Perhaps there was no Santa Claus even in this world – it was either Korky the Cat dressed up or Alfie the Air Tramp flying over the snowy rooftops with a sackful of golliwogs: but Xmas was Xmas; Lord

Snooty and His Pals brought home the yule log and there were twenty shillings in the pound.

One's memorable Christmas is always in truth a snowball of Christmasses – the year the Monopoly set arrived amalgamated with the year of the boxing gloves and the year the pond froze. My memorable Christmas Number is a wild nostalgic welding of all the Grand Yuletide Issues I have ever read, from *Playbox* and its simple dollies' tea-parties in the thirties, to the more sophisticated dorm feasts of the *Hotspur* in the forties, when the boys of Red Circle School were compelled by some handy plague to spend the hols in Conk House. The point is that it was always perfect Christmas. 'Everything is safe, solid and unquestionable. Everything will be the same for ever and ever,' wrote George Orwell about the reassuring world of boys' papers – but he never mentioned Christmas. And Christmas, or Xmas, or Yuletide, was the safest, solidest and most unquestionable season of all. Come poverty or pestilence, burglary, arson, legal proceedings, disease or Act of God, that higher being known as Ye Ed guaranteed that everyone, from the lowliest mouser in the *Dandy* to the top-hatted Western Brothers in *Radio Fun*, everyone in history as far back as Stonehenge Kit the Ancient Brit, should have a cracker, a friend to pull it with, and a slice of that perfect, spherical pudding.

Looking back, I am not so sure that the Bumper Xmas Specials were as Bumper as all that. Our Regular Features might have been augmented by half a page of Christmas Chestnuts, and possibly some character like Merlin the Magician, whom one regarded more as an executive of the paper than as a working journalist, might be encouraged to knock out a column of Party Teasers; but in general it was to enjoy a feast of fun with all your Old Favourites that you placed an order *now* with your local newsagent.

There were, however, certain characteristics and conventions that distinguished the Christmas Number from the ordinary or secular numbers and which kept one going, beyond the rather disappointing New Year Number, through the thin weeks before the Egg-citing Easter Special.

To begin with, there had to be snow. The masthead or title of the sheet had to be dripping with snow, each letter encrusted with it, crisp and even. If there was no snow it was not a Christmas number. Furthermore there had to be snow in every illustration.

The snow did not have to be *used* in the illustration (although a bit of background detail showing an old gent catching it in the back of the neck with a snowball always helped) – it just had to be there. And with robins on the sill and a log fire burning, the Editor's Chair creaked benevolently, Inky the Office Boy tapped out his Speshul Xmas Messidge, and the rules were relaxed.

The normally strict editorial quarantine was lifted so that characters could stroll at will from one page to another (or even, provided they were under the same management, from one comic to another). Thus Pansy Potter the Strongman's Daughter from the back page of the *Beano* could turn up at Desperate Dan's Christmas party on page three of the *Dandy*, and Big-hearted Arthur, having lost his latchkey somewhere in the pages of *Radio Fun*, might effect an entrance through the window of the wrong house and find himself enjoying a slap-up feed with his old playmates, Nan Kenway and Douglas Young.

For the more anti-social characters who could not be trusted off the page, those who outside the festive season usually got their come-uppance in the last frame, there was a general amnesty. Hungry Horace was allowed to eat three or four of those immortal round puddings without any resultant bellyache, and Keyhole Kate was rewarded for a year of voyeurism with a gigantic, holly-bedecked keyhole with the compliments of Mr Artist.

The rules were relaxed, but there were rules to be obeyed. The dramatic verities had to be strictly adhered to in the Christmas Number. Laurel and Hardy might be editorially described as Our Two Chumps; they might have suffered a year of crisis, buffeted week by week from mean uncle to miserly landlord, afflicted now with gout, now with objectionable nephews; even in *Film Fun*'s Mirth-packed Monster Number there can be no respite, and Eddie would not be a Happy Editor for long if he allowed them to sit down for their Christmas Tuck-in without first going through fire and water to get it. Convention demanded that before any character sat down at that famous groaning board in the last frame he should go through a Peer Gynt-like saga of misfortune and misunderstanding and misadventure, proving himself in the snowy world outside the Hotel de Posh. And so Our Two Chumps, at the beginning of their adventure (Laurel and Hardy in *Yule Be Sorry*), find themselves not only stony-broke but on the verge of being evicted by Mr Moneybags, a diminutive Rachman figure who seems to control all the *Film Fun* properties.

Now the Prize Pair find themselves out in the compulsory snow, singing carols in a pathetic attempt to keep body and soul together. An irate householder, mistaking them for cats, pours water over them. Drenched, hungry and homeless they turn in their anguish upon one another, each partner bitterly reproaching the other. 'I never want to see you again, if not sooner!' A lifelong partnership breaks up. And so the tragedy continues until Stan (or Olly), now bowed with remorse, happens to walk into a footpad who is holding Mr Moneybags at gun-point. The thief is routed, the Two Chumps are re-united, Mr Moneybags reforms on the spot and leads them to the Hotel de Posh where a table for twelve has apparently been reserved for him. Harold Lloyd, Claude Dampier, Old Mother Riley and Max Miller are among the guests.

It is *A Christmas Carol* without the ghosts, *The Mistletoe Bough* in which the girl finds a wad of fivers in the trunk and treats everyone to a munchful meal. 'Everything is safe, solid and unquestionable.' I have a dim memory that in the real world outside the mullioned windows of Thomson-Leng Publications and the Amalgamated Press it rained, not snowed; there were not really enough presents to fill a pillow-case, and the raucous carollers irreverently sang 'Hark the Herald angels sing/Mrs Simpson's got the King.' But in the real world of the Christmas Numbers the snowmen wore top hats, there were grapes and jellies, Laurel and Hardy were friends again and the plum duffs were as round as footballs.

YES, VIRGINIA, THERE IS A SCROOGE

Many years ago a little girl called Virginia wrote to an American newspaper to ask if it was the truth that there was a Santa Claus.

The editor's reply has become a classic. 'He exists as certainly as love and generosity and devotion exist,' wrote this good and simple man. 'Yes, Virginia, there is a Santa Claus.'

Well now, assuming that Virginia has not lost her sense of

curiosity over the years, she may by this time, having grown up and seen a little of the world, be wondering about another well-known Christmas character. Is there really, Virginia might ask, any such person as Scrooge?

This time it falls on me to give the answer.

Is there a Scrooge?

Virginia, you might as well ask if there is bad luck, or bad temper, or bad manners, or whether there is any such condition as a fit of melancholy on rainy mornings.

You cannot touch these things, Virginia, but you would not deny that they exist. And so does Scrooge.

What does it matter that no one has ever seen him? Have you ever seen the malevolent spirit who makes you miss the last bus or ladders your tights or causes the bread to fall jam-side downwards?

Of course you haven't, Virginia. But that's no proof that these things don't happen, for you know they do.

Virginia, if there is no Scrooge, who do you think is responsible for all the pettiness and callousness and lack of imagination that you find in the world? You're not to blame, and your friends aren't to blame, so who is?

When an old lady's pension is cut on a technicality, when the homeless are turned away, when the children's swings are chained up, when this or that event is banned in the public interest, when pets are forbidden and the kissing has to stop, there, Virginia, if you look hard enough, you will always find Scrooge.

Or there you would find him, I should have said, if he were not hiding behind the coat-tails of officialdom. And officialdom will always swear that he hasn't been seen today, or that he went the other way.

They will tell you, when you point out Scrooge's unmistakeable handiwork, that this was an isolated case or that it was the computer's fault or that there has been an administrative error, or that rules are rules.

Don't believe them, Virginia. A person of flesh and blood works the computer, and makes the rules and then enforces them, and that person is Scrooge.

Scrooge thrives on rules, Virginia. He believes in them, far more than you believe in him. And he believes in order, duty, and the small print in the contract. What he does not believe in is creating precedents, for when you create precedents it means that if one person has been made happy then everyone else might want to be happy likewise.

Virginia, this is a world of opposites. The opposite of joy is misery and the opposite of generosity is meanness and the opposite of charity is spite. But these things are intangibles and they can only be brought to life as parasitic growths in a human shell where love, kindness, humour and tolerance have long departed.

When an old-age pensioner is worried out of her mind, it is because some person is creating that worry. When a child is disappointed, it is because some person has caused that disappointment. When the music stops abruptly, it is not usually because the orchestra has run out of breath.

Not believe in Scrooge? You may as well not believe in January.

If there were no Scrooge, Virginia, there would be carol-singing all year long. Theatres would open on Sunday. Pubs would close at one in the morning, or when they pleased. There would be café tables on the pavement, and dancing without a licence, and no such thing as the law of obstruction. Post office clerks would smile.

But as long as the people's spirit can be quenched, and laughter can be stopped, and a regulation can be found to prevent innocent enjoyment or even ordinary peace of mind, then Scrooge will flourish.

He exists all right, Virginia. He exists as certainly as red tape and petty-mindedness and over-zealousness and pusillanimity exists.

Yes, Virginia, there is a Scrooge.

ALBERT AND THE LINER

Below the military striking clock in the City Arcade there was, and probably still is, a fabulous toyshop.

Once a year we were taken to see the clock strike noon, and after the mechanical soldiers of the King had trundled back into their garrison, we were allowed to press our noses to the toyshop window.

Following a suitable period of meditation, we were then supposed to compose our petitions to Father Christmas.

The centrepiece of the fabulous toyshop's window display was always something exotic such as the Blackpool Tower in Meccano, or a twin-track Hornby train running over a viaduct. None of us had to be told that such luxuries were beyond Father Christmas's price-range.

This year the window featured a splendid model of the *Queen Mary*, which had recently been launched on Clydebank. It was about four feet long, with real lights in the portholes and real steam wisping out of the funnels, and clearly it was not for the likes of us.

Having seen it and marvelled at it, we dismissed this expensive dream from our minds and settled down to list our prosaic requests for Plasticine, farmyard animals that poisoned you when you licked the paint off, or one pair of roller skates between two of us.

All of us, that is to say, except Albert Skinner, who calmly announced that he was asking Father Christmas for the *Queen Mary*.

None of us said much at the time, but privately we thought Albert was a bit of an optimist. For one thing, the *Queen Mary* was so big and so grand and so lit-up that it was probably not even for sale. For another, we were all well aware that Father Christmas's representative in the Skinner household was a sullen, foul-tempered collier who also happened to be unemployed.

Albert's birthday present, it was generally known, had been a pair of boots.

Even so, Albert continued to insist that he was getting the *Queen Mary* for Christmas, and sometimes when we went to his house to swop comics he would look to his father for confirmation.

'Dad, I am, aren't I? Aren't I, dad! Getting that *Queen Mary* for Christmas?'

Mr Skinner, dourly whittling a piece of wood by the fireside after the habit of all the local miners, would growl without looking up:

'You'll get a clout over the bloody earhole if you don't stop nattering.'

Albert would turn complacently to us. 'I am, see. I'm getting the *Queen Mary*.'

Sometimes, when his father was in a bad mood (which was quite often), Albert's pleas for reassurance would meet with a more vicious response. 'Will you shut up about the bloody *Queen Mary*!' Mr Skinner would shout. 'You gormless little get, do you think I'm made of money?'

Outside, his ear tingling from the blow his father had landed on it, Albert would bite back the tears and declare stubbornly: 'I'm still getting it. You wait till Christmas.'

One day the crippled lad at No. 43 was taken by the Church Ladies' Guild to see the military striking clock in the City Arcade, and when he came home he reported that the model of the *Queen Mary* was no longer in the window of the fabulous toyshop.

'I know,' said Albert. 'I'm getting it for Christmas.'

Then it was Christmas morning, and we all flocked out into the street to show off our presents, sucking our brand-new torches to make our cheeks glow red, or brandishing a lead soldier or two in the pretence that we had a whole regiment of them indoors.

No one expected to see Albert, but before long he came leaping, jumping, almost somersaulting, into the street. 'I've got it! I've got it!'

We clustered round him, and bubbling with pride he produced what seemed on first inspection to be a length of wood. Then we saw that it had been carved at both ends to make a bow and a stern, and that three cotton-reels had been nailed to it for funnels. A row of tin-tacks marked the Plimsoll line, and there were stuck-on bits of cardboard for the portholes. The whole thing was painted over in sticky lamp-black, except for the lettering on the port-side.

'ThE QuEEn MaRy,' it said in white.

Once again, we didn't say much. Albert's *Queen Mary* was a crude piece of work, but clearly many hours of labour, and much love, had gone into it. Its clumsy contours alone must have taken night upon night of whittling by the fireside.

Mr Skinner, pyjama-jacket tucked into his trousers, had come out of the house and was standing by his garden-gate. Albert, in a rush of happiness, ran to his father and flung his arms around him and hugged him.

'Look, dad! Look what I've got for Christmas!'

'Get out of it, you soft little bugger,' said Mr Skinner. He drew contentedly on his empty pipe, cuffed Albert over the head as a matter of habit, and went indoors.

6

SEE HOW THEY GROW

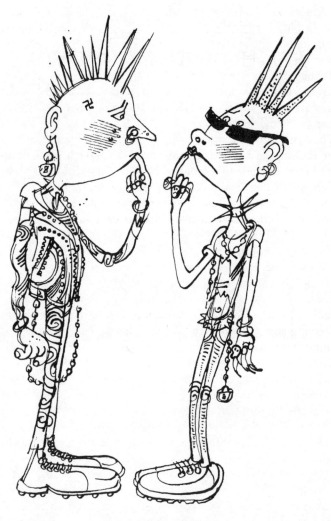

LEFT-HANDED KISSES

LEFT-HANDED KISSES

An American book just published over here, *Teenage Romance or How To Die Of Embarrassment*, reminds us how little the basics of young love – not to mention young love-bites – change over the years.

Teenagers may dress differently, dance differently, tattoo their heads and talk a language resembling Iroquois Indian but they still worry about their hands sweating when snogging in the back row of the pictures.

They still light the wrong end of the cigarette and realise only after flashing on a winning smile that they have a piece of apple stuck between their two front teeth, and they still hang about in the chemist's then leave without buying anything.

Or so we are told by Delia Ephron who has written this instructive compendium, which contains two valuable pages on How To Hide A Pimple and another two on How To Worry ('Worry that you have B.O. ... Worry that everyone hates you ... Worry that in a long kiss you have to breathe through your nose and your nose will be stopped up ...').

Some worries she doesn't mention. Nothing, not even the ordeal of Romeo and Juliet, can surely match the anguish of two shy young lovers wandering across a buttercup meadow in the shimmering sunset ... both of them dying to spend a penny.

Then when – on the excuse of having a sudden craving for a bag of crisps – they do re-reach civilisation with its welcome public conveniences (what if they're closed?), they both go into the wrong one by mistake.

Worry is to the under-sixteens as bad feet are to the over-sixties. Girl virgins still worry about being pregnant and boy virgins about being impotent ... and virgins of either sex still confide to the dressing-table mirror, 'I know you can't get it off lavatory seats but I think I'm going to make medical history.'

Lavatories, come to think of it, have always loomed large in teenage nightmares. It is more years ago than most of you have had hot flushes but I still remember the chest-gnawing embarrassment of coming out of the men's room in the Majestic Ballroom, Leeds, colliding with someone carrying a tray of lemonade and returning to my partner looking as if – well, as if I hadn't made it in time. There was nothing I could bring myself to say, there was nowhere she could bring herself to look, and we never saw one another again.

Beyond bathroom range, there are still traumas enough. There must still be the anxiety of waiting for a date outside the Odeon, knowing perfectly well that it was outside the Odeon where you said you'd meet and having a clear recollection of her/his last words being 'See you outside the Odeon' – but she/he is now a full one and a half minutes late and are you absolutely sure you didn't say the ABC?

Can left-handed boys kissing right-handed girls ever be absolutely sure that they're not going to move their heads the wrong way and get involved in a nasty nose-collision like stags clashing antlers?

Don't teenage girls still wrestle with the eternal and insoluble dilemma that they'll be thought too easy if they do and too hard-to-get if they don't? And don't teenage boys still hope for a disturbance from park ranger or peeping tom before they're forced to go further than they know how to?

Then there is the enduring suspicion that she reads out the choicest bits of his love letters to her best friends . . . that he told all his mates what happened on the towpath that night and that's why they're all giving her funny looks . . . There is the fear that the boil on his nose might not have cleared up by six o'clock this evening . . . and that the wisps in her comb are a portent that all her hair is going to fall out . . . There is the ever-present possibility that though her parents are supposed to be in Majorca, the hotel burned down and they are going to walk through the door and switch the light on any minute . . . and that when she smiled at him after that tender moment, she wasn't smiling at all, she was laughing at him . . .

Hideous, perspiring, stomach-clutching days. And what wouldn't you give to live through them all again?

AREN'T PARENTS HELL?

A heartfelt 'hear hear' rippled through the nation when the parents of runaway Christine – now happily restored to them – wrote in the *Mirror*: 'It's hell being the parents of a teenager today.'

In nine words they said it all. But there are two sides to a coin and it is equally true that it's hell being the teenager of parents today.

The trouble with parents these days is that they work at it so hard. If you're a teenager they won't leave off being parentish for a second. It's like being a budgerigar and having some clown say 'Tweet tweet' to you all day long.

It is reassuring to be tweeted at from time to time but you do not want it morning, noon and night.

Parents fume and worry and get themselves into such a towering parental state that they come out with bitterly wounding personal insults then say they are only telling you what you ought to know because they love you.

If they are not being insulting they are being mawkish. Every so often they will say something deeply embarrassing such as, 'Now I want you to promise me that if you're ever in trouble you'll come straight to us.'

Parents are congenital sneaks and liars. They search through your clothes while you're out and if you catch them at it they say they're just seeing if there's anything that needs to go to the cleaner's.

They have as much trust as a feral cat. You can't have a cold sore without them accusing you of sniffing glue, and when they come into your bedroom you can see their nostrils twitching like a tracker dog's. Sometimes you catch them staring at your eyeballs because they have read somewhere that this is how you can tell if someone is on drugs.

They are obsessed with the act of eating. If you do not put away your own weight in potatoes every meal they go to the doctor and tell him you have got anorexia nervosa.

They're terrible pessimists and are forever warning you of the lousy rotten things that are going to happen to you when you're older. The oft-threatened prospect of your coming down to earth with a bump one of these fine days seems to afford them keen pleasure.

Parents are always asking for things. Your father tells you not to forget Mother's Day and your mother tells you not to forget Father's Day, and both want a rundown on the birthday or Christmas present you have bought for the other, and will not hesitate to call you a little miser if they think it hasn't cost enough.

They talk about you in your presence as if you were the dog. 'Has he got any idea what he looks like?' one of them will ask the other. Whereupon the other will sigh.

Parents sigh a lot.

They have no sense of shame. If you find out that they've been reading your diary or private letters you would think they would run away to avoid facing you, but they don't.

They are incredibly nosey yet amazingly incurious. They want to know where you're going and where you've been and who with. But they never want to know what you think.

They believe the mere fact of being twenty-odd years your senior makes them well-informed, shrewd, understanding and intelligent. To hear them carry on it is plain they regard themselves as Dunroamin's answer to Robin Day and Marje Proops.

They want every experience to be a life sentence. If you pack up the guitar because you're getting nowhere with it after two years they say you never stick at anything for more than five minutes, and if you switch courses at your polytechnic they say you're forever chopping and changing.

They have absurd expectations. Just because you've got a few O-levels they think you could finish up as a professor of English if you'd put your back into it, and when you fail one of you A's they accuse you of throwing your life down the drain.

They're always complaining about the noise but never seem to realise that when they go on at you they can be heard three streets away.

And oh, how they *do* go on. And on. And on.

Aren't parents hell?

SURVIVAL COURSE

The *Mirror*'s School-leaver's Guide to Real Life is full of sound, but one-sided, advice. I thought I would redress the balance by presenting my Real Life Guide to School-leavers.

In thousands of British homes at this time of year, it is impossible to take four steps without tripping over one of these creatures.

Your astonishment, as you wonder how the expiring sea-lion draped across the sofa has evolved from the tiny moppet who used to call you Da-da, turns quickly to irritation when the apparition snaps its fingers, addresses you as Man, and asks you to fetch it a biscuit.

Short of doing a moonlight flit and not leaving a forwarding address, you have got to learn to live with the monsters you have created. I offer the following tips for what they are worth.

1 – All teenagers are idle. They have been so since Biblical times and there is nothing you can do about it at this late stage.

2 – But it is not because of their idleness that they will not get up in the morning, or, in some cases, the afternoon. Teenagers remain in bed because they stayed up so late last night that they finally keeled over. Treat their bedrooms as casualty wards.

3 – Teenagers eat when they are hungry, and not when they are not. They do not normally have breakfast. Just leave some bowls of food lying around, as you would for a large dog, and do not hassle them about meal times.

4 – A son who spends many hours staring into the bathroom mirror is not thinking of doing away with himself. He is watching his moustache growing.

5 – All teenagers are selfish. If they ever do anything for you, treat it as a big favour, because that's what it is.

6 – Girls of school-leaving age will burst into tears if you mildly criticise them. Do not feel guilty about this: if you didn't mildly criticise them, they would find something else to burst into tears about.

7 – Do not ask teenagers what they are planning to do tomorrow. There is no such day as tomorrow in the teenagers' calendar (except when they are asked to tidy their rooms).

8 – It follows from this that there is no point in asking them what they are planning to do with the rest of their lives. They do not know: if they did know, they would be doing it.

9 – But that is not to say they are not hatching some grandiose scheme which will involve you lending them a hundred pounds. In refusing this loan, do not ask what it is for. Nothing infuriates a teenager more than keeping a secret that no one wants to hear.

10 – You cannot have a telephone and a teenager in the same house without family rows. Get rid of one or the other.

11 – Girls bring home loutish boy friends on purpose. They pick them out specially to annoy their parents. You can annoy them right back by pretending that the latest lout reminds you a lot of Cary Grant.

12 – Boys who bring girls home usually just leave them lying about, like a cat that has brought home a mouse. There is no need to take on your son's social obligations by engaging these young ladies in small talk. Skulk in the bedroom and then they will put all the blame on him.

13 – If you are burdened with teenagers of both sexes you will find that they have entered into a financial arrangement of Byzantine complexity, whereby your daughter has lent your son all her money. Keep out of these negotiations altogether.

14 – Teenagers are great ditherers, especially at around seven in the evening when they cannot decide whether to stay in, go to the disco, see what Tom and Charlie are doing, or give the Blonde Bombshell a ring. Any attempt to arbitrate will end up in your parting with a fiver.

15 – A boy of sixteen who does not ask his father if he can have a motorbike is not normal. (The normal reply is, 'No, you can't.')

16 – Teenage boys are notorious liars when it comes to boasting how much they had to drink last night. Do not rise to the bait. If they'd really had as much as that, they would not yet be upright.

17 – School-leavers who are turned down for a job because they lack qualifications are inclined to round on their parents and ask: 'But why didn't you make me take another A-level?' There is no answer to that. Do not attempt one.

18 – If you find yourself walking around muttering the things you mean to say to your children, get a grip on yourself. By the time they turn up, you will have an entirely fresh crop of grievances.

19 – All teenagers are misunderstood. It is no use asking them why: they will simply tell you that you wouldn't understand.

20 – If, in spite of (or because of) this excellent advice, your teenagers threaten to leave home, do not panic. Teenagers who mean to leave home don't threaten, they just do it.

GOOD LORD, MR CHIPS!

There are stirrings in the cloisters of our great public schools at revelations by the wife of the headmaster of one of them, Mrs Daphne Rae.

In a book of reminiscences which could well have been entitled Good Lord, Mr Chips! she blows the gaff on some of the goings-on in these supposedly staid institutions during her early life.

The most notorious going-on concerns the beautiful wife of a housemaster who introduced one hundred boys annually to 'the various pleasures of sexual activity.'

News of this interesting variation on the traditional dorm feast at last reached the headmaster's ears, whereupon the services of the lady's husband, and thus of the lady herself, were dispensed with. She was so distraught at losing her annual fix of a hundred strapping lads that her marriage broke up. Nowadays, of course, she would probably take her case to the industrial tribunal.

I must say that when I read this story I wished for the first time in my life that I had had the benefit of a public school education. At my own particular academy (Leeds School of Hard Knocks, gravel drainage, prospectus on request) we were very strong on woodwork, chemistry and hanging upside down from the parallel bars, but lamentably untutored in a bit of the other.

This was despite the fact that because of the wartime staff shortage an unusually high proportion of our teachers were women. The fact that a majority of them looked like the back of a tram-smash might have had something to do with it.

But we could dream, couldn't we? Much of our playground talk revolved on speculations as to the sexual proclivities of Miss A. (history) who was alleged to have been seen walking hand-in-hand with Mr B. (geography) in broad daylight; on the supposed illicit liaison between Mrs C. (music) and Mr D. (science); and on the rumour that Miss D. (scripture), who was reckoned to account single-handedly for the rest of the alphabet, was in such an advanced state of clinical nymphomania that she was on the verge of being put into a home.

There the dream stopped. The idea that a member of the teaching profession, or lady wife of a teacher, might be capable of propelling herself into a leg-over situation with one of the boys (let alone the whole of 4A, 4B, and 4C) was beyond the realm of possibility. It was as unlikely a prospect as the vicar's wife doing a striptease by way of opening the jumble sale.

But the fantasy of being seduced by an older woman runs even more deeply in the mind of your average growing lad than the fear that he could contract a social disease that will make his nose drop off just by thinking about it. And that fantasy must have its outlet.

In an outwardly respectable council house with net curtains and nothing to suggest that it was in all essentials a free bordello – a red lamp, perhaps, and a flashing sign saying: 'Next please' – there lived a divorced lady of mature years who for the purposes of this narrative I had better call Mrs Smith.

Mrs Smith, it was said, was as partial to our age group as an anteater is partial to ants. The evidence for this was that pimpled youths were often to be seen leaving her house, combing back their hair and smirking. When asked at what they smirked, they tapped their noses and declined to give evidence.

Furthermore, Mrs Smith was a peroxide blonde. Need I say more?

The drill was that you were supposed to hang around outside Mrs Smith's house until eventually, if she fancied you, she would call you in from her window, take you up to her bedroom and give you what I believe is nowadays termed a right seeing-to. Spitting out your boot-laces, she would then take on the next in the queue.

Now I am an observant person by nature and I thought it would be instructive to observe Mrs Smith's house for myself. I once, indeed, observed it for five hours – without, however, seeing anything of remark.

Finally, one rainy evening when I was standing in a puddle outside her gate, observing like billy-o, the front door opened and Mrs Smith – stark naked except for shoes, stockings, skirt, blouse, cardigan and pinafore – asked me what I wanted. My heart leaped like a mountain goat, I blushed to the tip of my dripping nose, and I replied: 'Nothing'. Mrs Smith then advised me to take myself off and I did so, my observations concluded for ever.

Eventually I did learn what those smirking youths had to smirk about. It was, as I say, a time of wartime shortages. Mrs Smith was our local source of black market cigarettes. But even had she been the Every Boy's Own Libertine we were all longing for, I would still have been hopelessly on the wrong track.

I see now that I should have gone to Greyfriars.

BRIEF ENCOUNTER

Being an avid student of biography, I shall naturally tune in to ITV's essay on the life and works of Miss Phyllis Dixey next week.

Miss Dixey was as much a part of my youth as cork-tipped cigarettes, the back row of the Gaumont, acne, Brilliantine and the Moo-Cow Milk Bar. How odd that an age of such total innocence should be evoked most vividly by a lady who specialised in taking all her clothes off.

Actually, I tell a lie about the innocence being total. All my memories of Phyllis Dixey are tinged with guilt, this being due to the fact that whenever she appeared on the boards of the City Varieties, Leeds, I played hookey in order to catch her Wednesday matinée.

I am surprised, looking back, that the schools of Leeds found it worthwhile to remain open when the famous stripper was in town, since her audience on those Wednesday afternoons was made up almost entirely of goggling fourth-formers.

If the theatre had been surrounded by truant officers, yelling at us through megaphones to come out with our hands up, I suppose we could at least have had a shot at claiming that our visit was educational. For unlike downmarket productions such as 'Nudes of the World', 'Strip Strip Hurray' and 'We Never Clothed,' Miss Dixey's Wednesday afternoon soirées had so much class that they should have been subsidised by the Arts Council.

It is entirely due to my studies at the City Varieties that my grasp of the classics is second only to that of Lord Clark of 'Civilisation'. How else would I have learned that Aphrodite Triumphing Over Psyche is a lady with no clothes on, that Venus Rising From The Sea is also a lady with no clothes on, and that there is a second version of the famous Gainsborough 'Blue Lady' portrait, in which the model retains her hat but dispenses with her knickers?

But all this will doubtless be touched on in Thames TV's symposium about Miss Dixey's influence on literature and the arts. What might not be mentioned is that alone among those serried rows of spotty schoolboys up in the gallery, I – thanks to my extensive theatrical connections – actually met Phyllis Dixey in the flesh.

(When I say flesh, I mean a blue satin dress. When I say blue satin dress, I mean that she was wearing this garment, not me. At least I think she was. My impressions of the occasion, as you will see in a moment, are somewhat confused. But a blue satin dress was worn by one of us on this historic encounter, I am certain of that.)

My extensive theatrical connections consisted of a lad called Raymond whose uncle had once done some electrical work for Nat Gonella, the trumpet-player. This, for reasons I do not properly comprehend, somehow gave Raymond the entrée to the theatrical digs where Mr Gonella sometimes stayed. When it turned out one day that the celebrated, the fabulous, the one-and-only Phyllis Dixey was to be found under the same roof, Raymond kindly offered to introduce us.

After some formalities, consisting of my giving him all my money, my gun-metal cigarette case and some back numbers of *Health and Efficiency*, Raymond conducted me to this Mecca among boarding-houses, and left me to comb my hair in the living room while he fetched Miss Dixey.

A few light-years later Raymond and Phyllis Dixey appeared in the doorway, one of them wearing a blue satin dress. The goddess in human shape did not actually cross the threshold – I think she was on her way to the bathroom – but she certainly paused long enough for Raymond to present me.

'This,' he said, pointing in my direction, 'is Keith Waterhouse.'

The vision spoke.

'What a funny name,' said the most beautiful woman in the history of the world.

I searched for a reply – something witty, brief and sophisticated that would etch into her mind and be remembered for ever. 'It's better than Nicholas Ridiculous' I heard myself saying – that being the name of a character in a radio comedy show of the time.

But although I heard myself saying these words, Miss Dixey did not. Owing to my mouth having suddenly gone dry, all that I actually got out was 'It's better than Nicholas.' I think you will agree with me that this was perhaps the most pointless, goonish, stupid remark ever spoken by any human being since the first ape-man uttered the first grunt.

Miss Dixey evidently thought so too, for at that point she brought our audience to an end, leaving me feeling like Quasimodo. That night I wrote her a letter, explaining that what I had meant to say when she very kindly joked that I had a funny name, was 'It's better than Nicholas Ridiculous.' But I didn't post it. I wish now that I had. It might have been the beginning of a wonderful relationship.

THE CASE FOR ADOLESCENTRY

I once thought up a crime called adolescentry by which, as with infanticide and the French *crime passionel*, the offence would in itself be an indication of diminished responsibility.

The idea was that if you pushed your teenage offspring over a cliff in a moment of extreme exasperation, you got off.

The case for adolescentry came back to me while brooding over that immensely depressing Panorama report, The Battle Against Heroin, the other night.

Heroin addiction, from being the province of pop stars and Soho junkies, is now available to all. Youngsters yet to sit their O-levels can buy the stuff as freely and almost as cheaply as soft ice-cream.

Our run-down housing estates have produced such weird and wonderful mutations of the human teenager over the years that when you see those rag-tag and bobtail tribes of bald-pated or orange-crested grotesques shambling along their concrete walk-ways you wonder if you have perhaps stumbled upon some new Quatermass experiment.

But until lately they have drawn the line at systematically killing themselves, except in very small numbers.

No one can tell how many of the young are already hooked on heroin but an estimate of between 25,000 and 50,000 is bandied about. That gives us up to a hundred thousand agonised parents.

We saw some of them on Peter Taylor's programme. It made you long for that lost, innocent era when mothers had nothing to fear but that their daughters might be in the club.

Looking back on my own long involvement in the care and protection of teenagers I now see that my generation of fusspot parents had it cushy. All we had to worry about was whether they were smoking pot, about to join a commune, developing anorexia nervosa, taking up with the Moonies, dropping out of school, snorting cocaine, popping pills or falling into the company of gang-bangers.

Since those halcyon days, fathers and mothers have had care upon care heaped upon their drooping shoulders. As a matter of routine in our present civilisation, every teenager must be keenly examined daily for telltale signs of having adopted the hairstyle of the Amazon parrot or taken up the practice of wearing a safety pin through the nostrils.

One innocuous tube of glue, tucked away in a sock drawer and probably bought for the purpose of making model aeroplanes, can put a parent on tranquillisers.

Until now, though, every teenage excess, every youthful folly, every juvenile prattfall, has been something a determined parent could hope to do something about with the expenditure of a good deal of time and anguish. Heroin, however, beats the system. Heroin is catching.

It is, I suppose, only another craze – though for thousands it will be a craze until death, like being condemned to hula-hoop into eternity. The next teenage cult, no doubt, will be licking the polish off furniture or eating live rats.

One thing is sure. It's not getting any easier to be a parent. Fewer children are being born, notes the General Household Survey published this week. I'm not surprised. All that surprises me is that there aren't more cases of adolescentry.

See how they grow

Like a swallow in reverse one of my brood has departed these shores for the summer.

This migration – as far as any swallow has ever ventured – has induced maudlin thoughts on the tendency of children to grow up. One minute they are sucking lollipops and the next they are humping a rucksack over the far horizon.

The disconcerting thing is that you don't notice it happening. I have been told many times that old age creeps up on you – but I didn't know it was my children's old age they were talking about.

Apart from birthdays we have only our offspring's word for it that they are growing up. This is perhaps because we have not noticed the signs – or not wanted to.

I thought I could perhaps perform a useful service this morning by listing some of the ways in which you can monitor this beanstalk process. So:

Your children are growing up when they prefer half a lager to something with white rum in it . . . when you offer them the other half and they say: 'No, it's my round . . .' and when –

– they don't clean up dirty jokes for your benefit

– they don't roll their eyeballs and yawn elaborately when you tell your own stories for the hundredth time

– they say '*!*!' after tripping over the dog – but without giving you a quick sidelong glance to see if you're shocked

– they stop pretending they've never seen an X movie

– they no longer shove whatever they're reading behind a
cushion when you come into the room.

They're growing up when they keep an ashtray in their bedroom where anyone can see it ... and they put their cigarette ends
in it instead of in a matchbox ... and when –

– you're expected to knock on their bedroom door – *and wait* –
before you enter

– you ask them to turn the sound down and they say 'Sorry' and
do it

– they wipe their feet

– they change their underclothes without being told

– they prefer money on their birthdays

– they nag about your health ... and stop reminding you that
you promised to leave them your watch and lighter in your
will.

They're growing up when they don't hide their mail, when they
ask your advice, when you ask them what's wrong and there is
every chance that they'll tell you ... and when –

– they start asking what things cost

– they know how many calories in a slice of cake

– they say 'This is Charlie' instead of 'That's Kermit the Frog'
when introducing their friends

– and as for your own friends, they stop calling them Auntie
and Uncle.

They're growing up when they don't wait till you're out before
making their interminable phone calls ... and their friends don't
hang up when they ring and you answer.

They're growing up when you go on holiday without them –
and all you like to ask when you get back is whether they watered
the plants.

They're growing up when they stop asking you how you are
in French

– they sometimes let you win at chess

– they go to bed without falling asleep first

– they go to the doctor's on their own

– they no longer write blank-verse poems that begin 'Life has
no meaning'

– they occasionally buy their own newspapers

– they pay the milkman out of their own money instead of
calling you to the door

– they don't have to be told to take the dog out

– they can cook a meal in the oven as well as on the grill ... and it doesn't have baked beans in it.

And finally:

They're definitely growing up when they wander around the house opening and shutting drawers, and you ask them what they're looking for, and they say 'My passport.'

THE PARENTS' CHARTER

A couple of kids stopped me in Oxford Street and sold me, for five pence, a smudgy copy of the Charter of Children's Rights.

They'd run it off on a duplicator in flagrant breach, I suspect, of the original copyright.

Anyway, full marks for initiative. And full marks, too, to the Children's Charter which – although this particular copy of it was practically indecipherable – I happen to know is full of good sense.

'Children have the right to privacy of person and thought ... to freedom of expression ... to freedom from political indoctrination ...

'A child's personal appearance is his own and his family's concern ... Children have the right to such knowledge as is necessary to understand the society in which they live ... They shall have the freedom to make complaints about teachers and parents without fear of reprisal ...'

Fine. Agreed. Accepted. Right on.

But, dear children, has it ever occurred to you that parents have their rights too? I would be very surprised if this revolutionary thought has ever entered your heads, and for that reason, I have drafted, for your consideration, a Charter of Parents' Rights.

Run it off on your duplicator by all means but don't try to sell it to me. Sell it to each other.

1. Parents have the right to their sleep. If you've promised to be in by 10.30 they have no wish to be counting the flowers on the wallpaper at one in the morning.

2. Parents have the right to freedom from unnecessary worry. If it

takes you three hours to nip out and buy an iced lolly it will not occur to your parents that half-way down the road you decided to go to a pop concert instead. They will conclude that you have been raped, kidnapped or murdered, or a grisly combination of all three.

3. A parent's personal appearance is his own concern. He does not want to be told that his hair is too short or that turn-ups are out of fashion. Nor does he require a psychedelic kipper tie on Father's Day.

4. Parents have the right to be human beings. That is to say, they have the right to fall into irrational rages, to contradict themselves, to change their minds without reason, to be stubborn, dogmatic and bloodyminded, and in general to behave occasionally like children, who as you well know are the salt of the earth.

5. No parent shall be scoffed at, sneered at or in any way discriminated against for his opinions. If a parent takes the view that the popular ballad, 'Leap up and down, wave your knickers in the air' is not the greatest song since 'Greensleeves', that is entirely his own affair.

6. Parents have the right to freedom from political indoctrination. It may well be the case that the world would be perfect if all money were distributed equally, the police force abolished, pot legalised, and the factories turned into communes, but your parents are not necessarily shambling morons if they prefer to go on voting Co-op-Labour.

7. Parents have the right to the enjoyment of their own home. They are unlikely to enjoy their own home if one of the bedrooms appears to have been converted, without planning permission, into an indoor piggery. You may argue that your room is nothing to do with them. A glance at the rentbook will prove otherwise.

8. Parents shall have the freedom to make complaints about their children without fear of reprisal. The expression 'reprisal' includes sulking, screaming, slamming doors, making a motion with the hand as if winding up a gramaphone, and threatening to throw yourself in the river.

9. All parents shall have the right to expect a reasonable return for their labour. Having acted, over the years, as your unpaid nurse, teacher, cook, cleaner, nightwatchman, swimming instructor, banker, valet, hairdresser, boot-black, launderer, odd-

job man and general dogsbody, they are surely entitled to ask you to fill the coal bucket once in a while.

10. Parents have the right to such knowledge as is necessary for them to understand the society in which they live. This means that they should be told exactly why you have painted the words 'Screw the Pigs' in four-foot letters across the garage doors, what this inscription means, and how you propose to erase it.

11. Parents shall not be humiliated because of their own inadequacies. They shall not be addressed in O-level French, grilled on the subject of the principal rivers of Australia, or be required to make head or tail of the New Mathematics. At public dances, parents have the right to foxtrot without being mocked.

12. Parents shall have the inalienable freedom to nag, criticise, threaten, cajole, warn, scold, and offer gratuitous advice. They carry on in this boring way not because they enjoy it but because they have a duty to exercise their most precious right of all which is:

13. Parents have the right to be parents.

7

TEDDY AND THE
GEEZER

TEDDY AND THE GEEZER

TEDDY AND THE GEEZER

I am sorry that despite all protests, the long-cherished 'Listen With Mother' is to be taken off the air (or 'axed' as we say in this business, as if they were chopping down a favourite tree. Well, they are, aren't they?).

It is one more example of programme tinkering where the planners make it as difficult as possible to find a programme and then say that audiences have been dwindling.

I was intrigued, though, to learn that these days 'Listen With Mother' is heard by almost as many long-distance lorry drivers as tiny tots. Maybe it's on the particular wavelength that gives them the best reception – or maybe they just like to suck their thumbs and listen while roaring up the M1.

Anyway, as a service to those truckers who will soon be missing their favourite programme, here is a 'Listen With Mother' story to tuck into the glove compartment for a rainy day.

Are you driving comfortably? Then I'll begin. Today's story is called Teddy And The Geezer.

One fine morning Teddy wakes up, looks at his Mickey Mouse clock and leaps out of his cot with a cry of, 'Streuth! Look at the bleeding time!'

'Don't you start,' says Dolly, wiping sleep out of her eyes. 'You should have put the bleeding alarm on. I suppose you want me to get up and cook you a fried slice?'

'Elbow the breakfast, gel,' says Teddy. 'I got to drive all the way up Toytown with a truckload of ginger pop. But you needn't think you're going to stop in bed all day,' he says, struggling into his check trousers and yellow waistcoat. 'Because when that woofter Golly comes round for the rent this morning, I don't want him to find you poncing about in that shortie nightie.'

'Chance would be a fine thing,' murmurs Dolly throatily.

'Don't you give me none of your moody, gel, or you will get a right seeing-to,' warns Teddy. And with that he does no more but toes it down the depot.

Soon Teddy is driving his Matchbox 38-tonner up the Noddyland Freeway. He is just motoring past the Noah's Ark turn-off when he sees a Dinky 2000 on the hard shoulder with its hood up, and a geezer in a conical hat with stars on it flagging him down.

'Thank Christ you stopped,' says the geezer. 'I'm supposed to be up the Enchanted Castle turning a prince into a toad half an hour ago, but my wheels is playing me up.'

'You're a wizard, encha?' enquires Teddy, sucking a hollow tooth as he peers under the bonnet.

'Yes, but I'm not allowed to weave spells on nothing mechanical. Different union, see.'

'You have got a dodgy pedal,' says Teddy. 'Pass me that spanner and it should not take a jiff.' And in no time at all he has mended the geezer's motor.

'How can I ever thank you?' cries the geezer.

'Just give me a drink of lemonade and we will say no more,' says Teddy.

'I will do better than that,' says the geezer. 'As you have already sussed, I am a wizard. I am not wearing this conical hat just to pull birds with. I will grant thee three wishes.'

'You are on,' says Teddy. 'First off, I want you to turn my old woman into a mouse.'

'Say no more. What is your old woman's name?'

'Dolly,' says Teddy.

'Right,' says the geezer with a wave of his wand. 'Your Dolly is now a mouse. What is your next wish?'

'There is a woofter Golliwog what is our rent-collector. I want him turning into a cat.'

'Easy-easy. Golly is now a cat. What is your third and last wish?'

'I want Golly what is now a cat to call for the rent, see my old woman, what is now a mouse, and chase her all round the bleeding house, then sink his teeth into her neck.'

'Leave it out,' says the geezer. 'What do you think he has been doing every time you take a load of ginger-pop up Toytown?' And with a puff of smoke and a flash of his indicator, the geezer is gone.

And that's all for today. Next week our story will be Golly Gets Banged To Rights.

ALL THEIR YESTERDAY

Two elderly mayflies are hovering on a rain-puddle. They were born around seven yesterday morning. It is now getting on for two am. In a few hours they will pass away. It has been a long life.

'It is not what it was like when we were lads,' grumbles the first mayfly. 'There was none of this total darkness same as what you get now.'

'It was all light and sunny,' the second mayfly agrees. 'I can remember when you could see to the end of the road.'

'You're going back a bit there, Cyril,' says the first mayfly.

'I blame the Russians, Walter. You cannot tell me all them nuclear tests up Siberia do not have an effect on the daylight.'

'Artificial lighting they have, these days.'

'Street lamps,' says the second mayfly with scorn. 'Cheap Japanese technology.'

'You never saw artificial lighting when we were young,' says the first mayfly. 'We didn't need it. You got your light from the sun, and if the sun went behind a cloud, you did without.'

The second mayfly says: 'Street lamps! These youngsters today don't know they're born.'

'No, there was nothing like that in them days. And there was no glowworms to gawp at for minutes on end, neither. Isn't that right, Cyril?'

'Too true, Walter,' says the second mayfly. 'We had to make our own amusements.'

The first mayfly cackles reminiscently: 'Do you remember the time we flew into that cow-swamp?'

The second mayfly scratches its head. 'By bloody hell, Walter, you aren't half trotting down Memory Lane with that one! You're going back to ten past three, aren't you?'

'Either ten past three else a quarter to four – I forget. But one thing I'll never forget is chasing that blonde mayfly with the big thrusting wings through them bullrushes. A right little cracker she was. I wonder where she is now.'

'In the Old Mayflies' Home, most likely,' says the second mayfly unkindly. 'She was a bit long in the tooth, you know, Walter. She was twelve hours old if she were a minute.'

'I liked them mature,' says the first mayfly wistfully.

There is a tranquil silence. The time clock in the street-lamp overhead clicks, and then the lamp switches itself off.

'Do you know what? Cyril,' says the first mayfly. 'I can't see my flaming antennae in front of my face. I reckon I need glasses.'

'You've got to expect it at our age,' says the second mayfly. 'We're not getting any younger.'

'Still,' the first mayfly ruminates, 'we've had a good run for our money, Cyril. I reckon it was a golden age, what we lived through.'

'It's them what's just starting out that I feel sorry for,' says the second mayfly. 'I mean to say, look at the uncertain times they're living in. Fancy growing up in the pitch darkness with the constant threat of the owl hanging over you. No wonder we get juvenile delinquency.'

'And the frog menace, Cyril,' says the first mayfly. 'Don't under-estimate the frog menace.'

'I wasn't including conventional weapons, Walter. There's been a frog manace for as long as there's been mayflies.'

'Maybe so,' says the first mayfly. 'Maybe so. But at least we could see the buggers.'

The second mayfly says: 'I've heard tell that in hundreds and hundreds and hundreds of minutes from now, it should get light again. Something to do with the ice-cap shifting, I believe.'

'We won't live to see it lad. We'll be dead and buried by then.'

'Any road,' says the second mayfly, 'I've seen all I want to see. We've had some smashing times when you think about it, Walter.'

'Messing about on the council reservoir, eh?' remembers the first mayfly with a faraway look in its eyes. 'Mile after mile of shimmering water. I wonder if it's still there.'

'They'll have filled it in for redevelopment by now,' says the second mayfly.

'It seems like only yesterday, Walter.'

'It WAS only yesterday, you silly old fool,' the second mayfly says, but fondly.

PEACE AT HALF TIME

Paul McCartney's song 'Pipes of Peace' commemorates a famous World War One Christmas when the Tommies and the Huns are said to have laid down their arms and played football in No Man's Land.

It is a celebrated legend. What is not so widely known is that there were 127 arrests after the match, and so many injuries that it made World War One look like World War Two.

A German eye-witness told the *War Illustrated*: 'The English were like animals. I have never seen anything like it. They were throwing beer bottles, Christmas puddings, packets of fags, anything they could lay their hands on.'

An English private said: 'The bovver started when one of their side shouted 'Ello, Tommy!' No way was we going to take that from a bunch of Krauts. One of my mates chucked a toilet roll onto the pitch and it sort of escalated from there.'

A redcap said: 'Let's face it, a minority of our squaddies came into the trenches just looking for aggro. On the other hand, there was no proper supervision of No Man's Land, and no serious attempt by the Kraut authorities to prevent their lads from getting duffed up by the England side. So in a way they were asking for all they got.'

A German sergeant said: 'I was terrified. I only escaped with my life by disguising myself as a nun, and even then I got hit over the head with a flying mince pie. It is sickening. I came here to fight a war, not to be set on by a bunch of soccer hooligans.'

An English subaltern said: 'Since the score when the match was abandoned was 0-0, there will be a replay on New Year's Eve. We are conferring with our opposite numbers to make it an all-ticket game with the two sides segregated by barbed wire.'

TINKER, TAILOR, LIBRARIAN ...

Although these are bad times for the lads in local government, who don't know where their next penny on the rates is coming from, some town halls are still modestly expanding their activities.

The Borough of Hammersmith and Fulham, for instance, is advertising for a Senior Intelligence Officer at up to £9548 a year and an Assistant Intelligence Officer at up to £7248 a year.

It may come as news to you, as it did to me, that councils employ intelligence officers at all. It could be that Hammersmith is unique in running its own secret service. Or maybe it's quite usual for boroughs to have a flourishing spy network but they put it down in the books as street lighting or drains maintenance.

That Hammersmith has been up to its eyeballs in espionage for years is evident from its ad which continues: 'Hammersmith pioneered a Member's Intelligence Service in the late 60s ... We are now looking for two people with the skills to develop the service to communicate the right information to the right people at the right time ...'

What happened to their last two municipal Mata Haris, I don't care to ask. I do hope they haven't defected to Ealing. Perhaps the poor devils slipped over the Kensington border disguised as tourists to find out about the neighbouring power's deadly parking-permit deterrent, and are now held in the basement of a hostile town hall having splinters shoved up their fingernails.

It must be a thrill a minute, though, being an intelligence officer for the council. I suppose unlike most local government officials you don't get a desk and a hat-stand – they give you a hollow oak tree in the park. You don't file your forms in triplicate – you eat them. And when the Mayor, codenamed M, has a mission for you, he arranges an innocuous-seeming rendezvous in the council slipper baths.

'Well, Caruthers and Mainwaring, I expect you have a pretty good idea why I've sent for you. We've intercepted a coded message to Islington Borough Council that Tower Hamlets are massing social workers and mobile toenail-clipping centres on the Hackney frontier. We don't know what the cunning blighters are up to but we can't have them stealing a march on Hammersmith. Go to it, chaps.'

'What will our cover be, sir?'

'You, Caruthers, will go in as a weights and measures inspector. You, Mainwaring, will shave off your moustache and become a lollipop lady. Here are your papers and peaked caps. Your contact is a raffia co-ordinator at the civic leisure centre. He calls himself Ron. You may recognise him by his red hair.'

'Good God, sir – you can't mean Ginger Alladyce! But we thought after that Uxbridge Housing Department fiasco –'

'You thought he'd been downgraded to assistant librarian. That's what you were meant to think. In fact he was smuggled into Tower Hamlets and became one of their ratepayers. He's a very brave man. You mustn't let him down.'

'What's the password sir?'

'Alladyce will say, 'Cor blimey, this here is a right turn-up for the book, is it not?' to which you will reply, 'Never mind, matey, it will all be the same in a hundred years' time. And chaps –'

'Yes sir?'

'Should anything go wrong, you're on your own. So if your cover is blown, rather than allow yourself to be interrogated you'd better take one of these.'

'What is it, sir?'

'It's an application for early redundancy.'

LISTENING IN THE DARK

The BBC have kindly explained why my radio set keeps conking out at odd moments. It is all to do with Radio Four moving to 1500 metres on the Long Wave, and Radios One, Two and Three having something unpleasant done to their kilohertzes.

(No, I don't understand it either, except that I know it means I shall have to buy a new set. But apparently there are Boy Scouts roaming the country who will spell it out in full to old age pensioners. The moment a lad wearing headphones and garter-tabs appears in my street, I shall put on a false beard and look baffled.)

Apparently the conking-out process – which will get worse rather than better between now and November – is necessary while engineers get cracking on the switchover. I'm not clear how they set about this, but I imagine they are like those gangs of workmen you see on the railway lines on Sunday mornings, wielding pickaxes and wearing fluorescent orange jerkins.

I expect they have to turn off the electricity while they tie a granny-knot in a wavelength, hence the conking-out. But if you put your ear very close to the set during one of these periods you will probably hear a faint voice up in Droitwich calling, 'See if you can shift that rusty old megacycle with a crowbar, Fred!' And another voice echoing back along the ether, 'Daren't touch it, mate! It's the only fing what's stopping Desert Island bleedin' Discs from caving in!'

Presumably, as the gangers edge in nimble single-file down the narrow catwalk between 275 and 285 metres, a man with a whistle is on the look-out for approaching symphony concerts or party political broadcasts.

All that is straightforward enough. What leaves me utterly bewildered, however, is the BBC's statement that their biggest difficulty is carrying out work on Radio Two, because 'the network closes down between two and five am, allowing engineers only a few hours in the dark to carry out inspection and modifications.'

I simply don't understand why they have to work in the dark. Don't these gangs of workmen carry torches? Can't they hook up an arc lamp to the World Service so they can see what they're doing? You can just imagine the chaos: 'Have a feel of this, Fred. Can't make out whether it's a kilohertz or one of my bleedin' cheese sandwiches.'

Pretty silly the BBC will look if they connect Radio Two to the gas main by mistake, and only those with VHF frying pans or long-wave kettles can get the Jimmy Young prog.

What I suspect is that these fellows are not so much workmen as radio commandos, trained to make dawn raids on the Medium and Long Waves. With cork-blackened faces they crawl stealthily through the high-frequency undergrowth between 693 and 909 kHz. A sign from their leader (on detachment from Saturday Night Theatre) and they quickly overpower Radio Two by throwing a blanket over its head.

'If Waggoners' Walk makes a dash for it, Snowy, shoot to kill!' Then the wretched programme is frog-marched to a barn where Radio One, Radio Three and Radio Four are already held captive, trussed-up like chickens in aerial-wire. Later, at gunpoint, they will all be led to their new wavelengths and told to keep their mouths shut if they know what's good for them.

That is the only explanation I can think of. It certainly makes as much sense as any statement so far put out by the BBC. I hope you now understand more fully what is happening to the radio wavelengths.

BREAKFAST SERIAL

'Hello, good morning and welcome to your breakfast hour at No. 14, Sycamore Crescent. I'm Mrs Charles Robinson, you're Mr Charles Robinson, and here in the kitchen with us we have Master William Robinson and the dog Rover. Later on we hope to be joined by the incomparable Miss Wendy Robinson and we're expecting the postman, the milkman and our cleaning lady, Mrs Peabody. And we've lots more in store for you, but first a time check. Charles.'

'Eh? Good God, is it that already? What's for breakfast?'

'Charles, among the goodies we've got lined up this morning there's orange juice, corn-flakes, eggs, bacon, toast, marmalade and coffee, plus muesli and shredded carrot for Wendy who is now a vegetarian, and I'm sure we'll be hearing something more about that later in the breakfast. There'll also be an interview with the milkman about leaving one pint short yesterday and we're promised a telephone hook-up with Mother who has some pungent things to say about grocery prices, lazy workmen, immigration, her rates demand, crime, and a controversial plan for bringing back the stocks. I'll be asking what you'd like for supper and Mrs Peabody should be giving us an update on the shocking Tube service. But right now, homework. This report from William Robinson.'

'I'll do it on the bus.'

'And if I can just fill us in on the background to that, William, I think I'm right in saying you used to do your homework in the evening until you went against the general trend by getting hooked on Channel 4, when you switched to dashing it off before, during and after breakfast. But now that you're also hooked on breakfast television, you're planning on telling your teacher – I hope I'm not putting words into your mouth here – that you did your homework, but the dog Rover ate it. What would you say to that?'

'*Shush, Mum, I'm watching this.*'

'That report from William Robinson. And now the dog Rover is wagging his tail, the kitchen door's opened and I do believe – yes, will you welcome please the delightful Wendy Robinson who's come all the way downstairs to be with us this morning – just a little behind schedule but looking deliciously informal in her old dressing-gown and nightie. Wendy, a little bird tells me you've been held up in the bathroom for the last hour and a half but you finally made it, hello, lovely to see you back in the kitchen again, and what would you like for breakfast?'

'*Is that Selina Scott?*'

'Wendy's asking if that's Selina Scott. And I'm getting a signal now from William that Selina Scott is indeed who it is. This is your breakfast hour, the time now is coming up to eight forty-six, and here in the kitchen we've been joined by Wendy Robinson. Any particular reason for asking that question, Wendy?'

'*Is she a vegetarian?*'

'That's a fascinating question though not one I can answer off the top of my head but perhaps we can kick it around and maybe one of us will come up with the answer. If I can come back to you, Charles ... Charles? No, we've lost Charles. William? And answer comes there none. I'm afraid we're having some technical trouble there – as you can see, Wendy, they're both here in the kitchen but the TV set on the fridge seems to be affecting reception for the present. Let me throw the question back at you, Wendy. Why do you ask if Selina Scott is a vegetarian?'

'*Because if she is, she ought to use her influence to appeal to all the viewers to stop eating bacon. If she started every morning by saying, "Hello, welcome and please don't eat bacon," she could save the lives of millions of pigs. Are there any apples?*'

'That's an interesting point of view, Wendy, and the apples are in the fruit bowl. And I think your father wants to come in here, probably to tell you that's the silliest remark he's ever heard. Who knows, maybe we're on the brink of one of those lively family debates we used to have in the pre-breakfast-telly era. Charles.'

'Pass the marmalade.'

'We'll take a break there while I answer the doorbell. After the break, the schoolboy who hasn't washed his neck, and the worrying story of the daughter who's going to end up with anorexia nervosa if she lives on nothing but apples. Plus, we'll be taking a look at the morning post and I'll be passing father the marmalade. Back in a trice ...

'And welcome back to the breakfast hour. This is Mrs Charles Robinson and the time by the kitchen clock is eight fifty precisely. A slight programme change now: that wasn't the postman at the door as I assumed, so I shan't be bringing you the morning post until later in the breakfast. Sorry about that. In fact it was our next-door neighbour Mrs Thribble who's just been making a lightning guest appearance to complain about the noise. Mrs Thribble tells me, and I quote, "Your Selina Scott is interfering with my Michael Parkinson, I should think they can hear your telly at the other end of the street." Unquote. William, I believe you've been fiddling with the volume control, perhaps you'd like to comment on that allegation from Mrs Thribble?'

'I always have to turn the sound up when Wendy deigns to come down to breakfast – she makes such a din crunching her apple.'

'Wendy?'

'No wonder he can't hear – he's got carrots sprouting out of his ears.'

'Charles?'

'Not unless you're making some fresh.'

'I think we have a crossed line there, Charles. I wasn't asking if you'd like more coffee, I was inviting your comment on ... No, I'm afraid we've lost father again, and that's a pity, because I thought for a moment there we had the makings of one of those old-fashioned ding-dong family quarrels that used to enliven the breakfast-table before the TV set took over. Never mind – we'll leave that there and move on now to where Wendy was until after midnight last night after she promised to be in by ten, always a fascinating subject. This report from Wendy Robinson.'

'Is that Frank Bough?'

'That report from Wendy Robinson, and I'm afraid the burning question of whether Frank Bough is a vegetarian will have to wait till another breakfast hour, Wendy, because my latest guest has just walked into the kitchen. And will you give a big welcome please to Mrs Amanda Peabody, cleaning lady, raconteur and a leading expert on the London Transport system. Good morning, Mrs Peabody, and let me start by asking you, just how difficult was it getting here today?'

'Shocking, dear. I was twenty-five minutes waiting on that platform before a Wimbledon train came along. And even then it was only going as far as Putney Bridge.'

'The irrepressible Mrs Peabody. Mrs Peabody, you don't know what a tonic it is to have a real conversation here on the breakfast hour, and I hope you'll pay us another visit very soon indeed. And one final question, which only you can answer. How would you like to start on the bedrooms? Mrs Peabody ...?'

'Just a minute, dear.'

'Mrs Peabody, before we move on could I just set the record straight on your guest apearance here today? I am not paying you two pounds an hour to sit at my kitchen table watching Selina Scott and Frank Bough.'

'I couldn't agree more, dear. Switch over to David Frost.'

ILL WIND IN THE WILLOWS

The Mole had been working very hard all the morning, spring-cleaning his little home until he had dust in throat and eyes, and splashes of whitewash all over his black fur.

It was small wonder, then, that he suddenly flung down his brush on the floor, said, 'Bother!' and 'O blow!' and also, 'Hang spring-cleaning!' and switched on his little television set.

No sooner had the Mole settled down to watch 'Play School' than his string-and-cocoa-tin telephone rang. The Mole hastened to answer it.

'Hullo, Mole speaking,' said the Mole.

'Hullo, Mole,' said a familiar voice. 'Ratty this end.'

'Hullo, Ratty,' said the Mole.

'Hullo, Moley,' said the Rat again. 'This being the only pay-phone on the river bank which has not been vandalised, I thought while pasing I would give you a tinkle and confirm that you have not been re-cycled as the crutch of a pair of moleskin trousers.'

'O, don't, Ratty,' begged the Mole. 'Not even in jest.'

'Who is jesting?' said the Rat. 'You know half the Stoats in the Wild Wood have finished up in the House of Lords, don't you?'

'My paws and whiskers – you mean as ermine?' gasped the Mole.

'I was not suggesting they had been given peerages, my furry friend,' said the Rat. 'These are dodgy times we live in, Mole.'

'They are indeed, Ratty,' agreed the Mole wholeheartedly. 'That is why I have programmed myself, if you don't mind, to spend the spring watching telly in my snug little house, instead of trotting along the hedgerows getting my tiny paws caught in traps.'

'That's if there were still any hedgerows to trot along,' said the Rat darkly. 'It is like Kansas around here these days, I kid you not. But you have touched on the very subject I am giving you a bell about, Moley. Usually around this time of year when the flowers are budding, the leaves thrusting in the green meadow and all like that, a young Mole's fancy lightly turns to thoughts of picnics. Why don't you hotpaw it down to my place? There's cold chicken-coldtonguecoldhamcoldbeefpickledgherkinssaladfrenchrollspot-tedmeatsandwichesgingerbeerlemonade –'

'O, stop, stop!' moaned the Mole despairingly. 'It really is awfully kind of you, Ratty, to go to such trouble, but I have given up picnics for Lent, on the advice of a Health Education Council circular warning that they are high on starch.'

'There's Ryvita,' said the Rat temptingly.

'Thank you all the same, O generous friend,' said the Mole. 'But even supposing I did try to venture out for a jolly time on the river, I shouldn't be able to get through the door for Save The Mole campaigners who are holding their sit-down vigil above my little roof, and even if I could, I should probably get lost in the Wild Wood and end my days in a laboratory.'

'Don't talk to me about laboratories,' said the Rat. 'I came within a whisker of having an electric circuit stuffed up my jumper and my brain removed the other day. It is true. Scientist dressed up as a washerwoman – "Hello, deary, how would you like some free scent for the girlfriend in exchange for being strapped down on my ironing-board for only a few minutes?" I should cocoa. Yet you do not hear of Save The Rat campaigners, do you, Moley?'

'There was ever such a pretty gypsy caravan round this way yesterday,' said the Mole. 'The lady invited me to hop in and have my fortune told for nothing. Luckily I noticed it said H.M. GOVERNMENT RESEARCH CENTRE on the side in ornate fairground lettering, also that she had a very deep voice, so I contented myself with buying a few clothes-pegs.'

'There is a lot of it about,' said the Rat. 'Ah, well, Moley, if I cannot tempt you, I cannot tempt you. You are probably wise – we small furry animals have got to look after Numero Uno in this day and age.'

'Is it a lovely sunny day out there, Ratty?' asked the Mole wistfully.

'It is and it isn't,' said the Rat. 'There is this big black cloud drifting over from the nuclear waste disposal plant at present. Still, must not grumble. It was acid rain yesterday.'

'And how have you been busying yourself on such a fine spring morning?' asked the Mole as he longingly pictured the Rat's beloved river to himself.

'Oh, the usual. Just messing about in Boots.'

'You mean boats.'

'No, Boots. It is the toxic fumes from these oil drums floating down the river – they do not half make your eyes water. The doctor has prescribed these drops I'm taking.'

'Poor old Ratty,' said the Mole.

'It is better than having to be stomach-pumped on account of having consumed a poisoned fish, which is what happened to Otter,' said the Rat. 'Hang about, Moley. There is an animal just turned up who wants to talk to us both. Says he has got some news.'

'Of the gravest importance,' said a deeper voice, which the Mole instantly recognised.

'Hullo, Badger,' said the Mole. 'And how are you this fine spring morning?'

'Tolerable, tolerable,' said the Badger. 'Though you would think the Badgers Protection Act had never been passed, the hazards one has to face these days. You would scarcely credit it, Mole, my young friend, but a taxidermist disguised as a comic policeman attempted to take me into custody last night. I, Badger!

And on a trumped-up charge of nocturnal prowling with intent to commit a felony, if you please!'

'The very idea!' said the Mole, his fur bristling with shocked indignation. 'You sent him about his business, Badger, I'll be bound.'

'With a flea in his ear,' said the Badger. 'Now I hear you've been whitewashing, Mole. Have you also remembered to get in a stock of tinned food and your Sanilav refurbished?'

'O, Badger, I am as cosy as hot buttered toast,' said the Mole.

'Wise Mole. Mark my words, though, when the nuclear holocaust comes, a whitewashed burrow won't save you,' intoned the Badger. 'I don't agree with those Greenham Common Fieldmice breaking the law and so forth, but I am beginning to get very worried about some aspects of our defence policy, Mole. No good will come of this Cruise missile business, believe you me.'

'I'm sure you're right, Badger,' said the Mole. The Badger was right about everything.

'But that is not why I have come among you and Ratty here today,' went on the Badger. 'It is about Toad. You've heard about his new craze, I suppose?'

'O, my, whatever has Toad done now?' asked the Mole, agog for news of the irrepressible Mr Toad's latest exploit.

'Joined the Army. Saw a video tape of Trooping the Colour, and straight away nothing would do but had to sign up as a Colonel in the Coldstream Guards. Now I want you and Ratty to meet me at Toad Hall in half an hour. We have to buy the poor fellow out.'

'But Badger,' protested the Mole. 'It's awfully snug down here, and there are so many snares and dangers for a little furry creature travelling through the Wild Wood, and who knows, perhaps Toad *likes* being in the Army.'

'Likes having his kneecaps blown off? You don't know where he's been posted,' said the Badger.

'Where?' asked the Mole civilly enough.

'Would you believe Porton Down?'

BOARDER SKIRMISHES

Dear Captain Smallwood,

In thanking your good self, Mrs Smallwood and helpful staff for a most enjoyable stay at the Clifftops Hotel, may I take this opportunity of enquiring whether my spare set of teeth have turned up at all? My wife has now got it out of the twins that they could well be wedged down one of the traffic cones in the swimming pool.

I am returning the key to the third-floor landing linen-cupboard which has somehow found its way into our possession. I have done my best to straighten it again but was afraid of snapping it. I am informed that you would be well advised to open the linen-cupboard with care, as it contains a certain quantity of coke from the compound at the back of the hotel.

You will recall that wet Thursday afternoon when most of the guests including ourselves viewed your excellent video recording of *Psycho*. We had assumed that the twins spent most of the afternoon with their brothers in the games room. Most certainly – though undeservedly, as it now turns out – they were made to share the blame for the damage inadvertently caused to the pool table. (I trust you have been able to eradicate the Pentel marks by now. If this proves to be impossible, may I recommend dying the cloth purple? The boys tell me that unlike snooker and billiards where conservative green still rules the roost, bright colours are all the rage for pool. They still deny all knowledge of the missing balls.)

It transpires that the twins in fact devoted the afternoon to a game of 'Scabs and Pickets' with those children from the caravan site. (I was not aware until presented with a supplementary bill for their tea that they were from the caravan site. Had I known they were not hotel residents I should not have encouraged the twins to make friends with them.) This at last clears up the mystery of their being wet through, and my wife would like to offer her sincere apologies to both you and Mrs Smallwood for any suggestion she might have made in the heat of the moment that the twins had in any way been thrown into the swimming pool by your staff in retaliation for the traffic cone incident, in which incidentally they were by no means the ringleaders.

Unfortunately it is impossible to judge from the twins' garbled and fragmentary account how many times the 'scabs' succeeded in getting through the 'pickets' – the nearest estimate we have being 'ten trillion billion'. We have established that the coke was carried in the soup tureen that so mysteriously went missing (I believe a search of the caravan site would not go unrewarded). This, I recall, was only a medium-sized vessel, so even if they spent the entire afternoon humping coke up the back stairs and into the linen-cupboard – an unlikely eventuality, when you consider how quickly toddlers of that age become bored by their games – there cannot be more than a generous sackful in there.

Once again, I am sorry about the goldfish in the toilet. I expect you will have had a good laugh about it now, but I can appreciate that it gave quite a shock to the lady in Room 32 at the time.

Without any prompting from me, the eldest boy wishes it to be made clear that his tactless observation 'What a dump,' upon arrival referred not to the accommodation, which even with his limited experience of the world he was able to appreciate was superior to any comparable establishment, but to the resort itself. I am afraid the attractions of the Costa del Sol last year have rather spoiled him for the quieter delights of the St Clement's On Sea sand dunes. This also accounts for what you might have regarded as his generally surly manner, except on the night of the disco ball, which he thoroughly enjoyed. Of the gramophone records skimmed into or across the swimming pool, his claim is that it was a joke that got out of hand. I accept this, my one regret being that it put the idea of the traffic cone escapade into impressionable young minds.

The eldest boy is, of course, quite unused to anything stronger than draught cider (if I may say so, I do not think Pedro should have served him with Green Chartreuse, though in fairness your bar staff were not to know that he had already been drinking Margarita cocktail mix outside the caravan site off-licence), and I am quite sure that Mrs Smallwood appreciates that he would not have made the suggestions he did, even in jest, had he not lost all command of his senses. He does stress that the remark, 'What's a nice broad like you doing in a dump like this?' was meant only as a humorous parody of a Humphrey Bogart film, and that insofar as it had any significance at all, the epithet 'dump' referred once more to St Clement's On Sea in general rather than the Clifftops Hotel in particular. The eldest boy wished to write to Mrs Smallwood personally but I hope I have persuaded him to let sleeping dogs lie. If she does chance to get a letter in the post without my knowledge, and it is in verse like the one I caught him writing yesterday, I trust that you and Mrs Smallwood will make allowances for the fact that he is only an adolescent who is going through a difficult phase.

I trust the electricity supply has been restored by now. It is none of my business but in your shoes I would seriously consider having the hotel re-wired. I am no electrician but in my humble opinion one ordinary coat-hanger jammed into one ordinary thirteen-amp socket should not have fused more than one floor at the most, unless there was something seriously amiss.

You will be happy to know that the youngest boy's leg is on the mend. He wants me to ask whether to your knowledge any of the guests took snapshots of him on the roof, and if so could you possibly put him in contact with them as he would like copies (for which he is prepared to pay himself) to show his friends. I am afraid they are taking his hang-gliding exploits with a pinch of salt. Was there by any chance any reference to the youngest boy's adventure in the local rag – I believe the fire brigade and rescue services sometimes 'tip off' the Press, also I suppose it was all publicity for the hotel, so you yourself may have had a paragraph inserted? If so, I would appreciate a cutting. I see little point in returning the bed-sheet which is a complete write-off, I am afraid.

Reverting to the twins, they were telling my wife a strange story about a sheep – or 'baa-lamb' as they quaintly put it – at bedtime last evening. Whether or not their acount is coloured by the nursery rhyme 'Mary had a little lamb', I do not know, but they were talking in their prattling way about a sheep in the meadow next to the caravan site, with which they say they made friends, and which according to them used to follow them about. They were probably making it up or exaggerating, but no harm can come of taking a peep into the ballroom if you have not been in there since Friday.

Thank you once again for a memorable stay, and we look forward to seeing you and your charming wife again on some other occasion. I know that you are fully booked up for some years to come but you never know, there is such a thing as cancellations and, as you are already well aware, we should like to be first on the shortlist. How's that for a testimonial! What a shame, when you are deservedly doing such a roaring trade, that you are having to close for repairs and redecoration at the height of the season. Personally I would have had it all done in the spring but I am sure you know your own business best.

Hold the front line

> The Ministry of Defence is offering to train a new
> generation of journalists as war correspondents.
>
> *Observer*

Trainee War Correspondents Detail, ha-ten-HIPE! Stand hat HIPE! Ha-ten-HIPE! Stand hat HIPE!

Hall right, you orrible shower of acks, you might ave broke your heditors' earts but you won't break mine, his that clear?

I SAID HIS THAT CLEAR! You there, with the nancy-boy air growing arf way down is back. Yes, hit's you Hi'm talking to, laddy – the one what tried to put is Naafi break hon hexpenses. What paper har you hon hin Civvy Street? The *Sun*, har you? When Hi'm through with you, you hidle little newspaperman, you har going to wish you was hon the flaming Moon! Hand put your eels together while your sergeant-major his going blue hin the face, my lad, hor Hi will ave you hon Hold Bailey shorthand fatigues so fast your feet won't touch the ground!

Hall right, then, which hof you lot knows ow to strip down hay typewriter? Hi thought so. You ave no idea, ave you? You har hay shower. What har you? Hay shower.

Ham Hi urting you, my son? Yes, you with the Pelican book hin is hammunition pocket – henlisted from the *Guardian*, wasn't you? Hi shall ave my beady hi hon you, sunshine. Hi shall be your Guardian hangel, Hi kid you not. PUT THEM GLASSES HON STRAIGHT, YOU LOOK LIKE HAN ARF-DEMOLISHED GREENHOUSE!

Hi asked you hay question, you orrible little hessayist. Hi asked hif Hi was urting you. WELL HI HOUGHT TO BE, COS HI'M STANDING HON YOUR BEARD! GET HIT SHAVED HOFF, DO YOU EAR ME!

Hall right, ands hup heveryone what as eard hof the saying, Habandon ope hall you oo henter ere. Nobody. Hand hanswer came there none. Hi thought you lot was supposed to be big readers. Hit seems Hi was wrong. You har hignoramuses. You har han hignorant bunch hof beer-bellied media-ounds, what har you? Well hif you think you as come to han oliday camp, you his making hay big mistake, ham Hi getting through to you? By the time Hi ave finished you will be writing front-line despatches what will make Max Astings look like hay gardening correspondent. You will be polishing them pooled reports till Hi can see my face hin them. Heither that hor Hi will make you wish you was back running the Kiddies' Korner hon the Skibereen Heagle, DO YOU READ ME?

Now you as hall drawn your hequipment. Hanyone what as not been hissued with notebooks, shorthand, reporters for the use hof, one; typewriters, portable, one; pencils, standard Haitch Bee, one; sharpeners, pencil, one; dictionaries, Hoxford, pocket, one; hand Thesauruses, Roget's, one, heither speak now hor forhever old your peace.

You, laddy – har you with this hintake hor har you just han hinnocent hobserver? STAND HUP STRAIGHT, THEN – YOU'RE NOT LEANING HAGAINST THE BAR HIN HEL VINO'S NOW, YOU ORRIBLE ACK YOU!

Didn't you ear me hask hif hanybody adn't drawn their hequipment from stores? Where's your typewriter, then?

Ho, that's hay typewriter, his hit? Hexcuse me, hi thought hit was hay pile hof scrap metal. LOOK HAT THAT KEYBOARD, MAN – HIT'S FILTHY! HI COULD GROW POTATOES HOUT HOF THAT LETTER C – GET HIT CLEANED! Do hi make myself hunderstood? Hi want you back ere hat heighteen undred hours with hay portable Holympic Hi could heat my dinner hoff, hall right?

Trainee War Correspondents, ha-ten-HIPE! Hopen horder – march! GET BACK WHERE YOU WERE, YOU'RE LIKE HAY BUNCH HOF PREGNANT FASHION WRITERS! HI AVE SEEN ARF-PISSED SPORTS COLUMNISTS HIN HAY STRAIGHTER LINE THAN YOU LOT! Stand hat HIPE! Has you were! Stand hat HIPE! Has you were! Stand at HIPE! Trainee War Correspondents, ha-ten-HIPE! Right, now keep hit that way. Bags hof swank now – hopen horder – march! Hat hease.

Hall right, now heverybody pay hattention. Corporal Arris

will now pass hamong you anding hout your course timetables. Hi ham going to run through this timetable just the once, so read, mark hand hinwardly digest, because woe betide the poor bleeder what his lying hon is pit writing colour features when e should be down hon the reporting range, hor vicky verky.

Reveille his hat ho six undred hours. You will be hon parade, newspapers read hand boots polished, hat ho seven undred. Mondays, Wednesdays hand Fridays hat ho height undred hours his Basic Training. That his to say, helementary grammar, spelling punctuation hand learning the parts hof the harticle. The first part hof the harticle, hor news story has hit his known hin some regiments, his the hintro. Hi shall ave you word-perfect hin hintro-writing one week from today hor know the reason why.

NO FAINTING ON PARADE, THAT MAN! Put is ead between is knees, Corporal – hit's hall right, son, you've just got hay touch hof writer's block. No need to fear hintro-writing, laddy, you'll be doing hit hin your sleep before Hi'm done with you. Hall you ave to do his memorise, 'Hafter hay successful thrust hup Ow's-your-father Ill with only light casualties, British forces was last night celebrating hay decisive victory.' The hofficer will give you hany changes what's necessary.

Settle down now. Tuesdays hand Thursdays hat ho height undred hours we ave Hinterviewing Hunder Fire. This will consist hof aving live hammunition fired hover your eads while hasking hay squaddie for is name, hage, ome town, bird's name, bird's hage, whether e as hany plans to marry said bird when e gets back to Blighty, hand just ow nervous e felt while taking Ow's-your-father Ill. You will not repeat not wear elmets during this hexercise. GET THAT NANCY BOY HOFF HOF MY PARADE GROUND, CORPORAL, HAND PUT IM HON CROSSWORD-COMPILING DUTIES! HAT THE DOUBLE!

Mondays hand Wednesdays hafter dinner break we shall be aving typewriter drill, so Hi shall want them portables clean, bright hand slightly hoiled. STOP FIDDLING WITH THAT MARGIN RELEASE, YOU HAGGRAVATING LITTLE JOURNALIST! WHERE DO YOU THINK YOU HAR – YOUR FATHER'S TYPING POOL?

Hon Thursday hafter dinner break you will get fell hin for your Cliché Recognition Class hin your ut, hafter which you will be marched down to the Censorship Hassault Course, for which you will hall ave hay despatch ready for hinspection, written hup hin your hown time. Your task will be to get hacross the hassault course to the Telex machine hon the hother side, hat the same time havoiding the Ministry hof Defence censors what will be iding hin barrels hor down slit trenches like hay field full hof rabbits. Hanyone reaching the Telex without aving is despatch blue-pencilled hout hof hall recognition as to go back hand start hagain, hand e will go hon doing hit hagain hand hagain huntil e gets hit right, heven hif hit takes im till midnight. DO HI MAKE MYSELF CLEAR?

That man fourth from the hend, front rank – what's your newspaper, Sunny Jim? Ho, hit his, his hit? Hand does Sir David Henglish let you stand haround is newsroom with your hankles crossed hand your and hon your ip? THEN DON'T DO IT ERE, YOU ORRIBLE REPORTER YOU!

Right. Swindle Sheet Parade his Friday hafter tea, Mock Press Council earings is hon Saturday mornings before your thirty-six-hour pass, hand Mock Defence Ministry press conference his daily from 1700 hours to 1701 hours. Hany questions?

No, you cannot put in for redundo, laddie, this his Haldershot, not the Street hof Hink.

Hall right. Seeing has we ave hay few minutes hin and before kit hinspection – hand Hi opes for your sakes them pencils his well hand truly sharpened – Hi'll just try you hout hon hay routine harmy eadquarters communique hand see what you're hall made hof.

Trainee War Correspondents, ha-ten-HIPE! Close horder – march! Stand hat HIPE! Ha-ten-HIPE! Shoulder – TYPEWRITERS! Hin your hown time, release carriage-locks. By the left, hat thirty words hay minute rapid typing, quick . . . wait for hit, that man, oo do you think you har, James Cameron? By the left, quick – write!

LOG: JAM

> Britain's most land-locked city, Birmingham, is to
> sponsor a trimaran in this summer's *Observer/*
> Europe 1 Singlehanded Transatlantic Race.
>
> *Observer*

Going by Pole Star, this should be mouth of Southampton Water.
According to sextant readings, not to mention evidence of own
bloody eyes, it is more like mouth of Bull Ring underpass. What
took to be warning beacons on dredged channel off Gymp Foul
Ground are in fact lights of Top Rank Suite. Suspect that Pole Star
may turn out to be revolving neon sign of Pink Pussycat disco and
steak bars. Upon Great Bear abruptly extinguishing itself shortly
after commencement of middle watch, decided as emergency
measure to substitute conventional navigation chart with two-
colour map stapled into middle of 'Let's Wine & Dine In
Birmingham'.

Making good speed, now two days out of Harbour and approx 45
feet NW of Tesco's, where we took on supplies. If we can
navigate our way back out of bloody car park, all should be plain
sailing. Trouble is, take wrong exit and you pitch up aground
outside Holiday Inn, where we had to lay up last night having
caught our bulwarks in the revolving door.

We have lost our bearings. During first dog watch we passed
International Trade Centre for third time, though this time on
starboard side which makes nice change. We are also taking on
loose chippings v. badly. The way we are going, nightfall will find
us adrift on Spaghetti Junction. Have been dogged by ill-luck ever
since we slid off fork-lift truck in Corporation Street and our
historic voyage commenced. At three bells during last dog watch,
Force Six headwinds blowing up from West Brom forced us to
seek harbour at Little Chef. Will get caught by Neap Tides at this
rate: either that or will run into road workings on motorway.

Cones hoisted. They are all the way down bloody M5 – if it is M5.

Motorway being reduced to single-channel narrows, and craft unable to sail with current owing to temporary road surface, we were forced to throw line to caravan 'Doris' which v. kindly towed us clear of shallows. Unfortunately, when turning either NNE or SSW down slip-road to take on evening paper (compass not working, and cannot be sure that what looks like Dog Star is not Marilyn's Surf 'n' Turf Room, 'where Brum's elite go to drink and eat') we sighted more 'Men Working' signals and presently ran foul of a steam-roller, which despite our call of 'Ahoy there! Sail before steam, you ignorant berk!' so damaged our larboard hull that we had to put int West Midlands 24-Hr Garages & Recovery Service for repairs. Took minicab 'Re-Ly-Abel' ashore and relaxed to non-stop live music in friendly yet sophisticated atmosphere of one of Birmingham's swishest waterfront night-spots, previously thought to be Ursa Minor.

Woke at first light and persuaded skipper of French soft furniture tug 'Henri Duval & Cie, Meubles Magnifiques' to take us aboard and drop us at West Midlands 24-Hr Garages & Recovery Service nor'-nor'-east or sou'-sou'-west of M5. No sign of craft in dry dock: thinking it to have gone adrift, called manager, who signalled M42 branch which confirmed that they had vessel safely under tarpaulin.

It's now very plain that as suspected we were never on M5 in first place and that navigation chart in 'Let's Wine & Dine In Birmingham' is stapled in upside-down. Thank God for collision with steam-roller, otherwise we should have continued on course up M42, turned to starboard in direction of North Sea and finished up scanning bloody Skagerrak for Statue of Liberty. Got lift on United Dairies milk tanker which was docking hard by municipal bus station. Took bearings and found that we wanted to be at Lat 15° Long D°, going by chart references employed in Greater Birmingham 'A-Z Citimap' which we purchased at bus station chandler's. Engaged minicab 'Re-Ly-Abel' to convey us to our berth.

It's unbelievable. Minicab 'Re-Ly-Abel', after having cheek to charge over pound per nautical mile for our voyage, dumped us not at West Midlands 24-Hr Garages & Recovery Service off M42, but at West Midlands 24-Hr Garages & Recovery Service off

M6 half-way to bloody Coventry. Skipper carried no charts or navigational instruments and was so inept at reading our Greater Birmingham 'A-Z Citimap' that we had to pilot him out of city centre, which took getting on for two hours as wind was against us. Intend to report him to harbour-master when get back from crossing Atlantic. Meanwhile, was obliged to charter towing truck 'West Midlands 24-Hr Garages & Recovery Service' to get us to our rightful mooring. So late by then that having checked our craft was seaworthy again, decided to put in for night at Lotus Blossom Dining Experience West and leave on first tide.

Cruising steadily down M6, hope to link up with M5 nor'-nor'-east of Smethwick by nightfall and thus be back on course. At least we do not have to steer through middle of Birmingham again – would sooner take a Cortina 2000 through bloody Needles than go through all that again.

Must have taken wrong slip-road – will write to council about this: road signs do not have flashing lights, sirens, bells or any indication whatsoever that middle shipping lane leads straight back to bloody Bull Ring. After taking on keg lager at Peter Dominic's, returned to our vessel to find traffic warden slapping ticket on hull for mooring on yellow line. Warned that next time she sighted craft we would find Denver boot clamped to rudder. Is it all worth it?

After laying up for night at Top O' The Tower prime meat carvery and licensed go-go bars, set sail at first light with aid of new simplified chart forming gatefold of 'Where To Go – The Discriminating Nite-Life Guide to the West Midlands'. Man-oeuvring tricky Exit 7 which according to our readings should have carried us to M5, found ourselves carried instead to M6 and had to sail several miles off course before turning short round at Grotwood Services. Intend warning *Reed's Nautical Almanac* to accept no advertising from any firm purporting to supply pilot guides to Birmingham and environs. Managed by brilliant display of seamanship to find proper turn-off for M5 going south'ard, and so after five days before the mast are at last set on proper course.

Becalmed on hard shoulder. Mist came down and so it would have been hazardous to make attempt to get back on fast lane with our oars. Lit pipe and enjoyed mournful keening of gulls, or pigeons as they more probably are just off Smethwick, and rumble of passing juggernauts. Presently police car hove alongside and insisted on radioing towing truck 'West Midlands 24-Hr Garages & Recovery Service' to take us in for barnacle scrape and MOT test, despite our protests that we were hardly likely to set off across Atlantic in unroadworthy vessel.

Luckily master of 'West Midlands 24-Hr Garages & Recovery Service' was seasoned old hand who as soon as he saw colour of our money agreed to pilot us to Warwickshire border and set us on course for Southampton Water. Had mist not turned into fog and our pilot lost his bearings, we should have been just about off Lizard Point by now instead of hard by Ladbroke International.

Unhappily, we were just tying up when same police officers we had encountered out on open M5 came aboard and charged us with doing six knots in built-up area, cruising wrong way along one-way street and failing to heave-to at zebra crossing. As case does not come up until Thursday, this must end our present attempt to win Transatlantic Race. Nothing daunted, we shall set sail next week for Sheffield and get in training for Americas Cup.

CLOUD-CUCKOO-LAND

> Switzerland had only one strike last year.
>
> *Financial Times*

I'll tell you what the trouble with 'What do we want? Ten per cent!' as a slogan is, since you ask. You try yodelling it.

The same goes for 'President of the Swiss Confederation M. Fritz Honegger Out Out Out!' Beep that out on massed alpenhorns and it sounds like a dawn chorus of Morse transmitters that've had the operation.

Oh, and another thing. Next time you want to bring the lads in the shipyards out as a gesture of solidarity with the Amalgamated Society of Cuckoo-clock Operatives and Allied Trades' proposed sit-in, just double-check if we've got a bloody navy, right?

I mean to say you made me look a right nana, walking into that ski-lodge and asking please could anyone direct me to the Zermatt dry docks. I mean to say I've got to go on 'Good Morning Switzerland!' tomorrow and win the hearts and minds of that lot. What are all those waiters and commis chefs and barmen and apprentice ski instructors going to say when I appeal for one hundred per cent support for our brothers in the tourist industry? They're going to say, 'There's that stupid berk who thought that team of downhill racers were flaming rivetters coming off night-shift!'

Not that it would have made a Swiss centime's-worth of difference to our cause if I *had* found any shipyard workers. Because you do realise those 'One out all out' leaflets you gave me are all in Italian, don't you? I mean granted that is a very nice drawing of a cuckoo-clock mainspring overlooker fainting from lack of nourishment, but it does say underneath it, 'Uno fuóri, voi tutti fuóri,' doesn't it? You see, the point I'm making is that all our local branch membership happens to speak bloody German, right?

And talking of printed matter. That poster you've got stuck up all over the place, 'Keep Switzerland Out Of The Arms Race.' Frankly, if you want my opinion, I think it's a waste of our slender budgetary resources. It'll have as much popular impact as that last one you dreamed up, 'Swiss Guard Out Of Vatican Now.'

Oh, and just while I think to mention it: do me a favour, will you? Stop calling the Red Cross blacklegs. You know they're not going to come out on strike and I know they're not going to come out on strike, so we might just as well learn to live with it, right?

Do you know what I sometimes think? I sometimes think we're not cut out for industrial action in this bleeding country. All right, so I'm depressed at this present moment in time. I'm on a big low, owing to our total lack of success in trying to mobilise the condensed milk workers into a go-slow. I mean to say, why didn't someone tell me we had a condensed milk mountain? I thought it was just snow. But you see, even if I was the greatest trades union movement optimist ever born, what is there to pin my faith in? The May Day Right to Work march up the flaming Matterhorn – who's going to turn out for that? It's a bloody joke, isn't it?

One thousand years of uninterrupted exploitation of the masses and what is the best we have come up with by way of protest up to press? A seven per cent turnout for a day of action by the Association of Secret Bank Account Tellers – and even that had to be on a Sunday, seeing as how they couldn't get time off during the week.

You know what we want in this country, don't you? Coal mines. I've a bloody good mind to go out and dig one myself. A winter of dis-flaming-content, that's what we need, with the militant faceworkers of Berne in bitter mood and even the traditionally moderate open-cast miners of Geneva expected to vote a massive yes for head-on confrontation.

Steel mills, that's something else we could do with. Silver-paper mills they'd have to be, in our particular case, to provide the wherewithal for wrapping our own chocolate whilst incidentally creating ten thousand jobs. That's it: half a dozen silver-paper mills in every canton in Switzerland. And then we want the Government to get some bugger over from America to close them all down. That'd do it. That'd get the lads out. You wouldn't have the National Union of Edelweiss Pluckers whingeing 'Let's not rock the boat' then, believe you me. I can see the headlines now: LAUSANNE – CITY WITHOUT A FUTURE.

Talking of key industries, shall I tell you where we missed our big chance? Where we went wrong, strategywise? When the bloody Japs started flooding the market with digital watches. Instead of vainly trying to persuade the Federated Watch-hand Makers, Numeral Engravers and Cog Grinders to organise a cross-legged sit-in, also to refuse point-blank to wear their pixie hats for the benefit of coach-parties, do you know what we should have done?

We should have brought out the chocolate workers. Mass meetings, we should have called. We should have put it to the lads straight. 'All right,' we should have said. 'Just because the Japs have not yet mastered the art of making chocolate come to a point so they can start copying Toblerone, whereas they are running rings round our watchmakers, you think you're laughing and giggling, don't you? It is a case of pull the ladder up, isn't it? But just you wait till Christmas, when they start dumping chocolate digital wrist-watches in every kiddy's stocking in Europe,' we should have said. 'And it won't stop at that, if we don't take decisive appropriate action,' we should have said. 'Stamping out chocolate pennies will no longer be a sinecure for life. The chocolate yen already looms on the horizon.'

I sometimes wish I'd been born Belgian. Or Dutch. I do, truly.

That's how despondent I am. I mean, you can say what you like about the Low Countries, but when there is a lock-out compelling our Belgian and Dutch brothers to lie down outside the factory gates under a big banner saying, 'WE SHALL NOT BE MOVED,' their convener doesn't have to come round with a bulldozer a fortnight later and dig them out of a sodding avalanche, does he? It is very difficult to put across your message as a militant when the biased media depicts you as having your face licked by a bloody great St Bernard with a little barrel round its neck, I kid you not.

Also, these other countries are not cursed with Swiss roll plants. Why our boss-orientated TV news-readers find it impossible to utter the words, 'Angry Swiss roll workers' without smirking all over their faces is beyond me, but find it impossible they do. No wonder we encounter difficulty in mobilising the redundancy-threatened jam-spreaders and sponge-furlers for a protest steamer-trip across Lake Geneva.

It is the same with cheese. All right, admitted: the flat nations I have mentioned do have cheese-workers, but the commodity produced by their underpaid labour force does not have holes in it. Therefore, should it be announced on 'News At 2200 Hours' that a crisis blew up in the cheese industry today, you do not have the news-reader sagging to the floor clutching his stomach and gurgling like a mountain-bred Norman Wisdom. I mean to say, what is so funny about the skilled perforation crews who punch out the precision-drilled holes in Gruyère staging a lightning walk-out, you tell me? If you want my view, the biased media get secret grants from the Government to extract the Michael at every available opportunity, in order to underplay and minimise our industrial problems.

Still: onwards and upwards, eh? Don't let the bar-stewards get you down, eh? I have had my moan, now let's start thinking constructively. Listen, let me try this on you. I mean to say, bearing in mind some of our topographical problems, how does this grab you? *Ski-ing pickets.* No?

DECLINE AND FALL

Dear Autumn,

I am dropping you these few lines in the hope that you will take the hint, see sense and stop treating your job as a cushy number sent from heaven. There are only four seasons in the year and we cannot afford to carry passengers.

I think you know what I am getting at, Autumn. I do not need to spell it out. As a season, you are taking liberties. You have been getting away with murder. You have been pulling a flanker and letting others do the work. Admitted, you have fewer months to play with than some other seasons we could mention, but what do you do with them? The old falling leaves trick and that is about it. It is not good enough.

Consider what Spring, for instance, is able to manage. So as to be fair, we will not take all the three months this typical season has at its disposal but just one at random. We will take the month of March. For openers, it comes in like a lion. Noted for it. By comparison, your own prime-time month of September shuffles around like an armadillo that needs oiling. Then look at the other goodies March has to offer: mad hares and Ides, to name but two. Not to mention Spring lambs being thrown up in the air by press photographers. Be frank – when did a gambolling Autumn lamb last get into the papers?

All right, you will say, I have picked a month that has everything going for it. So let me give you another one – April. April showers. April fools. April in Paris. Whoever heard of September showers? October fools? Granted, April has got Paris sewn up, but has it ever occurred to you to put in a bid for September in Oslo? And before you start whining that Spring has the weather on its side, let me give you one more idea. October fill-dyke. And how is this for a slogan to go with it: October is the cruellest month. You see, Autumn, you are just not trying. You are not using your noddle.

You are also bone-idle. To get anywhere in this world you have to compete, and let us face it, Autumn, you are not going to topple the opposition out of the ratings just by starting those bloody leaves falling and then sitting on your backside. You have got to work at it.

Look at some of the publicity material you are up against. The hounds of spring are on winter's traces. Summer is icumen in, lhude sing cuccu. Now is the winter of our discontent. Be honest now, Autumn: even if you had Saatchi and Saatchi handling your account, what is the best you could come back with if you didn't want a knuckle-rapping from the Advertising Standards Authority? The hounds of autumn are rolling about in some fallen leaves. Autumn is icumen in, cuccu thinks about legging it to Africa. Now is the autumn of our slight discomfort.

This brings me to the subject of write-ups and plugs in general, lack of same in books and mags being one of your biggest headaches. You have only got to turn to the *Oxford Dictionary of Quotations* to see what you are up against. Summer gets no fewer than eighty-five mentions, and that is not counting references to darling buds of May and other spin-offs. Winter is in there with fifty-eight mentions, including the chart-busting 'Blow, blow, thou winter wind.' As for Spring, it is top of the league with a mind-boggling ninety-one quotes, ranging from the flowers that bloom in it tra-la to sweet lovers loving it with a hey and a ho and a hey-nonny-no. Every one a winner.

And Autumn? It is laughable. A grand total of eleven mentions – all right, call it fifteen if you are including the word autumnal, which you are not going to tell me is in common use, particularly among punters with false teeth. Also, without any exception whatsoever, all these are quotes that no one in the world has ever heard of, even big readers. The only reason they are there is that the Oxford University Press had to bung something in under Autumn to make up the four seasons.

I beg of you, just look yourself up in the index. You have got two Shakespeares, both written on an off-day; you have got a John Donne, a Milton, a Browning, a Tennyson, likewise routine stuff; and you have got four Shelleys. All right, admittedly one of these is a full-blown ode beginning, 'O Wild West Wind, thou breath of Autumn's being,' but as this happens to be the very same one that ends 'If Winter comes, can Spring be far behind,' I am sorry to say that at the death you are once again left with egg on your face.

And that is it as far as big-name quotes are concerned. Once past Shelley we are down among the rubbish with the likes of James

Thomson (1700-1748), Charles Reade (1814-1884) and John Logan (1748-1788) who you can bet is known to the Poetry Circle as John Who? It is pathetic. I am sorry to say this, Autumn, but when your competition is 'In the Spring a young man's fancy lightly turns to thoughts of love,' and all you can offer – and by the same top-class author, mind: I am not talking about riffraff like your Matthew Arnolds (1799-1845) or your Thomas Hoods (1799-1845) – is 'Tears from the depth of some divine despair, Rise in the heart and gather to the eyes, In looking on the happy Autumn-fields,' then it is time to pack up and go home. I mean to say – happy Autumn-fields? It does not even make flaming sense. Still, I suppose we can be grateful that friend Tennyson did not make that Autumn-woods, because then we would have been back with those bloody falling leaves again.

Fair enough, you will say, but talking of odes as we were earlier, what about Keats's 'Ode to Autumn'? To which I will reply, go on, then, what about it? Because I hope you realise that inasmuch as this poem is addressed to you personally, you are referred to as thee and thy throughout, with the word Autumn not getting so much as a look-in. Whereas the other seasons are given free plugs by name. I mean to say you have only to look at the billing – Spring, Summer, Thee and Winter – to see what that ode does for you. No, I will agree that Keats was one of the governors, in fact as a poet he was chairman of the board in my book, but when it comes to P.R. I am sorry to say that his 'Ode to Autumn' is on a par with 'You are never alone with a Strand.'

All right, I will give you that, point taken, I can hear you saying next: but if your long-haired poets don't want to write about Autumn by name there is no way of making them, short of bunging them an Arts Council grant or fifty in oncers slipped into the back trouser sky-rocket. It that were only true, Autumn my son, your troubles would be over. You would be laughing and giggling. A quick crate of champagne to Sir John Betjeman and before you could say Joan Hunter-Dunn he would have knocked you out a right little cracker about how autumn leaves are falling golden now on tarmac recreation grounds in Slough, no questions asked and Bob is your uncle. But strange to relate, that is not how these rhymesters operate. Your Philip Larkins and similar of that calibre do not churn this stuff out to order. They have to wait for inspiration. And that is where you are definitely letting the side down, Autumn. Because let us face it, up to press you have provided them with about as much inspiration as my backside.

What you want is a completely new image – one that has got nothing whatsoever to do with things falling off trees. You have got exactly a year to think about it.

Yours etc,
God

EGGING THEM ON

Do you mind if I express some concern about the baby? I am assuming, of course, that that chocolate-coated blob in the corner, resembling some shapeless thing from Outer Space that has just oozed itself under the door, is in fact, the baby.

My concern for the baby is that if it has to be rushed to hospital and X-rayed, as well might happen before this day is over, an examination of its innards will reveal that it has turned into a human Smartie.

Have you any conception how many Easter eggs, whether milk or plain, that child has consumed since breakfast time?

And while we are discussing family affairs, may I ask why you appear to have adopted a small Nigerian boy without consulting me?

I am never sarcastic. I genuinely mistook the lad, whom you now claim is my son, for a young shaver of West African extraction. He looks as though he has been held by the heels and dipped in a vat of melted chocolate.

About the rest of my children I will say nothing. I merely inform them that at bath-time tonight they can report to me in the back yard, where I shall swill them down with a hose-pipe.

Certainly I will come to the point I wish to make instead of ranting and raving. It gives me no pleasure to rant and rave, I can assure you.

The point I wish to make is that this Easter egg business has got completely out of hand.

When I was the same age as that walking, talking cocoa-bean you are trying to pass off as my son, the giving of Easter eggs was a simple, unostentatious and rather moving little ceremony.

You clustered round the breakfast-table on the morning of Easter Day, where you were each handed a small, hollow chocolate egg with instructions not to eat it all at once, on pain of being kicked around the house until your backside was blue.

Note that I used the singular form and that I employed the adjectives 'small' and 'hollow'. A chocolate egg means one solitary chocolate egg. A small chocolate egg means one of substantially lesser proportions than a rugby football. A hollow chocolate egg means one not containing enough marzipan and nougat to stock a confectioner's shop.

Since we classed ourselves as higher than the beasts of the field, unlike certain babies I could mention, the injunction not to scoff this modest ovoid all in one go was obeyed. We did not chomp, we nibbled. We did not slurp, we sucked. A single Easter egg, in those far-off unsophisticated barefoot days, could last us well into July.

A glance at this household, which looks to me as if you have just brought off a successful take-over bid for Cadbury-Schweppes Ltd, reveals how very much the times have changed. Where, I ask myself, did we go wrong?

Please do not interrupt. The question was of a rhetorical nature, I will tell you where we went wrong.

We allowed the supply of Easter eggs to accumulate on a scale unprecedented since the Great Powers began to stockpile nuclear weapons. That glutinous, wobbling mass in the corner, which yesterday had the appearance of a baby, is an indication of what such insane escalation can lead to.

First of all, I bought the children an Easter egg apiece, and then *you* had to go and buy them an Easter egg apiece. And then they went out and bought each other an Easter egg apiece, making three Easter eggs per capita for openers.

Thereafter, they were bombarded with Easter eggs by aunts, uncles, grandmothers, godparents, friends and neighbours. For all I know they were stopped in the street and had Easter eggs thrust into their sticky hands by complete strangers. The result, as you can see, is the chocolate mountain which is the cause of my remarks.

I do not wish to alarm you, and I don't know whether there is any medical evidence to support me, but it is my belief that consuming the better part of a hoard of eighteen Easter eggs in less than two hours can soften a child's brain.

Because you know what our youngest son did the moment he received his pocket money this morning, don't you? He promptly waded through this knee-high dump of silver paper and fancy wrappings until he reached the front door, then belted off to the sweet-shop and bought a bloody Mars bar!

Yes, I have now quite finished.

No, thank you, I don't like chocolate.

Just a small piece then.

Hmmm. Not bad.

All right, seeing it's Easter – another tiny piece and then no more.

Not as tiny as that, damn it! I'll tell you what, why don't you sling over the whole egg while you're about it?

LOOKING FOR AN ORGY

I, Charles Septimus Parkin of 23A Jubilee Mansions, Norwood, make this statement voluntarily in the presence of Detective-Sergeant William Cooney and PC Throstle of 'E' Division. I am forty-three years old and a clerk in the employ of British Fat Products Ltd. I am married in name only. I do not wish to add to that.

I first became aware of the permissive socictly on or about September 5 1969. I remember the date because it is the birthday of my niece Avril, and I had bought her a Kooky-doll as a present. I do not know why the Kooky-doll is still in my possession, or why she was in the cistern cupboard. I cannot explain why she is wearing fish-net tights, see-through bra and a PVC mackintosh instead of the après-ski outfit depicted on her box. The Action Man produced by Det. Sgt. Cooney from the cistern cupboard in my presence does not belong to me. I do not know why Action Man is wearing only his boots. The Polaroid camera is for the purpose of taking holiday snaps. The photograph which I ate before being cautioned by Det. Sgt. Cooney was a holiday snap.

On or about September 5 1969 I read in a Sunday newspaper about a wife-swapping ring in Mauncey Road, Birmingham, together with an exposé of certain magazines 'for swingers only', also photographs allegedly taken at a drug party in Leeds before the reporter made an excuse and left. It is not true that from that day on I became obsessed by the permissive society, although what I read was certainly an eye-opener. I did not suggest to my wife Noreen that we should engage in similar activities. The phrase, 'Let's get some fun out of life while we're still young, or are you too frigid?' is not one that I would normally use. I did not place an advertisement in the *Swapper's Digest*. I have never heard of the *Swapper's Digest*.

I now recall that I did place an advertisement in the *Swapper's Digest*. The fifteen back numbers of this publication under the towels in the airing cupboard are for my own use. The advertisement was a joke. It has been put to me that 'Virile husband-and-wife duo wish to meet AC-DC couples, no prudes' does not sound like a joke, but I do not agree. It was an exercise in parody. I know nothing about an accommodation address in Soho. I received no replies to my advertisement.

I have never been in Mauncey Road, Birmingham.

I now recollect that I went to Mauncey Road, Birmingham, on September 9 and spoke to a woman now known to me as WPC Hawkins. My purpose in journeying to Birmingham was to visit an old army friend, 586 Cadger McNally, whose address I cannot at present remember. I asked WPC Hawkins to direct me to New Street Station. I did not employ any words such as 'Are you a swinger?' I recall employing the phrase, 'Where is the action?' This is an idiomatic expression indicating that I was looking for New Street Station.

I did not deposit a suitcase in the left-luggage office at New Street Station. I identify a suitcase produced by Det.-Sgt. Cooney as my property. I confirm that it did not fly to Birmingham of its own volition. The mask, riding-crop and length of rope are all my property. I purchased the mask at a novelty shop in Paddington in case my friend 586 Cadger McNally was giving his annual fancy-dress party. The riding-crop was a present for my married niece June, who is a keen horsewoman. I have no recollection whatsoever of proposing to my married niece June that I should be her gee-gee and that she should ride me around her living-room. The length of rope was in case of fire. I have always carried a length of rope in case of fire ever since reading that Hans Christian Andersen did likewise. It has been put to me that Hans Christian

Andersen is the same 'Fancypants' Andersen who is now doing bird at the Scrubs for thieving lingerie off of clothes lines. To the best of my knowledge Hans Christian Andersen was a writer of fairy tales. I have been informed what the expression 'fairy' means in common parlance. I have never been that way inclined. I have never been to Hampstead Heath.

It is not true that I was wandering about Leeds in a polka-dot dress and steel-blue nylon stockings on the night of September 9-10. The polka-dot dress produced by Det. Sgt. Cooney was purchased at Selfridge's for my friend 586 Cadger McNally's fancy-dress party. I regard flushing clothes down the lavatory as a normal method of disposing of unwanted property.

Having been shown certain photographs, I now wish to correct any suggestion I may have made that I was not wandering about Leeds on the night of September 9-10, but I deny that I was looking for a so-called drag party. I was in Leeds for the simple reason that I got on the wrong train at Birmingham New Street Station. I was suffering from flu and had taken some tablets shortly before drinking a glass of beer. This must have made me light-headed. I was definitely not wearing the polka-dot dress, except for a short period.

I admit to having knocked at a door in Victoria Hospital Avenue, Leeds, between 12.30 and 12.45 am. I deny asking the lady now known to me as Mrs Jeannette Henderson if there was room for one more. I deny suggesting to Mrs Henderson that nobody would take her for a sailor. My purpose in knocking at the door was to ask for a glass of water. I was not wearing the polka-dot dress. I had recently drunk a carton of milk which must have splashed over my overcoat, giving it a polka-dot effect. I did not raise my overcoat to thigh level while in conversation with Mrs Henderson.

Having been given an opportunity to reconsider that portion of my statement relating to the *Swapper's Digest*, I now believe that there may have been one or two replies to my advertisement. There may have been 1753 replies. Certain parcels which Det.-Sgt. Cooney removed from under the floorboards in my presence may contain replies to my advertisement. I have not read any of them. I do not recognise a typewritten manuscript entitled *Kitty's Awakening*. I do not know of any invitation to attend a party in Tulse Hill for sex fun.

I am familiar with Tulse Hill. I may have been there on the evening of December 18. An important invoice had blown out of my office window on that day and I thought it might have landed in Tulse Hill. I may have been wearing a shortie nightdress under my raincoat. I often wear a shortie nightdress in the privacy of my own home as I understand there is no law against it. I wear it because it is convenient. At approximately 10 pm, on the evening of December 18, I remembered that I had not taken the dog for his usual walk. I put on a raincoat over my shortie nightdress and took him as far as the pillar box. The dog having slipped his lead and been run over by a coal-lorry I thought that rather than waste my outing I would proceed to Tulse Hill and look for the invoice.

I may have approached several householders in the Tulse Hill district with the words, 'Have you a French kitten for sale?' I was not aware that this was a password. Owing to the accident to my dog I was anxious to obtain a new pet as quickly as possible. I do not know why I asked for a French kitten. I now think that I may have asked for a *fresh* kitten, meaning one that was only a few days old.

After a conversation with my wife Noreen I now recall that I have never owned a dog. I have been taking pills for a severe migraine and these, swallowed in conjunction with beer or wine, sometimes induce a sensation of owning a dog.

I deny hailing a taxi at Tulse Hill Station at 1.43 on the morning of December 19.

Having been assured that nobody is going to get their collar felt for taking a cab, I now remember hailing a taxi at Tulse Hill Station, but deny asking the driver if he knew anything about blue movies.

The taxi took me to my home. I deny saying, 'Well, here we are at Iceberg Manor.' I deny offering the driver double fare to take me to Hampstead Heath.

Certain evidence having been shown to me, I admit to being on Hampstead Heath at 3.16 on the morning of December 19 and approaching the gentleman I now recognise as Det. Sgt. Cooney. I regret having prevaricated about this matter, but I was of the impression that wearing false moustaches went out with Sexton Blake. I concur that if I had stuck to false moustaches instead of polka-dot dresses I would not be in the situation in which I now find myself.

I confirm that I mistook Det. Sgt. Cooney for a sex maniac, and that I asked him for information about any lewd, filthy, degrading and obscene parties that might be going on in the vicinity. I agree that I falsely represented my wife Noreen as being available for sex fun in the event of Det. Sgt. Cooney being able to assist me in my depraved endeavours. I now understand that my use of the words 'sizzling,' 'versatile' and 'hot pants' in respect of my wife Noreen was an offence under the Trades Description Act, and I wish to express my regret for any embarrassment, distress and disappointment caused both to my wife and Det. Sgt. Cooney.

ELECTRICITY I HAVE KNOWN

You learn something new every day. With no thought of self-improvement, for example, I was reading that story of Thurber's in which he recalls his mother's belief that electricity leaks out of any empty light socket if the switch has been left on. From this I gathered – going by the general context, and the known fact that Thurber was a humorist – that it doesn't.

I picked up another piece of electrical knowledge in 1951, while working as a drama critic on the *Yorkshire Evening Post*. Wanting to imply that a certain actress had given a muted performance, I wrote that while undoubtedly she had an electric presence, on this occasion it was as if the electricity had been immersed in water. A kindly sub-editor explained to me that when electricity gets wet, by some miracle of the elements it intensifies rather than diminishes. I have never seen the sense of this, but I conceded the point and have only used gas-driven metaphor since that date.

I was never taught electricity at school, nor was it often a topic of dinner-table conversation among my parents. What I know about the subject I have mastered the hard way. Take, as an instance, television, an electrical device of awesome complexity. Unlike more privileged students, who are able to go running to m'tutor every time the framehold goes wobbly, I have had to learn in the School of Life that on the large rented model the knobs are on the front whereas on the HMV portable they are on the side. Similarly with electric irons. When I bought my first electric iron

231

there was no plug attached, presumably in case I wanted to wind the flex around my neck and jump off Westminster Bridge with it. There was a leaflet explaining how to get the plug on, but this was of course in German, the international language of the household appliances industry. Only by putting my natural intelligence to the problem did I eventually work out the solution – find a German-speaking electrician.

And so, what with having perforce to change a light bulb here and tune in a transistor radio there, I have picked up a pretty sound working knowledge of electrical matters. It is not comprehensive, God knows – I still can't fully understand why you can't boil an egg on an electric guitar – but when I jot down a summary of what I have learned, I marvel that I have never been asked to write for the *Electrical Journal*:

1   Most electricity is manufactured in power stations where it is fed into wires which are then wound around large drums.

2   Some electricity, however, does not need to go along wires. That used in portable radios, for example, and that used in lightning. This kind of electricity is not generated but is just lying about in the air, loose.

3   Electricity becomes intensified when wet. Electric kettles are immune to this.

4   Electricity has to be earthed. That is to say, it has to be connected with the ground before it can function, except in the case of aeroplanes, which have separate arrangements.

5   Electricity makes a low humming noise. This noise may be pitched at different levels for use in doorbells, telephones, electric organs, etc.

6   Although electricity does not leak out of an empty light socket, that light socket is nevertheless live if you happen to shove your finger in it when the switch is at the 'on' position. So if it is not leaking, what else is it doing?

7   Electricity is made up of two ingredients, negative and positive. One ingredient travels along a wire covered with red plastic, and the other along a wire covered with black plastic. When these two wires meet together in what we call a plug, the different ingredients are mixed together to form electricity. Washing machines need stronger electricity, and for this a booster ingredient is required. This travels along a wire covered with green plastic.

8   Stronger electricity cannot be used for electric razors. Electric razors make a fizzing sound when attached to a power plug.

9   Electricity may be stored in batteries. Big batteries do not necessarily hold more electricity than small batteries. In big batteries the electricity is just shovelled in, while in small batteries (transistors) it is packed flat.

10   Electricity is composed of small particles called electrons, an electron weighing only $1/1.837$ as much as an atom of the lightest chemical element, hydrogen, unless the *Encyclopaedia Brittanica* is a liar.

Incurious people are content to take all this as read. They press a switch and the light comes on, and that is all they know about the miracle in their homes. This has never done for me. I have to know how things work, and if I cannot find out from some technical handbook – the *Every Boys' Wonder Book* series does an advanced manual on electricity – then I combine such information as I already have with simple logic. Thus it is very easy to deduce that the light switch controls a small clamp or vice which grips the wires very hard, so that the electricity cannot get through. When the switch is flicked on the vice is relaxed and the electricity travels to the light bulb where a bit of wire called the element, is left bare. Here, for the first time, we can actually *see* the electricity, in the form of a small spark. This spark is enlarged many hundreds of times by the curved bulb which is made of magnifying glass.

Why, is our next question, do these light bulbs have a limited life? As any schoolboy knows, heat converts oxygen into moisture. When all the oxygen in the light bulb has become liquefied in this manner, it naturally quenches the electric spark. Some years ago a man in Birmingham invented an everlasting electric light bulb which, since it contained no oxygen, would never go out. The rights in it were bought up by light-bulb manufacturers who keep it locked in their safe.

Now we come to electricity as a source of power rather than a source of light or heat. Why, when you plug in an electric iron, does it get hot, whereas when you plug in an electric fan it does not get hot but whirrs round and round? The answer is that when light or heat is required we use bare electricity, whereas when power is required we keep the electricity covered up. The constant flow of sparks, unable to escape, is converted into energy. This energy is fed into a motor which makes things go round and round.

I have not yet touched on fuse wire. It has always amazed me that an industry which is so enterprising in most respects – the invention of colour electricity for use in traffic lights and the harnessing of negative electricity for refrigeration are two examples that come to mind – should still, two hundred years after James Watt invented the electric kettle, be manufacturing fuse wire too thin. I pass on a hint for what it is worth. There is available from hardware shops a sturdy wire used mostly for making chicken runs, and this is far more durable than the stuff sold by electricians (who must, I appreciate, make a living). By using chicken wire I now have a fuse box which – even when the spin-dryer burst into flames due to too much booster electricity having been fed into it – has for six months been as impregnable as the Bank of England.

But why have fuse wire at all? I completely understand that the fuse box is the junction at which the wires leading from the power station join, or fuse with, the wires belonging to the house, and that these two sets of wires have got to be connected with each other somehow. But what is wrong with a simple knot? Perhaps I might make this the subject of a paper for the *Electrical Journal* which, I now see from the *Writers' and Artists' Year Book*, welcomes electro-technical contributions not exceeding 3000 words.

In some respects, I reiterate, my knowledge is imperfect. I have not yet explored the field of neon signs – how do they make the electricity move about? And the pop-up toaster – how does it know when the toast is ready? With an electronic eye, presumably – and this brings us to another fruitful area. What is the difference between electricity and electronics? Or is there a difference? Is electronics now just the smart word to use, like high-speed gas? How can an English computer speak French, which requires a different voltage? Logic would answer these questions too, and many of a more technical nature, but the light over my desk has just gone out. A valve blown somewhere, I expect.

8

NOT ONLY IN AMERICA

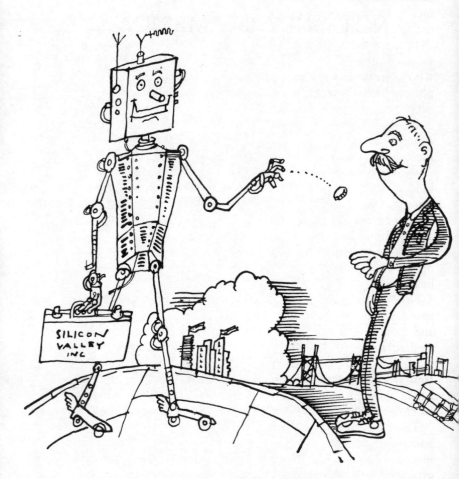

UPSCALE AND THE UNDERCLASS

UPSCALE AND THE UNDERCLASS

On each visit to these inventively articulate United States, a shoal of dazzling new words swims into my vocabulary. My latest catch includes a brace of opposites as bright as cold steel, which I will define for you – 'Underclass' and 'Upscale.'

Beneath the canopies of the swishest hotel in San Francisco's swishest square loiter four or five young men in their twenties, who accost the well-heeled with the same politely apologetic phrase: 'Would you have a little change so I can buy something to eat?'

It does not have the same poignant lilt as 'Brother, can you spare a dime?' but set to music it would be the song of the Underclass – the consumer society's human leftovers.

Dispossessed from the working class, because nobody needs the kind of work they can do, excluded from the unemployment figures, because to say they were out of a job would be like saying the dead were out of a job, the unskilled, uneducated Underclass are to America's new computer-based, computer-programmed, computer-owning economy what clinker is to coal. Used up. Not on the scrap-heap, for scrap can be reclaimed, but on the slag-heap.

Now watch the black-briefcase-toting corporate hustlers passing through the hotel's bronzed doors. The odd one, now and then, will toss a quarter into the palm of one of the lucky Underclass.

See how the coin glints, as if fresh from the mint. Actually, it's fresh from the laundry. Here's job creation for you: the hotel pays a man full-time to wash all its coins and iron its dollar-bills so that its clients' hands will not be sullied by dirty money.

This pampered, clean-fingered class, living ritzily on the plump harvest of Silicon Valley and suchlike new-tech vineyards, is identified now as Upscale: a definable, sizeable socio-economic group whose spending power is on the up and up and up.

It's those two nations again – the haves and have-nots. It was ever thus, of course, but now it is more noticeably thus than it was – and getting chillingly thusser by the day.

America's monetary tea-leaf readings suggest that happy days may be here again – for some. The graphs are on the upturn. Judging by my own infallible prosperity indicator – the abundance or absence of free bar-room bookmatches – recovery is in the offing. I have collected enough classy bookmatches to burn down San Francisco.

But when President Reagan spoke of expecting recovery, he never mentioned whose. It is only just dawning on the Underclass that this time there was no promise of a chicken in every pot. There are only selected, corn-fed chickens for particular pots – those of the Upscale two home-computer families with the new-world know-how. There's no steam-driven software in this new world, no coke-fired word processors – and no vacancies for blue-collar programmers.

The chasm between Upscale and Underclass may be seen almost anywhere for the price of a couple of bus rides. Each of the great cities has its Upscale and Underclass satellite towns or suburbs – a place in the sun for the upwardly mobile, a populated moon for the downwardly going nowhere.

San Francisco has Richmond and Marin County, out-staring one another across the bay. Richmond once had shipyards: now it has men sitting on walls. Marin County had yachts: now it has bigger yachts, thanks to a population of decision-makers whose really smart decision was to plug themselves into information technology and all that.

Both places have big problems. Richmond holds all local records and some national ones for illiteracy, unemployment, drug abuse, violence. Marin County has more drunken driving cases than the courts can cope with, and more money than it knows what to do with – in the shape of a legacy, now worth £200 million, left for the exclusive community's exclusive use by a local oil baroness.

Richmond's very own windfall is the promise of a yacht marina to take Marin County's overspill. Good news for redundant platelayers.

Alongside the syndicated etiquette columns in the papers, there is now a security column offering hints on how to remain unmugged and unmurdered. It has no advice on how long, or how, the Upscale Marin Counties and Underclass Richmonds of America can go on living side by side.

The pundits predict unheard-of upheaval – revolution, even. I don't know about that, but the prospect is worth a shudder. Looking down at night from the penthouses and rooftop piano bars of San Francisco, you can see a flickering glow from the giant bonfires in a slum park, where great mobs of the Underclass gather for warmth. At first glance it looks as if the city were in flames – and you think of all those classy bookmatches lying around.

CITY FRIGHTS

During a particularly dreary debate at last week's Labour Party Conference, I was leafing through the local paper when this paragraph leapt out at me from the agony column:

'The other night I had a terrifying dream,' writes Mrs T of Portslade. 'I dreamt I was in Leeds ...'

Now fear of going to Leeds (or Leedsophobia, as psychiatrists call it) is quite common among citizens of neighbouring towns – particularly those from Bradford, in whom a glimpse of the famous covered market (their own was sacrificed to a traffic scheme) induces blind fits of jealousy. But this is the first reported case from as far afield as Sussex.

The story gets stranger. For it transpires that Mrs T of Portslade has never even set foot in Leeds. She has just experienced this terrifying 'Northern Nightmare' (as the headline puts it) of being there. It appears that in her dream she was walking up a hill when Something hit her – probably a crow from Pudsey: they have to fly backwards to keep the soot out of their eyes – and she awoke screaming.

Mrs T's dilemma is that her husband is a traveller, and has suggested that she goes with him up north for a week. She would like to, but is terrified that he will take her to Leeds, even though he has promised that he won't.

The reply by the Brighton *Evening Argus*'s answer to Marje Proops is not, in my view, satisfactory. She advises Mrs T to go north and put all thoughts of Leeds out of her mind. 'If your husband does have to go there,' she writes, 'couldn't you remain in the place you are staying just for that day?'

Now I am no agony aunty but that is certainly not the advice I would give. There is only one way to get over the fear of going to Leeds and that is to do what I did when I suffered from a paralysing, sickening fear of going to Birmingham – grit your teeth, get in your car and deliberately set off there.

In the case of Birmingham, I have to admit, the cure didn't work. That was because my own nightmare – that the city had been converted into a gigantic concrete plughole that would suck me down into oblivion – as near as dammit came true. But Leeds, although it did go through a spasm of road-worship when it boasted of being 'the motorway city,' offers no such terrors.

I do suggest to Mrs T of Portslade, however, that she should take it in easy stages. If I were here I would set up base at some convenient resort such as Pontefract or Dewsbury, and make daily excursions into Leeds over a period of about a week, staying for a longer and longer stretch as fear of the place recedes.

On the first day, I advise her to go no farther than the bus station. Just get the bus into Leeds, have a look out of the window at the parish church – where local belief has it that if you dig up one of the old gravestones you will start a fresh outbreak of the Black Death – and go back at once to Pontefract.

On the second day Mrs T might venture as far as the handsome town hall, where, she will be surprised to learn, a kestrel has its nest in the dome. It is simply not true, however, that the kestrel once swooped down on a baby in its pram and carried it off to Ilkley Moor.

On the third day I recommend that Mrs T has a wander round the splendid Victorian shopping arcades, with their elaborate striking clocks. There is a legend that at midnight the moving figures which strike the hours come to life but – of course, by midnight, Mrs T will be safely back in Pontefract.

And so, day by day, she should embrace the city in ever-widening circles, culminating, I suggest, at the haunted art gallery out at Temple Newsam. Mrs T may then return to Portslade secure in the knowledge that her absurd fear of Leeds is conquered for ever. And when her husband next suggests a trip north, instead of writing to the papers about it she will simply reply: 'By gum, lad, that'll be champion.'

NOT ONLY IN AMERICA

There is nothing quite so good as a convention city when the last balloon has been popped and the parade's gone by. So since there was not much doing in Detroit after the Republicans had gone, I thought I would try ringing up Canada and find out if things were any livelier over there.

I did not have a Canadian telephone directory about my person so I rang the Canadian operator and asked if she would put me through to Canada.

'Canada? You mean Canada the country?' asked the operator civilly.

'I mean Canada the country,' I said.

'Hold the line, please.'

Seconds later a charming female voice came on and asked if it could help me.

'Is that Canada?' I inquired.

'Speaking,' said the charming female voice.

'Would you be so kind as to tell me,' I asked, 'whether Canada is open this weekend?'

'Sir,' said the C.F.V., 'Canada is open all year round.'

'Thank you. I will be right over.'

So I took a taxi to Canada, which is all of 5168ft. away through a tunnel under the Detroit river. I stayed only long enough to have a pleasant lunch, so there is little I can tell you about Canada except that it looks like America, but with Boots the Chemists and Marks and Spencer.

While I was there, however, I got to wondering whether the United States would be such a nice country to ring up from Canada as Canada had been to call from the good old USA. I decided to give America the golden a tinkle.

The American phone book was another one that I did not have on me – I really must start carrying these things around in my briefcase – so I rang the Detroit operator.

'Could you tell me,' I asked, 'whether America is on the telephone?'

'America, sir?' She sounded as if she wanted me to spell it.

'Yes. America.'

'Hold the line, please.'

After a moment the operator came back to me and reported courteously: 'There is no country listed under that name, sir.'

'It may be listed as the United States,' I suggested. 'Try looking under the US.'

'We have several thousand numbers under that heading, sir. Which one do you require at this time?'

'The United States itself. Or themselves, if you prefer it.'

'The United States Government?'

'No, just the United States. The Land of the Free.'

'The United States is not listed as a country, sir.'

'Are you telling me,' I demanded, 'that God's Own Country is ex-directory?'

'That's the way it looks, sir. Is there any other way I can help at this time?'

'Just tell America I rang,' I said.

WIGAN MARKET

It rates not a mention in *The Road to Wigan Pier*. It is, in the words of one of the council visionaries who boast of leading Wigan into the twenty-first century, 'definitely not an historic building in the technically accepted sense'. The inspector appointed by the Secretary of State for the Environment was decidedly sniffy: 'Neither visually pleasing nor functionally safe.'

And in truth, for all that Wigan's covered market manifestly has a special place in the affections of the town, few would class it among the architectural jewels of the north, leaning as it does towards the municipal abattoir school of design.

Yet once you have swung through the insitution-green doors set into that uncompromising brick façade under the penny-plain legend '1877 MARKET HALL' inscribed in a stone lozenge, you find beneath its glass and girdered roof an Aladdin's Cave, an enchanted grotto of rolls of lino, bolts of satin, ribbons and bows, humbugs, herbal remedies, skeins of knitting wool, soft toys, cards of buttons, caged birds singing sweetly, and such a groaning wealth of pies and pasties, cakes and fancies, pickles and crumbly cheese that you might imagine Wigan to be preparing for the greatest Sunday School picnic in history. Nowhere else, not even in heaven or Harrods' Food Hall, could you encounter such a blissful, waist-thickening cornucopia of barm cake, Long John cobs, Dunster spiced loaf, iced buns, cream hearts, treacle parkin, currant teacakes, gingerbread men, Sally Lunns, and twelve kinds of slab cake; of pork pies and Aintree pies and whist pies and stand pies, bacon fry, Cumberland sausage, chitterlings, belly pork, Yorkshire ducks, polony, honeycomb tripe, pickled onions, pickled beetroot, pickled gherkins, piccalilli; of chocolate nougat, cough candy, licorice torpedoes, fifteen varieties of slab toffee, buttered almonds, and the speciality of the region, Uncle Joe's Mint Balls, whose slogan ('They Keep You All Aglow') is also available on T-shirts.

It is all that a covered market should be: a bazaar of individual scenes and sounds, laid out in a pleasing grid of indoor wood-paved boulevards, with avenues of fruit and veg, of meat and game (Green's the Butcher's, famous for their home-made sausage and black puddings, have been there for five generations), of fish, of flowers, of lace and linens, of odds and sods, where Wigan can buy anything from a collar stud to a cure for barber's rash; plus a periphery of outdoor stalls, all plying their wares within a wider perimeter of pubs, fish and chip saloons, cafés, barbers, knife-grinders, tattooists and suchlike ramshackle establishments that have always clustered around these great northern souks, as did the tents of pedlars around the walls of medieval towns.

There is a boisterous and anarchic chaos about the place, in cheerful defiance of Market Bye-law No. 11: 'No tenant of any Shop, Stall or Standing shall throw about or suffer any Rubbish, Paper, Litter, Garbage, Oyster Shells, or Refuse of any description whatever, or suffer the same to remain under or about the same . . .'

Not to mention Bye-law No. 15, which is to do with the wanton throwing down of orange peel. The market is mutinously ankle-deep in orange peel. It is alive with noise and people, all of whom seem to know one another, and there are pushchair traffic jams at fruit-stall junctions where the young mothers gossip.

Grannies in hats like the creamy whirls on Norman's Home Made Sweets stall amble arm-in-arm along the produce-spilling thoroughfares, not shopping but socialising, perambulating, in the manner of Italian matriarchs taking the air in the lofty gallerias of Milan or Rome. You have only to drink in this bustling, eucalyptus-and-glycerine tinged tableau on a raw Friday afternoon, with fog-wisps swirling in the arc-light brightness to realise that the old covered market is the living, beating heart of Wigan.

But now a heart transplant is proposed, in the form of a spanking new market housed in an up-to-date £30 million scheme complete with car stacks, two-level shopping complex, super-market, underground service area and suchlike amenities. Wigan-ites fear that the patient may not survive the operation.

At Gibson's Whist and Domino Prizes and Wedding Presents stall, Bill Worsley presides over serried rows of pottery clowns and crinoline dolls, helped sometimes by his eighty-three-year-old mother, one of the many market dowagers whose corporate memory goes back as far as the day King George V and Queen Mary paid a state visit to Wigan Market and the apples and pomegranates were burnished as never before or since. What was good enough for royalty then, they aver, is good enough for Wigan still.

'These new precincts are all the same,' said Bill Worsley glumly. 'You won't know whether you're in Wigan or where you are.'

It is a common prognostication, of traders and shoppers alike. Paying her weekly instalment on a giant teddy bear under the sign that reads 'TOYS LAID BY FOR XMAS', Mrs Irene Hough says: 'It'll be like they are down south – and you're talking to someone what's been to these places and knows. I've got relatives all over the shop and the first thing they always say is "How's Wigan Market, our Nan?" You're never going to catch them saying "How's that new shopping centre?" because they've got their own – Brent Cross and that.'

To be sure, the old market hall has been showing its age of late. The rain gets in, it could do with a lick of paint and, according to Her Majesty's inspector, it suffers from 'fundamental defects arising from its design in a different historical period'. Among these is that, as a lady stallholder fastidiously put it: 'There are no Gentlemen's Facilities. Gentlemen have to take themselves across to the bus station.' But most Wiganites you meet believe it could have been put right for a fraction of the £7½ million they are spending on the new market hall (the old one cost all of £17,000).

At least, unlike some towns hellbent on rolling up the carpet on their own history, Wigan is not banishing its ancient market (there has been one there for seven hundred years) to a disused airfield or even – the fate of its cobbled wholesale market, now a car park – to an access road on the M6 motorway. The new market-cum-shopping centre will be where the old market stands now.

There was 'consultation', of course – that municipal version of the find-the-lady trick where the townspeople are presented with the option of four different schemes but not with the option of leaving well alone. The fact that petition against demolition attracted 50,000 signatures – equivalent to a quarter of the whole Wigan area's population – hurt the planners no end. The wording, Wigan's forward thinkers maintain, could have been more constructive.

And indeed, looked at constructively, it does seem from the developers' elevation and plan that the town could have gone further and fare worse. 'We are looking,' ran the council's brief, mindful of the market traders' wrath, 'for a new hall which is typically Victorian.' And that, or something like it, is what Wigan will be getting – complete with mock-medieval clock tower and a cluster of outdoor stalls with pretty striped awnings. There will be a lot of glass and red brick and natural slate, but somehow it does not seem a place for collar studs and cures for barber's rash.

'It's a burning shame,' says Mrs Bentham of Bentham's Quality Fruit, arranging her boxes of sweet pomegranates and Marjorie seedlings. 'Why can't they have spent a bit of money in keeping things as people want them? And what kind of fancy rents are they going to be charging? That's what we'd all like to know.'

That's the question two hundred market traders are asking and it's one the Metropolitan Council, four years before the new market looks like being optional, is for the present inclined to duck. 'The blurry Metro tell you blurry nowt,' declares an outdoor sweet stallholder who wishes to remain anonymous ('I don't want no blurry publicity else they'll have me out on my blurry ear'), viciously attacking a clump of treacle brittle with a toffee hammer. In clear breach of Bye-law No. 20 ('No person shall make use of any cursing of swearing or of any violent, abusive, obscene, offensive or disgusting language') he continues:

'They'll have to charge the blurry earth to get back what they'll be blurry spending – then they'll blurry wonder where all the blurry stallholders have blurry getten to.'

And what, in the new paradise of plastic fascias, will become of the sturdy, hand-painted slogans and mottoes that adorn almost every stall in the old market – 'Dependability,' 'Reliability Our Aim,' 'Quality fruit,' 'High-class meats,' 'Compare these prices anywhere,' 'Choice dairy produce,' 'Civility and service at all times'?

Victorian values – and, in truth to tell, no small quantity of quite Victorian-looking merchandise. 'Some of these little odd-ments and knick-knacks are possibly years out of date,' noted the *Wigan Observer* at the time of the market's centenary. 'But then, most Wigan folk are a bit old-fashioned themselves in some ways, and if they want something, the Market Hall will stock it.' Not, you feel, quite the image the 'blurry Metro' will be looking for in its new showplace.

That's what tends to worry Wigan's market shoppers, espec-ially the older ones like Mrs Murial Comstock, seventy-three, who cannot see the grand new hall stocking her liniment. 'It'll be all these boutiques that you get,' predicts Mrs Comstock darkly.

Mildred, among the bottles of bee salve and prune and senna preparation at Mrs Knight's Wigan Health Foods, doubts that the old market's atmosphere is transplantable. Going by the fancy arcade across the street, Wigan's first advance excursion into the twenty-first century and a place of standardised shopping units that might equally well be in Wimbledon or Westcliff-on-Sea, she may be right.

Today, beneath the raffishness and raucousness of the old market, there is an air of pained resignation – 'The blurry Metro'll go their own blurry way so there's no use blurry worrying.' Some, indeed, believe that the great days of the covered market are over anyway. Jesse Cooper, trading in paperbacks, remembers when punters came from as far afield as Liverpool. 'I had an old lady spending seven pounds a week – I'd give her a reduction, she spent that much. There's none of that now.' He blames it on the recession and the rival attraction of Bolton, which offers free car parking. 'They're killing Wigan – just driving the punters away.'

It is the Metro's earnest desire to get the punters back, plus an obsession with keeping up to date and dragging Wigan into the future, that has landed the town with the new development, which in an era of suburban shopping centres could well be out of date before it is even built. Some Wiganites look enviously to the example of Chesterfield, which ten years ago was faced with a similar fate. The people of Chesterfield served a writ on the council and now the town centre is thriving with the old market hall meticulously preserved.

'The historian of the future will tell how the thousands of inhabitants of this town and the neighbouring district came to see the opening of this beautiful hall and rejoiced in the work of their hands,' said his Worship the Mayor when he opened Wigan Market Hall with a silver key on 21 May 1877, in the presence of cheering multitudes, civic dignitaries from all the surrounding cotton towns, the 21st Lancashire Rifle Volunteers, representatives from the Oddfellows, Foresters, Boilermakers and Templars Lodges, three brass bands and 'numerous fife and drum bands'.

The *Wigan Observer*, on a more subdued note, commented recently: 'With the demolition men about to move in and rip the town centre apart, all we can do now is to keep our fingers crossed and hope that this time the planners have got it right.' Some would hold that they hadn't got it wrong in the first place, back in 1877.

SPINDLE CITY, USA

If you will imagine a Lowry millscape, but with all of the matchstick men in baseball caps, it was like that. Lowell, Massachusetts: known once as the Manchester of America, though the Salford of America would have been nearer the mark. Or any of the northern mill towns, with Sears Roebuck instead of a glass-roofed market. Main Street in clogs.

Spindle City – that was another name Lowell gave itself. So it was, in its loom-clattering Victorian heyday. One hundred and seventy-five mills, as satanic if not as dark as any on either side of the Pennines, and churning out the product of both – cottons and woollens.

A man could grow rich on statistics, then – or rather, richer than he was already. The streets around the mills are named after the Boston merchants who put the money up and made the statistics happen.

There were 932,600 of those hurtling spindles in Spindle City, and 13,358 millgirls sweltering over 28,139 looms, and 4,676,000 yards of cloth to show for their industry at the end of each seventy-five hour week.

All done with now, of course. The spindles are 'collectables of yesteryear' in the converted-barn antique stores out in the patchwork-quilt New England countryside, and you can buy the bobbins that fed them at four dollars apiece from the novelties boutique in a downtown reclaimed factory. Or a Monopoly-based board game called 'The Old Mill Town'. If it's their Spinning Jack that improved on our Spinning Jenny you want to see, anyone will direct you to the textile museum. Spindle City lives on as the name of a liquor store, a limousine hire firm, a company selling computer hardware.

And the Merrimack River on which the town stands – and from whose Pawtucket Falls came the energy that turned the water-wheels and powered the turbines that drove the belts that worked the looms that shuttled the spindles that put the warp and the weft and the wealth into all those statistics – now drifts green with duckweed where once it swirled purple with dye, as do the five and a half miles of factory canals, still maintained by the company that dug them with Irish immigrant labour, the felicitously named Proprietors Of Locks And Canals.

It was no less a travel writer than Charles Dickens who put me on to Lowell, back in knee-mottling days when I crouched over a council house fireside reading most of Leeds Public Library. Here he is, in his *American Notes*, arriving at the Boston and Lowell Railroad Depot (built, incidentally, by Whistler's father, who remains somewhat more of a local celebrity for his engineering genius than does Whistler's mother for her aptitude for portrait-sitting. James McNeill Whistler himself, who left Lowell at the age of three, steadfastly denied ever having even heard of the place).

'I was met at the station at Lowell by a gentleman intimately connected with the management of the factories there; and gladly putting myself under his guidance, drove off at once to that quarter of the town in which the works, the object of my visit, were situated.

'Although only just of age – for if my recollection serve me, it has been a manufacturing town barely one-and-twenty years – Lowell is a large, populous, thriving place. Those indications of its youth which first attract the eye, give it a quaintness and oddity of character ...'

I was already casting the movie. Dickens made Lowell sound like all the bustling little American home-towns I had seen in countless Hollywood epics at the local Paramount; yet cross-pollinated with the chimneystack-pierced Yorkshire industrial landscape I was growing up in. To a young romantic soaked in trouble-at-t'-mill novels and marinated in Andy Hardy pictures, Lowell seemed to offer the best of both old and new worlds.

Many years on, another and later account of Lowell was to impress me: 'If at night a man goes out to the woods ... and stands on a hill, he can see it all there before him in broad panorama: the river coursing slowly in an arc, the mills with their long rows of windows all a-glow, the factory stacks rising higher than the church steeples ...'

It could be J. B. Priestley describing his native Bradford, fictionalised as Bruddersford in *The Good Companions*. In reality it is the Beat Generation's Jack Kerouac describing his native Lowell, fictionalised as Galloway in his first novel, *The Town and The City*.

My kind of town, then. But by the time I was in any position to make a pilgramage to Lowell, the textile industry had been manmade-fibred and import-dumped out of business, the mill towns were completing their rags-to-rags life-cycle – and John L. Kerouac who used to shoot pool in the Pawtucketville Social Club on Textile Avenue had long ago gone on the road. I feared that if I ever did get to Spindle City, it would only be to discover, like Gertrude Stein reaching Oakland, California, that when I got there, there would be no there there.

What should I find? Empty mills at best. But demolished

mills? An inner-city wilderness of parking lots and corrugated-iron boulevards? An Arndale Centre?

It could have been so and nearly was. Indeed, had I gone when I was first able, I should have been dismayed to find it rapidly becoming so.

The end of the King Cotton era came far earlier for Lowell than for Lancs, and for different reasons, with most of its looms silenced long before the end of the 1940s by cost-cutting competition from the industrially burgeoning Sunbelt which, not content with growing the cotton for the North, was now manufacturing its own cotton goods.

The mills closed. The canals stagnated. The freight trains whistled forlornly back to the Boston marshalling yards, empty, and the railway lines through back alleys silted up. In a fit of depression as spiritual as it was economic, Lowell began to dismantle its industrial past. Let it all come down.

After that came the genteel horrors of 'urban renewal', with pretty Victorian shopfronts and handsomely proportioned red brick factories swathed in plastic cladding as if they were sores that had to be bandaged, while the high windows of the remaining, abandoned mills became a target range for vandals.

Then the decay stopped. The plastic cladding came down and the scrubbing-brushes and brass polish came out. Lowell, a little late in the day, had remembered what Lowell was: the first industrial city in the United States, the cradle of the modern American dream, where capital, labour, power and machinery (aided and abetted, it has to be said, by the slave-owners of the South) came together for the first time ever to create the big business baronage that made America rich.

Downriver all neat and trim stand the historic townships of Concord and Lexington where the American Revolution began with a militia captain's cry of: 'If they mean to have war, let it begin here!' Nothing much of a battle cry was recorded when the first mill-wheel began to turn on the Merrimack River – only a laconic entry in the diary of Kirk Boott of the Merrimack Manufacturing Company on 3 January 1824: '10 bales of goods sent off to Boston – being the first lot sent off.' But the American industrial revolution had begun.

A heritage, then. Like a *grande dame* on hard times whose dull old family portraits in the attic turn out to be Gainsboroughs, down-at-heel, post-industrial, poor old Spindle City found that it had something of value left after all. Thus, with a little help from its friends in Washington, the town was designated a National Historic Park, like Gettysburg and Valley Forge, by a law signed by President Jimmy Carter. You could no more pull down a mill in Lowell now than you could shoot a Yellowstone bear.

Not all Americans yet know Lowell's story – though 400,000 of them took the guided tour last year, when many of them, like me, would doubtless have retained a broad comprehension of the turbine principle for a full half hour – but everyone within city limits does.

The story starts with the personal experiences of one Francis Cabot Lowell, a Boston merchant of that celebrated talk-only-to-God ilk, who in the year 1810 cast an envious eye upon the Industrial Revolution going on in the old country and said to himself, like an entrepreneurial transatlantic Blackstuff Yosser: 'I could do that.'

Mr Lowell sallied forth to study our factories and their machines. As to the form his studies took, the town named after him tends to this day to be delicately euphemistic. He 'acquired a knowledge' of our methods while touring the mills of Manchester and Scotland. He 'memorised' our technology. He 'obtained all possible information'. And then returned to Boston retaining such a 20:20 vision of what he'd observed that he was able to commission America's first power loom from the blueprint in his head.

To the outsider, even the admiring outsider, it is quite plain that we have yet another first here: Mr Lowell pioneered industrial espionage.

The Industrial Revolution at that time was virtually the registered copyright of Britain. Its manufacturing machines were not for export, its plans and patents were not for sale, the emigration of skilled mechanics was not encouraged. The embargo applied particularly to America where although we had lost a bunch of colonies we had gained an important customer for our textiles. Thus Mr Lowell, being escorted around our factories where the new power loom was practically a state secret, must have pined for yet one more invention – the microdot camera – before hurrying back to his lodgings to scribble down what he had seen. He had, says today's received opinion, 'little to aid him except his remarkable memory' – plus, what received opinion now omits to mention, a batch of drawings of a dressing frame, the patent of a Mr Horrock of Stockport, which he had somehow 'obtained'.

It has to be said for Mr Lowell that he not only re-invented the power loom but improved on it no end; that he thought up the concept of the 'total mill' with all the processes contained within four high walls: and further, that so distressed was he by the slums and the squalor of our Hindle Wakes cotton towns that he determined that should his experimental factory work, the American industrial revolution should be something else again.

So, for a while, it was. The most remarkable Cottonopolis relic to be found in present-day Lowell is not the imposing Boott Mill where it still stands stark and square on the Merrimack River; nor the surviving dormitory blocks where the mill-girls lodged two to a bed, and whose matrons were required to impose a ten o'clock curfew and 'report the names of such as are guilty of any improper conduct, or are not in the regular habit of attending public worship'; nor yet the bell towers, as common once as church steeples, that summoned them to wake, and to work, and to eat, and back to work, and to leisure, and to bed. It is a little literary magazine called *The Lowell Offering*, which flourished between 1840 and 1845: 'Will compare advantageously with a great many English Annuals' – C. Dickens.

And the remarkableness of *The Lowell Offering*, which at first glance looks conventionally like all the multitudinous *Ladies' Realms* and *Wreaths* and *Garlands* that flourished on both sides of the Atlantic in that period, lies in its subtitle: 'A repository of original articles, written by Factory Girls.' (In Bootle and Bradford, a mill-hand was considered a scholar if he could write his own name.)

'Pleasures of Factory Life', 'Plants and Flowers in the Mills', 'A Weaver's Reverie', 'Musings On The Leisure Hours of the Mill Girls', 'The Western Antiquities', a typical contents list might read; while a typical article – 'Chapters On The Sciences' – begins: 'Alice, Bertha and I went out this morning for the ostensible purpose of getting air and exercise, but in reality to inspect the cliffs and hills above the river, to collect some minerals for examination ...' And every word was written by girls who had put in a twelve-hour day drawing in warp ends or winding shuttle bobbins.

'From whence originated the idea, that it was derogatory to a lady's dignity, or a blot upon the female character, to labour? And who was the first to say, sneeringly, "Oh, she *works* for a living"?' writes one of the 'fair operatives' (as they were gushingly dubbed in the *Boston Mercantile Journal*). 'Surely . . . to be able to earn one's own living by labouring with the hands, should be reckoned among female accomplishments, and I hope the time is not far distant when none of my country-women will be ashamed to have it known that they are better versed in useful, than they are in ornamental, accomplishments.'

Mr Lowell couldn't have put it better himself. His conception of mill work was far removed from the drudgery he had seen in Britain. In the first place, the factory as a prison, whose inmates served a life sentence, would never be seen in New England (or anyway, Mr Lowell's portion of New England. There were in fact a few primitive wooden mills up and down the river which advertised blood-chillingly for 'Men with growing families' – as bland a request for child labour as could be framed). Mr Lowell's girls, recruited from the farms of Massachusetts, Maine and New Hampshire, would serve at the looms for only three or four years – just long enough to salt away a nest-egg from their $1.85 to $3.00 weekly earnings (more than a teacher made).

They would be, in the words of one mill-owner, 'a fund of labour, well-educated and virtuous' – their virtue being secured by the requirement upon them to live in custom-built, strictly regulated, properly supervised boarding houses in the vicinity of the mills. Their leisure hours would be devoted to self-improvement, attending lectures and lyceums, compulsory prayer, and chaperoned walks along the river.

Mr Lowell's ideas worked, the experimental model factory he had set up flourished sufficiently to encourage the idea of a entirely new city of model factories, but he did not live to see his New England Jerusalem. It was a bunch of his cronies, calling themselves the Boston Associates, who a dozen years or so after their colleague's profitable tour of our textiles towns and four years after his untimely death at the age of forty-two, went out to the community of East Chelmsford, Massachusetts, inspected the 30ft drop of the Pawtucket Falls, and declared it the perfect site on which to develop the 'Lowell System' of mass production and enlightened management, while incidentally making themselves immensely rich.

Derby, Kirk Boott wanted to call the new industrial settlement, after his family's home town. There were, and are, many English place names, on and off the Merrimack and Concord rivers: Andover, Winchester, Bedford, Carlisle, Leominster. But Derby, East Chelmsford in Middlesex County next door to Cambridge was not to be be. The Boston Associates decided to honour their late friend and benefactor, Mr Francis Cabot Lowell.

And so there now, 160 years on, pop. 91,177, established 1822, incorporated 1826, municipal motto 'Art Is The Handmaiden Of Human Good', stands this city of Lowell on that gushing ninety-degree loop of the Merrimack River, down the Lowell Connector from Route 495: with its drugstores and delis and bars and shoeshine stands and the five-cent savings bank and the bowling alley and Rotary, and 'Bon Marché', still brick-engraved on the front of the spruced-up department store, and the ice cream parlour, and the public library, and the barber college, and Lowell High with its handsome projecting clock subscribed by the classes of '38, '39 and '40: and with all those zillions of bolts and bales of fabric and all that long tapestry of history behind it.

Old-timers populate the benches of those aimless little tree-infested civic-improved corners that you get in cities these days – the ordered dross of 'urban renewal' – which in New York would be pocket-handkerchief parks for winos and bag-ladies. Here they peacefully puff their corn-cob pipes and josh and howdy the leaf-fluttering, birchbroom-sweeping fall days along, with only the tall chimneys behind them as a reminder that Lowell once hummed and belched and spewed with factory din and factory steam and factory effluent, and trainloads of cotton goods clanged through the streets while pigs were still snuffling about in the farmyards of what is now Manhattan's garment district.

More Norman Rockwell than Lowry, these days. The paper-boys stream out of the *Lowell Sun* office with the City edition, fanning out to the lawn-sprinkling, porch-and-rocking-chair clapboard suburbs; and a late sunbeam catches the bronze statue outside the police station of a kid looking trustingly up into the eyes of the cop with the hand on his shoulder.

Babbit would have felt at home here. The short happy life of

The Lowell Offering notwithstanding, and the Lowell Opera Co Inc notwithstanding, and the Marshall Sisters' Dancing Academy on Central Street notwithstanding, and art being the handmaiden of human good notwithstanding, Lowell does not over-burden itself with culture. Indeed it has some reputation for out-and-out hostility to the arts.

Jack Kerouac, by some, is remembered merely as the town drunk. By most, remembered not at all. A leaflet put out by the public library regrets more in sorrow than in anger than though he rebelled against 'the grey industrial spirit' of 'the city that is being glorified as the birthplace of the American Industrial Revolution', he has remained Lowell's best-kept secret. There's a shelf of Kerouac paperbacks in the book store but the bestseller in the time I was there was a book on how to get rich.

But despite all that – or perhaps because of all that? – very much an Our Town sort of town.

That's at third glance. On the second you might be in Rochdale. On the first, anywhere, or nowhere: for following the Dickens route into Lowell these days you arrive not at Whistler's father's Boston and Lowell Railroad depot on Market Street, but at an antiseptic 'transportation terminal' on the edge of town, designed apparently by a computer.

The heart sinks: no there there? But if it is a northern heart, it rises at once at the sight of the old C.I. Hood & Co manufactory beyond the car-park, with its flaked legends –

HOOD'S TOOTH POWDER
HOOD'S OLIVE OINTMENT
HOOD'S VEGETABLE PILLS

– painted on the brick and the name spelt out again vertically down the tall chimney. As cheerfully bleak a sight as anyone born above the Trent could wish for. Patent medicines and sarsaparilla were Spindle City's first exercise in diversification when the profitable nap began to rub off the textile business, and you can still find fading advertisements for nostrums and pectorals on the high blank walls. I'm at once reminded of terrace-ends painted with BILE BEANS and the magnificent slogan that tells the traveller he is in deepest Lancashire: UNCLE JOE'S MINT BALLS: THEY KEEP YOU ALL AGLOW.

Looking down from the Hood Manufactory you can see the town there below you all compact and neatly framed by the canals, the Concord River, and that great arc of the Merrimack, where huckleberries still grow along the far bank on the verge of the Veterans Of Foreign Wars Highway.

The Merrimack wraps a cycloramic backcloth around the clustered mills, each uniformly of five storeys to incorporate all the processes of cleaning, carding, combing, spinning, spooling, weaving, bleaching, dyeing and printing under one slate roof, as laid down by Mr Lowell's concept of the 'total mill'.

And dotted about and in between and in the long looming shadows of the mill walls, reminders of how Mr Lowell's girls lived: the Corporation Boarding House, no more than a brick barracks really, yet at least accommodating a parlour where they would sing round a jointly owned piano; the bell towers that called them back to toil for another long day; the Lowell Institution For Savings where deposits by mill-girls (amounting in 1833 to an unheard-of $100,000) established the wage-earning woman as an economic force in America; St Anne's church (named after a relative newcomer to the calendar of saints, the beatific Mrs Boott) where they compulsorily prayed; and the straggling path to the Pawtucket Falls where they took their Sunday afternoon walks.

A far cry from *Hard Times*. 'These girls,' raved Charles Dickens, 'were healthy in appearance, many of them remarkably so, and had the manners and deportment of young women: not of degraded brutes of burden.'

But some of the young women in their National Park Service Ranger uniforms who may be encountered on that same path today take a less rosy view of Lowell's early days. Not to put too fine a point on it, they reckon that Dickens and other VIP visitors – who came in shoals – had the cotton pulled over their eyes.

This distinctly pragmatic version has it that what those paternal, philanthropic gentlemen from Boston were really doing was selling the idea of industry to a predominantly agricultural nation which still believed that its prosperity depended on what could be grown in the soil rather than what could be mined or processed from it. President Jefferson, with his insistence on the rights to life, liberty and the pursuit of happiness, and his preoccupation with farming, was not much help. The Boston Associates had to find a cheap labour force and persuade it that living year-round by the mill bell was preferable to living by the farmers' almanac.

Poor farm girls came cheap (half as much as men), they were plentiful, and they were used to long hours. They were anxious to earn – either to save for a dowry, support their families, or simply to have money to spend for the first time (Dickens reports that a visiting hero 'walked through three miles and a half of these young ladies all dressed out with parasols and silk stockings'). Above all they craved the excitement and the freedom of living in a city. 'Sarah, don't I feel independent of everyone!' wrote one girl to her sister back on the New Hampshire farm.

As for the lectures and the lyceums, *The Lowell Offering*, the curfews and church attendances, and the strictly supervised boarding-house system dreamt up by Mr Lowell – all (runs this theory) public relations: rural parents, suspicious of goings-on and gallivantings among the bright lights of Spindle City, had to be reassured that their daughters would return to the nest as virginal and pure in mind as when they left it (and on the whole they did).

Well, there is probably a good deal in all this; but I prefer to recall that there was an era when philanthropy was a fact – our own Titus Salt, after all, didn't build his model wool town of Saltaire merely to become richer, otherwise he would have built a model slum – and self-improvement was a fact – every English mill town had its mechanics' institute – and the virtues of industriousness, cleanliness and godliness, not to mention virtue itself, were a fact. And at the very least, being dependent on water-power rather than on an exclusive diet of soft coal, Mr Lowell's New England Jerusalem was a sight less grim and grimy than the older New Jerusalem over here.

Whatever the ins and outs of the Lowell Experiment, it couldn't and didn't last. Utopias don't: especially when idealism eats into the profits.

With cut-throat competition in the over-expanding cotton industry, conditions had been getting worse; the girls now sleeping three to a bed instead of two, working three or four machines instead of one or two, and for longer hours. They were inhaling not only 'the sweet perfume of the rose, the lily and geranium' as formerly described by the pioneer militant Sarah Bagley, but also cotton fibres and the whale-oil lamp fumes that swirled through the stifling, steam-heated rooms. There had already been one or two short strikes: now the girls began to organise.

That did it. Troublemakers were fired and blacklisted. The Lowell Female Reform Association, hindered by girls who were prepared to put up with a few years of long hours for the sake of having their own bank book, got nowhere. Then a slump came along, thousands were laid off, and those who were left found themselves working harder and harder for less and less.

When recruiting started again, the farm girls stayed on the farms and their places were taken first by Irish immigrants who'd originally come over to dig the canals; then French-Canadians, Greeks, Portuguese, Poles ... each new wave welcomed by the mill-owners, so long as they'd work for less, or in worse conditions, than the wave before.

Ghetto tenements as festering as any Coketown back-to-back replaced the orderly boarding houses, and no one trilled at the parlour piano, 'And now we sing with gladsome hearts, The theme of the spinner's song, That labour to leisure a zest imparts, Unknown to the idle throng.' The Lowell Experiment was over.

There is no trace of a mill town dialect in Spindle City. Mr Lowell's girls never had one: their accents were gentrified, rather than coarsened, by upward mobility into the city. The immigrants spoke their own languages, then melting-pot American. Now Lowell's voice is US standard have-a-nice-day and hey-how've you-been. If they'd gone on pulling everything down you would never have guessed there was ever a cotton mill here.

Lowell, having dabbled in the odd spot of diversification since those old sarsaparilla days, got into electronics early and is now on the magic high tech circuit – hardware, software, microcomputer systems and all that.

Being a national historic park helps. It was a shrewd move: your floppy disc firms and printed circuitry outfits can move their potted-plant office room-dividers into all that lovely big space which a century ago the belligerent Ms Sarah G. Bagley compared originally to a flower garden and subsequently to a slave plantation; and they can claw back a lot of tax on steam-cleaning the once steam-dripping brick walls and restoring all those handsome bits and pieces Mr Lowell's young ladies wouldn't have noticed in their hurry to get out of the mill and into the lecture hall to catch Ralph Waldo Emerson. Keeps costs down no end.

Never mind. I should have liked to have known Spindle City in all its phases: Cotton Garden of Eden, Cotton El Dorado, Cotton Hell's Kitchen, and Cotton Ghost Town; and I am happy to know it now in its brick-mail revival.

'I saw [the factories] in their ordinary working aspect, with no preparation of any kind, or departure from their ordinary everyday proceedings – I may add that I am well acquainted with our manufacturing towns in England, and have visited many mills in Manchester ...' wrote Charles Dickens, in what does read, come to think of it, like the testimonial of a gullible traveller who thinks he's been allowed to see China or Russia as it really is. Maybe Lowell duped him after all. If so, the trick still works. I'll go back.

LONDON BY THE SEA

Although I have never heard it called such, except on the inn-sign of a famous seafront pub, I will take the guidebooks' word for it that its nickname really is 'Dr Brighton'.

And a singularly inappropriate one it is, for if Brighton were indeed a doctor, it would have been struck off years ago. Here, it is evident to the visitor before he has progressed more than ten yards out of the station, is a resort to scandalise the neighbours. (Hove, one feels, would feel far happier on the Newhaven side of Roedean.) Brighton clearly smokes too much, drinks too much, eats too much, keeps undesirable company, is a shocking lecher, and stays up too late for its own good.

'London-by-the-sea' is its other nickname and a more accurate one, since beneath the provincial patina of tea shoppes, clock tower, corn exchange and rambling department stores there does seem to be a watery metropolitan borough trying to get out. Perhaps 'Earls Court-by-the-sea' would be nearer the mark, though: much of Brighton perfectly mirrors the SW5 postal district's atmosphere. They share an atmosphere of grandeur run to seed, of flaked stucco terraces carved into bed-sits and cheap hotels, of restless comings and goings, and fleshy retired barmaids and ladies of the chorus living alone in basement 'garden flats'.

When I think of Brighton, it is its populace rather than its piers and pleasure domes that first drifts into my mind. The former gown manufacturer tucking into his lobster thermidor and complaining that he has to go up to Town tomorrow because his son doesn't know how to run the business. The cat-feeding cloakroom lady who looks as if she has been something theatrical in her day. The port-sipping lady wearing fishnet stockings who is really a gentleman wearing fishnet stockings. All human life is there.

And it is the people who have stamped their personality upon the place, rather than the place upon the people as in (or so it seems to me) say Cornwall or Edinburgh. Or is it that they were attracted towards Brighton from London or wherever (native Brightonians seem thin on the ground) because they were, in the first place, natural Brighton material? For there is a distinctive, recognisable Brighton type; faintly roguish, hedonistic, the suggestion of having a bit of a past. Max Miller lives. So, come to that, does his female equivalent. This is Merry Widow country.

'Brighton was full of disappointed and bad-tempered visitors,' writes Paul Theroux in *The Kingdom By The Sea*. A slur. When did Brighton ever let anyone down? There are some places – Venice, New York, Paris – which on a first visit are almost exactly as one anticipated. No matter how much they have structurally changed they remain intrinsically unchanging, fixed on a remembered picture postcard. Brighton is in that league.

Despite some hideous self-inflicted wounds in the way of 'up-to-date' – ie, already dated – leisure complexes and suchlike excrescences (there is hardly a landmark in the town, including the Royal Pavilion itself, that developers have not at one time or another wished to raze to the ground in favour of something in ferro-concrete), it is still recognisably the Brighton of *Brighton Rock*, of spins in the jolly old roadster and illicit hotel weekends under the name of Smith. (After the IRA outrage at the Grand Hotel – now being meticulously restored to its former wedding-cake glory – police appealed to guests using false names and addresses to come forward in confidence).

Its crescents and colonnades, its marzipan Taj Mahal domes and turrets, its birdcage bandstand and its pair of Victorian piers – one being spruced up, the other, alas, still anxiously waiting for a conservation lifebelt to be thrown to it as it slips inch by inch into the sea – give Brighton its particular appearance, but what gives Brighton its peculiar flavour is harder to pin down.

Although commanding its fair share of rock false teeth, comic postcards and pintable saloons, it is not as other seaside resorts. Indeed, once away from the promenade it is easy to forget that you are in a seaside resort at all – particularly in winter when its bustling streets are exuberantly lacking in that Sundayish, washed-out, end-of-season gloom that afflicts other English watering-places when the visitors are all gone.

The fact is that although tourism is its bread and butter, Brighton somehow gives the impression of secretly tucking into cake, and one is intrigued to know where it came from. Here, the outsider feels, is a town with a private life, a town, you feel sure, that is *up to something*.

Like London-on-the-Thames, London-by-the-sea is really a series of linked villages, but on a Lilliputian scale, with dis-tinctively separate neighbourhoods consisting of only a cluster of little streets, a shop or two, and a tiny terrace-end pub. These pubs, of which there seem to exist more to the square mile than anywhere else in England, are very much a feature of Brighton life. Accommodating hardly more than a dozen regulars, with the barest minimum of house-room left over for the toleration of strangers – ie, nosey-parkers from as far away as the next street but one – they range from simple, plain-penny boozers to ex-quisitely-decorated twopence-coloured gin cabins, all red plush and flock wallpaper. What they have in common (apart from ubiquitously delicious crab sandwiches) is the sense of intrigue, of murmurings in corners, of being 'in the know' about matters from which the casual visitor is excluded. Whatever Brighton is up to, it is up to it in these little pubs. I would not wish to suggest that here is a town which could assist the police in their inquiries, but there is certainly a whole lot of wheeler-dealering going on.

Dealers, of course, antique and otherwise, play an important part in Brighton's economy. Most visitors make for The Lanes, a prettified rabbit warren of narrow streets where gift boutiques and smart clothes shops seem gradually to be gaining the upper hand over the many small antique shops that have traditionally dominated the area. The untarted-up and indeed downright raffish North Laines (not a mis-spelling: its the geographical name of a stretch of seedy-looking streets between the station and the Dome) is more to my taste. This is Brighton's Casbah: bric-a-brac and cast-offs, second-hand books and records, a Saturday flea market, antiques and ephemera, old fireplaces and old furniture, fruit and veg, gossip and tittle-tattle – and, overall, that very Brighton feeling of deals being done, of arrangements being made, of something happening.

Not all these mysterious arrangements, to be sure, are financial transactions. Brighton is at once the most gregarious and the most secluded and secretive of communities, a colony of party-givers who passionately respect one another's privacy. All through the town, slotted in behind the grand crescents and the Regency squares or tucked away up the long pebble-and-flint-walled alleys or twittens as they are known, are little nests of doll's-house cottages where the fishermen once lived, and which now, washed in pretty pastel colours and decked out with coachlamps, are the very private homes of very private people, many of them commuters in the creative professions who have chosen Brighton because Brighton leaves them alone.

But should anyone feel like company there is always a party, always impromptu Sunday morning drinkies at this or that flat, always the corner pub where everyone knows everybody, always the network of wheeler-dealers, always a nosh at a friendly restaurant.

As with its pubs, Brighton has probably more restaurants to its name than any town of comparative size and indeed many a good deal bigger, from the baroque, baronial and fishy splendour of Wheeler's Sheridan with its oak-panelled walls and green banquettes, to the candle-lit room the size of a gingham tablecloth which two friends thought it would be rather fun to open, one of them doing the cooking while the other chats up the customers, and which serves kiwi fruit with everything. Here, too, there is that indefinable air of exchanged confidences, of everyone being in on the same conspiracy. Only in Brighton, I feel, would the dinner-jacketed *maître d'* of an upper echelon restaurant, having asked if the service has been satisfactory, go on to recount, in his discreet, professional murmur, how the cantankerous ghost of the establishment's previous owner pushed him down the cellar steps against last night.

Less exotic eating places abound: bistros, trattorias, pizza joints, steak houses, Indian and Chinese, upmarket hamburger houses and of course fish and chip saloons.

Which brings us, though not necessarily the residents of Brighton, to the seafront. Here we have a population that is somewhat schizophrenic about that portion of its catchment area consisting of shingle and salt water. Brightonians are sharply divided about the beach. Some of them never set foot on it, regarding it with scorn as the preserve of trippers. Others spend every waking hour sunbathing on it (there is a famous, or notorious, nude sunbathing area) – which is why the archetypal Brighton face is either the texture of a pickled walnut or the colour of the chalk cliffs of Beachy Head which glimmer whitely beyond the Marina.

The same goes for the promenade: retired folk, particularly retired folk with dogs (the Brighton dog, is, naturally, the clipped poodle), take their morning constitutional along it: working residents tend to leave it, too, to the tourists and to derive their exercise from flitting along the twittens on mysterious errands.

There is a case to be made for both camps. The seafront at Brighton has its high Victorian moments with some delightful ironwork filigree confectionery in sugar-almond blue, but at the end of the day (when some quite pretty fairy lights come on) it is just a seafront much like any other of its period. Brighton the seaside resort could be Bognor or Bridlington – whereas Brighton the town, the part they never did sing about in the old music hall ditties, could be nowhere else but Brighton.

The Brighton of *Brighton Rock*, Grahame Greene wrote in an introduction to a new edition, 'may in part belong to an imaginary geographic region'. And he added: 'I must plead guilty to manufacturing this Brighton of mine'.

No: *not* guilty, Mr Greene. Brighton was manufactured by itself, and it is in its own exotic and exuberant imagination that it truly exists.

Brighton, true Brighton, abounds. Brighton is Brighton race-course, no longer the resort of race gangs but still looking as if it is going to burst forth into an English production of *Guys and Dolls*.

Brighton is the plush and gilt of the Theatre Royal, with ladies in black bombazine dispensing champagne to theatrical agents with camel-hair overcoats thrown across their shoulders, down to inspect their clients in pre-West End tryouts.

Brighton is a lunchtime sherry at the Cricketers, and a dozen oysters at English's. It is a Saturday morning spent truffling through the delicatessens and patisseries of Kemp Town – Hampstead-by-the-Sea, this elegant and expensive section might be called – and Sunday reading the papers on a canopied verandah with a glimpse of the Newhaven-Dieppe ferry on the horizon.

Brighton is – but there is no point in trying to piece it together like a mosaic. Brighton is simply one of those regions that awakes each day full of promise. The sun rising over Palace Pier brings with it an excited feeling that something is going to happen today, that there is adventure in store. The same sun setting over Shoreham power station conveys the same sensation of adventure ahead this evening. Nothing much does happen, of course. Then why the euphoria?

It's because Brighton *is* the adventure.

CHAOS IN CAIRO

A town planner who died and was sent to purgatory would expect to find himself in Cairo. It is everything a city must not be by the modern urban rulebook – yet by all the yardsticks of the incorrigible city-dweller, all that a city should be.

One's first impression, upon being tipped into this teeming megalopolis, is that this time the forces of chaos have gone too far. It is like an ants' nest. Observe an ants' nest long enough, though, and you note that every ant has a task and every ant is going somewhere, however purposelessly it seems to be running around in circles.

So it is with Cairo. That terrified horde of American tourists, zig-zagging crazily across the local Spaghetti Junction in peril of their lives, are taking the only route out of their hotel alternative to whistling up a cab whose driver would want to make a detour to his brother's handicrafts shop in the outer suburbs. Those six-abreast cars hurtling towards them are trying to knock them down. This is, after all, traditionally the meeting ground of East and West.

That shepherd swathed in deck-chair material who has single-handedly congealed the rush hour into a motionless, hooting mass by driving his flock the wrong way up Cairo's answer to Bond Street is, like everyone else, merely trying to get home for lunch. That devout Moslem prostrate in the dust has left his lorry obstructing the tram-lines not out of cussedness, but because the pavements are already full of parked vehicles.

And the noise: the mullahs are obliged to bellow the faithful to prayer through an echo-ricocheting public address system because otherwise they could not be heard over the car horns. Every Cairo motorist drives on his horn because otherwise the rattling trams he is overtaking on the wrong side would not hear him coming for the sound of their own bells, the wailing of street-vendors and the clatter of freelance scavengers in their squashed-petrol-tin donkey carts. It all makes sense.

Cairo, considered from an environmental health point of view, so hugely needs something doing to it that all attempts at doing anything to it, short of flattening every minaret and market stall and starting again, must fail.

The holes in the road where the underground railway system is being dug add mightily to the traffic snarl-up it is meant to relieve (and when the underground is finished, if that day ever comes, it will only be to add a subterranean, Faustean dimension to the confusion). New flyovers serve only to decant the cars more quickly into the Sargasso Sea of stalled traffic.

As if the rickety fabric of the city is aware of its own problem, every so often there is a mushroom cloud of dust as a building shudders, sighs and then disintegrates, thus saving the bulldozers the trouble.

Cairo's charm eludes the guide-books. The murky Nile runs bank by bank with a highway that has all the glamour of the Hammersmith flyover. The Pyramids, as plagued with touts as the camels are with flies, are parked on the fringe of Cairo's equivalent of Dagenham, like giant paperweights.

Less plugged in the brochures, and extraordinarily difficult to find considering that it sprawls over half the city, is the Khan al Khalili, the great complex of Eastern bazaars that is the beating heart of Cairo. (If lost, ask a member of the Tourist Police, recognisable by his badge which reads Tourist Police – in Arabic. Or, easier, follow your nose until it picks up a pot-pourri of spices, coffee and camel dung.)

It is here, in this labyrinthine, wheeler-dealering honeycomb of Aladdin's caves, that a horrified city planner might see, in seething, smelly microcosm, how a working city actually does work.

A carpet-seller lays out his wares then goes across to a goat-dealer and bargains for a goat. The goat-dealer buys a recycled sewing machine. The sewing machine re-cycler then buys a carpet.

Everyone has made a deal, including the straggling, jostling, Mother Courage entourage of itinerant boot blacks, barbers, beggars, olive-vendors, tea-carriers, money-changers and renters-out of hubble-bubble pipes who service all this entrepreneurism.

At the top end of the market they sell gold by credit card to Americans – at the bottom end they sell, or try to sell, restored paraffin cans to one another. It is worth pushing through the human tide to where the Khan al Khalili so wretchedly peters out to experience (so long as you put your camera away) the touching friendship of Cairo's poor.

Unlike most of the hundred or so warm-hearted souls who will greet you on any given day, they do not have brothers who run a jewellery shop at most advantageous prices – they want only to welcome you to their mean alleys where all they own is a tethered goat.

But don't let on if you chance to be a planning officer.

QUEEN'S FLOAT

A glance at a map of New York City and environs, any time between the scheduled hour of departure from Southampton and the year 1934 when the QE2's stately grandmother the *Queen Mary* was launched on British Movietone News at the Tivoli Cinema, Leeds, would have shown that I was dreaming the impossible dream.

The Statue of Liberty does *not* rise from the sea like Venus on the half-shell, her upraised right arm giving an outsize impression of Excalibur on the shimmering horizon. It is a geographical impossibility. The first distinguishable landmark, I have to record, is the water tower of the Coney Island amusement park.

The ship – boat? it? she? Even after five days afloat the correct nautical terminology refuses to trip off the tongue with sufficient jauntiness – does not even set its compass due west and aim directly across the Atlantic like a migrating Blue Riband dolphin, as I had always imagined. For navigational reasons beyond my understanding, she heads for Newfoundland and then turns sharp left. Right hand down a bit at the Nantucket light vessel and straight on along the featureless coast of Long Island.

I never suspected that when I finally did make it across the ocean in one of the legendary liners, it would bring me into the New World sideways.

But between four and five on the fifth morning at sea or the 113th hour of sailing, the Coney Island water tower recedes into the grey background of dawn and the sharp end of the ship (not more landlubber's gauchery: it's the expression all the officers use with self-conscious inexpertise) begins to fill up with yawning, shivering, lens-focusing passengers, several of whom ask if that is Brooklyn Bridge looming before us. (This hour, by the way, does not officially exist. On the east-west voyage – or east-northwest-south voyage as it turns out to be – all the clocks are stopped for an hour at 4 am, to catch up on the time difference. What greater luxury, on a luxury liner, than a twenty-five-hour day?)

No, it is not Brooklyn Bride, it is the almost unheard-of (to the British) Verrazano Narrows Bridge which links Brooklyn and Staten Island and divides Lower New York Bay from Upper New York Bay. We are there. We have arrived – huddled masses yearning to take snapshots.

As one colossus of engineering passes beneath another, an early traffic-jam of trucks overhead sounds a welcome on hooters only fractionally louder than the QE2's own foghorn. And then, suddenly and unexpectedly and like all celebrities looking smaller than one had anticipated, there, only a couple of hundred yards away, is the Statue of Liberty posing most prettily for her photograph.

My forty-six-year-old dream, of standing on the deck of a Cunard liner and watching the land of bubble-gum and gangsters and East Side kids and back-stage musicals take shape before my very eyes, has come as close to coming true as it ever will. The sun, as perfectly red and round as an Edam cheese, slides up behind the breathtaking skyline of Manhattan and a woman beside me, clutching the boat-deck rail and looking transfixed with awe at the beauty of it all, says to her husband without taking her eyes off the glimmering spires of Gotham, 'What time d'you think the shops open here, Eric?'

But I have begun this saga stern before bows. I must go back to the point at which the seedy boat-train from Waterloo – which has so far held all the promise and romance of the last tube to Ruislip – rumbles self-importantly across Canute Road into Southampton Docks while a man with a red flag holds up the traffic. What until this moment looked like a trainload of squashed, disgruntled season-ticket holders with plastic macs and carrier-bags is instantly transformed into a cosmopolitan throng of international travellers with sets of matching pigskin luggage in the guard's van – for there, alongside us on the platform, where you would normally expect to see Post Office vans and perhaps a chocolate machine or two, is the immense black whale-like flank of the *QE2*.

A departure hall queue of 1815 souls for check-in, immigration formalities and security frisking, which makes Heathrow look like a country bus station, should guarantee to get the bile flowing again – but the exuberance of our surroundings keeps our spirits up. The Southampton Ocean Terminal is an art deco confection, all mirrors and maple and fluted columns and rounded corners, of such Jack Buchanan and Jessie Matthews movie-set extravagance that one can only marvel that it has not been torn down and replaced by something nasty in ferro-concrete.

This sensation of stepping back into the 1930s lasts only as far as the gangplank. When we go aboard, my instant impression – later confirmed – is that where the *Queen Mary* was a floating Ritz and the *Queen Elizabeth* a floating Savoy, what we have here is a floating Inn On The Park or a floating – name any top-grade hotel in any major American city. That is to say, comfortable without being extravagant, luxurious without going raving mad. No marble baths or Tudor fireplaces. Decor which is the visual equivalent of Musak.

My first-class cabin, which the management prefers to call a stateroom, is like dozens of hotel rooms I've stayed in – but with an excellent view of a lot of water. On the ship's radio, the ship's DJ twitters on about tomorrow's activities: 'Even if you're not into flower arranging, girls, go and see the wowy things they do with flowers.'

For security reasons, and much to the relief of the crew, *bon voyage* champagne parties and cries of 'All ashore who's going ashore' belong now only in the world of old movies. No doubt some passengers are sipping a glass or two in their cabins while reading their greetings telegrams and arranging their flowers, but most of us are milling around the place like kids on their first day at boarding school.

So much to do. One's allocated restaurant to be found, the bars (seven of them) to be located, deckchairs to be reserved, hairdressing appointments to be made, library books to be borrowed, travellers' cheques to be cashed. (The ship's currency is the dollar. Though sterling is supposed to be equally welcome, the casino and some of the shops offer a poor rate of exchange.) As three tugs tow us away from port, to the strains of 'Land of Hope and Glory' through the Tannoy, all eight public decks are busy-busy with the to-ing and fro-ing of 1815 passengers doing absolutely nothing of any importance.

The ship's officers, I am to learn before long, are a fund of useless information, much of it statistical and of the well-I-never or did-you-know? variety. No wonder the Cunard liners figured so largely on cigarette cards in the golden age of Atlantic crossings. Did you know that the *QE2* carries 2000 bottles of pickles and sauces, 600 jars of baby food and 50 pounds of 'Super Crunchies for Hungry Doggies'? Well I never. Did you know that the *QE2* spends $66 a mile on oil? Fancy that.

One or two of these statistics, meant to impress, faintly alarm me. We are carrying 120 bottles of vodka and 150lb of caviare. I am a vodka drinker and I propose to eat caviare until it comes out of my nostrils. What if everyone else is of like taste and like mind? Did you know that this works out at less than a spoonful of caviare a day each, with the merest sniff of the barman's apron as accompaniment?

Luckily many passengers turn out to be pink gin drinkers with a preference for *foie gras*. The *QE2*, I am assured, never runs out of anything, and by way of proof I am escorted to the refrigerated bowels of the ship where I am shown, among other rations, 79,200 eggs. Well I never.

Some facts are harder to come by. What every transatlantic passenger who has never been on anything bigger than a Channel ferry wants to know is, am I supposed to dress for dinner and who do I tip and how much? Before embarking I rang Cunard, who said I would find all that kind of information in a booklet in my cabin.

I said that left it a bit late for sending my dinner jacket to the cleaner's (it turns out there is a dry cleaner's on board. But of course), and what proportion of the first-class passengers would be dressed up? They reckoned fifty per cent. On my count it is eighty per cent, and about twenty per cent in Transatlantic class. (Also, about half a per cent wear evening dress on the first night out, thus breaking the only rule of naval etiquette every Englishman knows by heart, so naturally we know-alls titter at them up the sleeves of our blazers.)

This first-class business, by the way, applies only to cabins and restaurants. The rest of the ship is liberty hall. 'People graduate to the parts of the ship where they feel most at home,' is the way Cunard put it with elephantine delicacy, meaning that some play bingo while others don't. In fact there are no observable class extremes – most passengers are decent middle-of-the-road people who tend to greet each other with, 'Not too hung over after the festivities of yester-eve, it is to be hoped?'

On the tipping front, all the booklet had to say was, 'There's only one rule about tipping. You give precisely what you want, to whoever you want, just as you would ashore.' It would be more helpful to say that you tip your cabin steward, your two restaurant stewards, the wine butler if you use his services, the *maître d'* if you have regularly called on his talents for flambéing everything in sight, and the nurse if you have left your children in her care. You bung them what you would bung if you were snowed-up in a first-class hotel for five days and unable to eat out. Barmen you tip as you go along, as you would in a hotel cocktail bar.

As for the restaurant service that is the main cause of all these mental calculations, it turns out to be brisk and efficient – yet friendly to the point of chirpiness. Four-star Dickensian coaching inns must have known chaps like this, I reflect, as a South London steward urges me confidentially to order whatever I like, whether it is on the menu or not (how about a 79,200-egg omelette?) and his Liverpudlian colleague chips in with, 'Just so long as he doesn't have the boeuf stroganoff, because it's not up to its usual scratch.' The semi-joshing approach keeps everyone happy. The man at the next table remarks that it comes as news to him that the English make such good waiters. So they do, so long as you call them stewards. And fortunate for us it is too.

But I'm surprised to be asked for my dinner order at lunchtime – 'so that everything can be cooked for you personally. The roast Long Island duckling, sir? A very good choice, you'll like it. And your dessert order?' – 'You mean you're going to cook the dessert?' – 'We would like to take your dessert order, sir. How about the chocolate cream pie? Be a devil.'

Lulled, I suppose, is the word for my condition as I accept this preposterous routine without a murmur. Sea travel, I am to find, is a lulling experience all round. At dead of night, when the only sound to be heard at 28.5 knots is the soothing rattle of the forty coathangers in my fitted wardrobe, I lie in bed and dwell on the tasks for tomorrow: the brisk walk around the boat deck, breakfast, a game of quoits, the daily flutter on the ship's position, the eleven o'clock bouillon, the twelve o'clock Bloody Mary . . . I am asleep long before I have reached the rigours of the afternoon such as the lecture in the Q4 room on 'How To Discover Undervalued Stocks' by a Wall Street broker.

One day merges with another, one small excitement with another. Soon I will not be able to remember whether it was a whale that was sighted near Seal Island or a seal near Whale Island. Fog descends. In the bars, old hands reminisce about those old transatlantic days and say, apropos of the *QE2* which now has to go Caribbean cruising to make a living, that there will never be another. The bell of a lightship tinkles, and a detective play crackles over the BBC World Service. 'One moment, sergeant. I don't think you appreciate who I am.' It beats flying.

IN THE WOODSHED

Herman was the man who was going to explain to me why Boston, which likes to call itself the cradle of liberty or the Athens of America or both, seems hell-bent on turning itself into the Little Rock of the north.

Herman was to meet me in the lobby of the Statler-Hilton. He would be wearing a red blazer. And that was the snag.

There were, in the lobby, at least a hundred men wearing red blazers. A minimum of sixty shades of red, ranging from salmon pink to claret. A few dozen wore green blazers, other blue, purple or chequered. Some wore no blazers at all. There were easily a thousand people present.

Most, if not all, were singing.

Four men (in red blazers) marched up to the reception desk and pinged the bell for attention. It sounded in the key of G and, as if on cue, they launched into a perfectly-harmonised rendering of 'You Can't Convict the Mother of the Girl I Love'. The receptionist waited politely until they had finished.

Over at the cashier's grille, another group sang 'Beautiful Isle of Make Believe' as they signed travellers' cheques. By the bookstall, four browsers were giving their version of 'I Want a Date at a Quarter Past Eight'. In the bar (appropriately) they were delivering 'Nellie Dean'. The mingled strains of 'Cousin of Mine', 'Goo-Goo Eyes' and 'God Made a Wonderful Mother' floated down from the mezzanine.

If you saw, a few months ago, a fascinating TV documentary on American barber-shop quartets, I won't need to explain the term 'woodshedding'. If you didn't, woodshedding is what happens when four men come together – as it might be in the lobby of a hotel in Boston – and find, by happy chance, not only that one of them is a tenor, one a lead tenor, one a bass and the other a baritone, but that they all know the words of 'Shine On Harvest Moon'.

Looking for Herman, I had gatecrashed a convention of the Society for the Preservation and Encouragement of Barber Shop Quartet Singing in America. And they were woodshedding like mad.

There was a long winding queue for the dining-room. To pass the time, an impatient tenor began to hum 'In The Good Old Summer Time'. A neighbouring baritone took up the refrain. A couple of bases joined in. Soon the queue of would-be diners, a hundred or so strong, sounded like a Welsh choir. While in the dining-room itself they were lingering over their coffee with 'Love Me and the World is Mine'.

Well, it was all good clean American fun. But not far away, in South Boston, white youths had earlier been roaming the streets singing a less innocuous song: 'We'll hang all the niggers from the nearest apple tree'. The walls were chalked with slogans. The National Guard was on stand-by. An airborne division – remember Little Rock? – had been on temporary alert. There had been stabbings, street riots, arrests.

Boston, where the anti-slavery movement began, was facing the issue that not many years ago nearly brought the Civil War back to the deep South – the bussing of school-children in the cause of racial integration.

There was no sign of Herman. Maybe he was practising 'Sweet Rosie O'Grady' in the men's room.

Still, if I was looking for a cross-section of American opinion on this explosive topic, I reckoned a couple of barbershop quartets would be as good a sounding-board as any.

I approached an earnest group of crew-cuts who were wood-shedding 'Carry Me Back to Old Virginny'. Excuse me, what do you think about Boston's bussing problems?

'We're here to barbershop, pal, not to talk politics.'

I asked 'Sweet Adeline' the same question.

'Boston has problems, we all have problems. That's why we sing barbershop – it brings back those good old days.'

I turned to 'My Old Kentucky Home'. Excuse me, but do you know the American Nazi Party has moved into Boston in force?

'No, but give us an "A" and we'll sing it.'

By now the woodshedding groups were breaking up and they were drifting into the hotel convention hall where a jamboree of harmonising, the main purpose of their visit, was about to take place. I joined them.

The hall was packed with happy, shining, expectant, innocent faces. About two thousand of them. All of them white. Four lithe young men (in red blazers) bounded on to the stage. They were white too. The pitching pipe gave them a note. And they sang a haunting negro spiritual.

That's barbershop.

That's America.

STREET SCENE

Capri. An open-air terrace restaurant in the shade of an orange grove. A perfect day. The scent of bougainvillaea mingles delicately with the aroma of cannelloni.

A Yorkshire couple pause and study the menu. Below the expanse of white tablecloths is a steeply-sloping vineyard, and far below the harbour is the Bay of Naples, and far away on the shimmering horizon, like a brush-stroke in a Chinese picture, is a smudge of purple which is Vesuvius.

The lady tugs her husband's sleeve.

'Come on, Ronnie – you don't want to eat out in t'street.'

9

THIS SEMI PARADISE

THIS SEMI PARADISE

THIS SEMI PARADISE

Further evidence that we live in an era of one damn thing after another may be gleaned from the news that the Great British Semi is in decline.

It's Dunroamin we're talking about. More and more home owners are switching to terraced houses and flats, while fewer and fewer are buying semi-detached and bungalows, so the building societies are saying. They have figures to prove it.

Next, I suppose we shall hear that the garden gnome has been superseded by the polystyrene rabbit.

I had noticed in a vague sort of way, that they are not building semis any more – or not, at any rate, the kind of traditional semi I would award the Dunroamin seal of approval to, with a sunburst gate, a porthole window by the front porch and a diamond-shaped flower bed cut into the lawn.

What I had not realised was that the semi is going the way of the bakelite wireless set, the Tin Lizzie and the cigarette card. It is becoming a period piece, a bit of Thirties kitsch like the circular cocktail cabinet.

When the last semi crumbles into a heap of pebbledash, it will be not so much another precious bit of England we are losing as the whole shooting match. The semi *is* England. This royal throne of kings, this scepter'd isle, this semi paradise, as Shakespeare meant to write.

Coming back to these shores from even the briefest trip abroad, the first thing you notice is how endearingly like Legoland our country looks, with its ring roads and frying-pan-shaped cul-de-sacs of neat little sloping-roofed brick boxes, all so identical yet all so different behind their privet hedges.

The semi is uniquely British. The Coronation Street-type terrace you can find in Baltimore, the Edwardian villa in San Francisco, the bungalow in Alice Springs. But nowhere else will you find the semi as we know it. There is no corner of a foreign field that is forever Ruislip.

I have never myself had the good fortune to live in a semi. No, that's not strictly true. I've had the good fortune but not the good sense. But when I was a snotty-nosed yet upwardly-mobile urchin, Dunroamin was my goal.

There was a ribbon development of private semis just up the road from our council estate and I used to go and stare at them, marvelling at the lifestyle of these multi-millionaires with six hundred quids-worth of bricks and mortar around them, a Ford Popular in the garage and a sunflower in the front garden. One day, Keithy lad, I used to tell myself, all this will be yours.

By now, I suppose it is time to realise, I must have missed the boat. But I have always had and shall continue to have a soft spot for our suburban answer to the cuckoo-clock Swiss chalet.

If the semi-detached is pining into oblivion, so must semi-detached life. What then will become of those fine old English institutions such as washing the car on Sundays, walking the dog as far as the pub, and going up the wooden hill to Bedfordshire?

The answer is that they are going up the spout like so much else, as lifestyles and what the social engineers call leisure patterns shift and change like snowflakes. Only this week it was revealed that the traditional roast beef Sunday lunch, which a million Dunroamin dwellers used to sleep off on a million uncut moquette settees in a million front rooms with three million flying geese on the walls, is virtually a thing of the past, having been replaced by the Chinese takeaway and suchlike.

It is all, in my view, part of a dark, deep plot to turn these islands into a kind of offshore Australia where everyone swaggers around in a vest with a Walkman clamped to his ears, swigging fizzy drinks straight from the can which is then left on top of a pillar box or spiked on my railings.

(A Sheffield reader gives me the ultimate in can disposal which I wrote about recently: he saw one stuffed into a boot on display outside a shoe shop.)

All things must change, and we with them. But I wish they would leave us Dunroamin.

NUCLEAR VIDEO AND THE PLANNERS

As a part-time student of our labyrinthine town and country planning regulations – as rich a territory to a professional jester as a Gruyère cheese to a professional mouse – I am interested in a development (or as it may turn out, non-development) in Peterborough.

A small consortium of businessmen have acquired a one-acre site on which to erect a £2 million nuclear fall-out shelter for 250 families. They are looking for 1000 canny souls to shell out reservation fees of close on £2000 apiece. They are also seeking planning permission.

And there is the rub. The lady chairman (or chair, as lady chairmen are known these days, preferring to be equated with four wooden legs rather than two trousered ones) of the council planning committee has said, very properly, that the application will be considered on its merits.

She is then quoted as adding, with rather less detachment, 'But if you want my personal view, I think it is a non-starter. As I understand it, they only want professional people who can afford £2000. That is no good for ordinary people.'

Now I happen to feel quite strongly that if there are any survivors of the holocaust if and when it comes, ordinary people should be of their number. But I believe the professions should be represented also: a doctor or two, a few engineers, an architect, an advertising consultant. All these would play their part in attracting human life and light industry back to Peterborough.

Mix 'em up a bit, that's what I say. A bunch of ordinary folk, a sprinkling of professionals, two cats, two dogs, a couple of giraffes and a dove, and we're in pretty good shape for the post-nuclear millennium.

Alas, on this isolated occasion my view carries no weight. For when considering a planning application, a planning committee has to follow the spirit and letter of planning law. And while planning law has a great deal to say about the rights and restrictions placed upon professional people – particularly those in such professions as animal charcoal manufacturer, glue boiler, bone grinder and so on – it makes no provision whatever for ordinary people.

I have gone over the various Town and Country Planning Acts with a magnifying-glass and I can find no mention of ordinary people. In the supporting case-law there is the odd reference to 'the reasonable man,' but all my experience of ordinary people suggests that reasonable is the last thing they are – and they are likely to become even less so when the missiles are dropping and the fall-out shelter commissionaire won't let them in because they're not wearing a tie.

So unless Peterborough wants a six-month public inquiry and an appeal to the House of Lords on its hands, it will have to find some other way of blocking this potential blot on the landscape.

Happily, there is a way. These communal nuclear shelters are a bit of a growth area these days, which means that to attract the customers and relieve them of large sums of money, you have got to offer them something the other nuclear shelters haven't got – double-glazing, say, or a money-back guarantee.

What the proposed Peterborough bunker offers is an amenity area.

This amenity area will feature, among other facilities, a video room – and if that's not in breach of the planning regulations I will convert this column into an illegal hot-dog stand and push it off Southend Pier.

What about your residential zoning, then? Nice middle-class neighbourhood, albeit fifty feet under the ground, and there's a bloody video parlour plonked in the middle of it? That's not what you pay your rates for.

Then there's your nuisance factor. What about the ordinary people crawling about in the ruins outside? Haven't they got enough on their plate turning black in the face and then dying, without having to listen to the next-door neighbours playing endless repeats of 'Yes, Minister', and their flaming space-invader machines pinging away at all hours?

If that objection is over-ruled, there is the old change-of-use ploy. Recreational facility slap-bang in the middle of an industrial development area, or what used to be an industrial development area before it became a very large crater. Not on.

And if all else fails, there is always precedent to fall back on. Two years ago Peterborough council had a similar application, for a nuclear shelter at Orton Longueville. They turned it down. On the grounds that it would create parking problems.

THE TOWN HALL GLIDE

It is not often that I literally dance up and down with rage – certainly not more than twice a day – but if you had slapped a number on my back this weekend I could certainly have qualified for the Foaming At The Mouth section in the National Ballroom Dancing championships.

The cause of this tango of fury was nothing world-shattering such as Russia leaning on some small country like a Soho protection racketeer, nor anything particularly mind boggling such as Sir Keith Joseph.

What moved me to charge four steps to the side, reverse turn, forward lunge then promenade chasse up the wall, was a casual, almost throw-away statement in the middle of a routine news item about a marathon reading of all Shakespeare's plays in Covent Garden.

'Originally we wanted to have a non-stop reading,' said the organiser. 'But the local authorities thought that all-night readings were not a good idea.'

The thought that percolated the red mist as I went through the basic movements of the Apoplectic Two Step (leading with left foot, traverse ceiling and pirouette around light fitment. Pas glissade and gnash teeth) was WHAT THE BLOODY HELL HAS IT GOT TO DO WITH THE LOCAL AUTHORITIES?

Since an all-night reading from Shakespeare is not a permanent structure or a timber dwelling resting on concrete it presumably does not come within the labyrinthine provisions of the Town and Country Planning Acts, which local councils have a duty to enforce.

Since an all-night reading from Shakespeare cannot be placed between two slices of bread and eaten, it is unlikely to be subject to one of those sinister-sounding Night Cafés Orders, which are also administered by the council.

The Shakespeare marathon is part of a shopping-precinct book fair and so it may be that it falls under the umbrella of the Shops

Acts, the dual purpose of which is to prevent shoppers shopping at the hours that most suit them, and to provide gainful employment for council inspectors.

But what is more likely is that some nervous council official riffled through his files for the heading, 'Readings, all-night, Shakespearian,' found that there was no precedent for any such wild orgy of blank verse, and at once broke out in bleak smiles and declared: 'You can't do that there 'ere.'

Now there is, of course, nothing new in local authorities interfering with innocent enjoyment. I can remember the golden age of municipal watch committees, when posses of councillors in bowler hats, their walrus moustaches trembling with indignation (or some such powerful emotion) would descend on any tatty vaudeville theatre where it was rumoured that the nudes were moving about on the stage, contrary to the Cor! Look How They Wobble! Act of 1934.

What is relatively new – it dates from the disastrous reorganisation of local government, when councils became too big for their boots – is the obsessive meddling in people's everyday (or everynight) lives that this Shakespeare business typifies. By now there is hardly any public activity at all that doesn't need council permission – or, if it doesn't, that the council will not muscle in on by virtue of owning the street, assuming responsibility for 'leisure amenities' or otherwise demanding a slice of the action.

Much of our present economic plight may be laid at the door of local authorities who have killed off whole areas of trade and industry by their wholesale disinclination to mind their own business. (Their own ventures into commerce are nearly always disastrous.) Of the vast sums being overspent by councils, which Mr Heseltine is so exercised about, hundreds of millions are squandered on departments whose only function is to see what the ratepayers are doing and make them stop it.

There was a time when it was the role of the town hall to lay drains, repair the holes in the road, keep the buses running on time, mow the grass on the park bowling green, unveil the occasional statue and little else. Those were simple days indeed, and we live in a much more complex age now. But it would be a damn sight less complex if we didn't have the local government albatross clinging to our backs twenty-four hours a day.

I feel itchy feet for that dance of rage again. Do you suppose I need council permission to use premises in a residential zone as a temporary private ballroom?

OF GRAVE CONCERN

Let us, this blackbird-singing Springlike morning, consider the topic of graveyards.

It is one on which I can claim some first-hand knowledge, though not, of course, as first-hand as some – as for instance the subject of an epitaph in Frome churchyard, Somerset: 'Reader, Death took me without any warning. I was well at night and died in the morning.'

As an undertaker's clerk in the employ of J. T. Buckton and Sons ('We never Sleep') Ltd. I spent much of my time in graveyards where it was my solemn duty to record the names of mourners.

As a moonstruck adolescent I did most of my courting in the local cemetery under the smirking gaze of a choir of stone angels.

As a young reporter, attending funerals was a part of my daily round; and to this day I retain an affinity with those melancholy acres where the dear departed enjoy their eternal sleep within the safe embrace of municipal spiked railings.

Or did. For graveyards are not what they were. In these secular, cost-cutting days, so many of them are neglected and overgrown, their plinths askew, their slabs and statues defaced, their gravel paths scattered with the seedy paraphernalia of the glue-sniffer and the meths-drinker. It is very sad.

Where cemeteries and churchyards are well kept – like the vast yet excellently maintained Brompton Cemetery just around the corner from me, a granite and marble city of Baroque tombs and gothic citadels, some of them like miniature St Pancras stations – it is like stepping back into Victorian times.

They are not only mausoleums, they are museums of local history. Nowhere, paradoxically, does your home town come more alive than in these compounds of the dead and gone. The stonemason, in a few chiselled letters, can conjure up as poignant a family saga as was ever set down by the likes of Arnold Bennett.

Well now. In Leeds, where my disposition towards the necro-politan way of life first took root, the city's Civic Trust has just made a study of down-at-heel churchyards and of one of the big municipal cemeteries which has now become a slum.

On the churchyard front, Mrs Barbara Roberts writes in her report: 'I want to be able to see what a Victorian churchyard was really like, not just now, but in the future, and not just for myself but for generations to come.'

On the municipal cemetery, the Friends of Beckett Street Cemetery argue against proposals – presumably instigated by the Enemies of Beckett Street Cemetery – to remove a large number of memorials and create an aimless grassy area, which is what municipalities usually do with their run-down cemeteries. The Friends want to conserve the place as an attraction in its own right.

Other cities please copy. And if you cannot conceive of a graveyard being an attraction in its own right, you have probably not taken a walk in one recently.

Do so today, and you may be surprised by its glum, surrealistic and tranquil beauty. If you are, do me a favour, would you? Pull up a weed.

CASTLES AND CRATES ...

Driving through leafy Hertfordshire this weekend I came across what looked like a huge stockpile of bricks in the middle of a field. Closer inspection revealed it to be a new factory, devoted to some inscrutable branch of electronics.

It is good news that here and there investors are still putting their money into industry rather than into Old Master drawings or enamelled medallions. But I have to say that this was the ugliest building I have ever seen in my life, not excluding the National Theatre.

Correction: I can't really describe it as a building at all. It was more in the nature of a large brick crate. Presumably the architect was told what was needed in the way of space and he worked out the measurement on graph paper and drew a thick line around it. The absence of design was total.

It is very strange that while we are getting increasingly concerned about the buildings that come down we show practically no interest at all in the buildings that are going up. So long, that is, as they are tucked away in the countryside – or 'green-fields' as current industrial jargon has it. And that is where new factories get built these days.

There was a time when architects were allowed to splurge themselves on factory design. In some of the northern towns, you can still see examples of their going raving mad on the drawing board. There are mills and warehouses up there that look like the Temples of the Pharoahs. And on the outer ring roads of London, the gleaming white razor blade and toothpaste factories are like picture postcards of the streamlined thirties.

Caring about what factories look like seems to have gone out of the window when the process of selling goods was separated from the process of making them – in other words, in the post-war era of the prestige office.

Nowadays you have a glass castle in Park Lane for the paperwork and a brick packing-case out in the wilds of Essex where the profits are actually made. It reveals an odd sense of values.

The planning authorities that gave us Centrepoint (as attractive a monument as Cleopatra's Needle, in my view, though just as useless) would not look twice at the kind of designs that are passed automatically by their rural cousins. So why is the countryside being pock-marked with these excrescences?

I don't suggest that every new factory should look like the Ovaltine Farm. But you would think that the cost-accountants could allow a little on the budget for pride and confidence in the product being made within.

THE TARTS COUNCIL

The proposal to allow licensed brothels in certain selected parts of our cities, in all other respects as loony a scheme as has been hatched by a Government committee for many a long day, has one redeeming feature that shines out like a red light on the Marseilles waterfront.

These municipal houses of ill-fame, it stands to reason, would have to be supervised and administered by local authorities. The prospect of council-controlled knocking-shops promises hour upon hour of unalloyed pleasure – and I don't mean what you mean.

Watching the council set about regulating the disorderly houses of the township would be almost as much fun as watching its workmen dig holes in the road.

The first thing to be settled is the thorny question of zoning. You cannot authorise a red lamp district where it would affect rateable values, cause a nuisance, set a precedent, or occupy premises designated for a road-widening scheme. The consultation process, that's what the siting of our friendly neighbourhood Strumpet Centre calls for.

A councillor in Southampton, I note, favours the end of the city's royal pier for a projected 'licensed brothel and centre for erotic entertainment' but she is probably right in anticipating objections from the amenity societies. Much nearer the mark is a former mayor of Wolverhampton who believes 'An area like a light industrial estate might be suitable.'

I think that is a most constructive suggestion and if I were on the district council's Parks, Recreation and Whorehouses Committee it would get my vote. The sodium-lit trading estate with its empty service roads and its forlorn brick boxes behind their wire-mesh perimeter fences is exactly and precisely where you would expect to find a British house of pleasure. ('Want a good time, dearie? We're next to the glue-works.')

There are some planning problems. Converting a disused soft-toy factory or sludge-refinery into a bordello probably counts as a significant change of use under the Town and Country Planning Acts. A public notice inviting objections to any proposal to instal a torture dungeon and mirrored ceilings would have to be hung from the railings for the statutory period.

Then there is the licensing procedure itself. Where there are licences there must not only be licensing applications ('State precise use to which circular bed will be put') but licensing regulations ('It shall be a condition of this licence that the licensee shall not wear laddered net stockings') and an inspectorate, presumably wearing peaked caps and brothel-creepers, to see that the regulations are carried out. There must also be consumer protection whereby the dissatisfied punter can complain to the weights and measures department.

All in all I can see job creation for not less than five hundred council employees on this one, including a highly-paid Brothel Executive occupying a flash new suite of offices complete with two-way mirrors.

One or two councils, passionately opposed to enterprise zones in any shape or form, would perhaps decide to run the brothels themselves as an essential social service. They would be the first cat-houses in the entire history of the world to lose money.

IN THE SWIM

A recent page in *The Times* boosting those flash new swimming complexes that so many cities have taken to running now that they all have leisure directors instead of parks superintendents, was decidedly snooty about the municipal baths of old.

'Gone are the days when a visit to a public pool was acutely depressing if not positively frightening. No longer is the hapless swimmer forced to shiver in the changing rooms, weep from the chlorine and cower from humourless lifeguards only too anxious to enforce the long list of rules ...'

It makes the old Bog Street Baths sound like Pentonville Jail (*'I sentence you to seven lengths on the first charge and five on the second, to run concurrently,'*) but I'm afraid that's not how I remember it at all.

I did not know much of the world when I was first permitted to sally forth with my cozzie rolled up inside a ragged towel – I didn't even know enough to keep my mouth shut under water – but I am pretty certain I would have been aware of being acutely depressed, positively frightened and hapless.

The only time I recall being positively frightened was when I was dared, on pain of being thrown in, to jump into the six-foot end off the iron-railed balcony. Come to think of it I might well have been acutely depressed and even hapless at that particular moment. Luckily the humourless lifeguard with his long list of rules came to my rescue.

There were minor fears, it's true: fear of having your clothes thrown in the water, fear of cracking your head on the bottom when you dived in, fear of drowning, fear of being humiliatingly refused entry because of your dirty feet, fear that – as mythology firmly had it – if you idly spent a penny while swimming, the water would indict you by changing colour (what colour, I always wondered. Purple?) But these were routine anxieties that any backstreet ten-year-old could cope with.

What I do clearly remember about those white-tiled, voice-echoing days is that they were a lot of fun – as much fun (if not more fun) as can be derived from the spraunciest clover-leaf-shaped heated leisure-centre pool complete with water chute.

For all that it was like swimming in a bottle of Dettol, and you had to traipse through a kind of sheep-dip arrangement before you were allowed in the water, and the changing cubicles were like police cells; and that in their iron-girdered austerity the corporation baths had much in common with the corporation workhouse, yet no one who ever took a Saturday morning dip in one will ever forget the shivering, slithering, splashing, diving-board-spronging, whistle-blowing joy of it.

Never mind that you could never get quite dry afterwards, or that you always dropped a sock in a puddle and trapped your fingers in the mangle while wringing out your bathing trunks. There was always the comfort of a thick beaker of Bovril, and the scramble around the slot machine for a penny bar of Ovaltine chocolate to take away the lung-searing aftertaste of a gallon of swallowed chlorine.

That *Times* piece quotes the manager of the fancy new Fulham pools on what swimming is all about these days: 'The big difference between the old municipal pools and pools like these is that we have applied marketing techniques. Swimming pools are competing with other forms of entertainment. To make them come here we've got to make them attractive.'

What he didn't mention, or may have forgotten, was that to make the people of Fulham come to the new pools they first had to stop them going to the old one, which was the subject of an enormous petition and which was occupied and run for a while by locals who knew what they would be losing.

The new-style leisure pools as they insist on calling them (to distinguish them from typing pools?) are certainly a huge success, at least in terms of the numbers of punters using them. Yet I'm not sure they haven't poshed and pampered some of the delight out of the municipal swimming experience.

Wave machines we did not have, but Bog Street Baths had all

the pulling power of Tom Sawyer's swimming-hole on a hot and dusty school-day.

PLOUGHMAN'S QUICHE

Easter is when the English customarily emerge blinking from hibernation, switch off the telly, and like Mole in *The Wind In The Willows* are drawn irresistibly to the Great Outdoors.

Easter, weather permitting, is when even the most dedicated city-dwellers turn to ancient rustic pursuits such as visiting National Trust properties, attending vintage car rallies and chuffing around on narrow gauge railways.

Anyone who thinks that country life is being urbanised out of existence should just try finding a space in a village pub car park on an Easter Monday. As for getting a go on the video game in the taproom inglenook, forget it.

Far from the simple rural pursuits dying out, they are more popular than ever, as the chart ratings show.

Village cricket for instance, which you might expect in these sophisticated times to be watched only by a handful of yokels and the village bobby (or in the case of pit village cricket, by two thousand village bobbies) nowadays attracts an audience from far and wide – as do village hang-gliding, village drag-racing, village water-skiing and village American football.

Village crafts flourish. You can buy a traditional glazed bunny-rabbit flower vase at the village pottery, or traditional horse-brasses imported from Hong Kong at the village smithy and DIY centre. Traditional plastic matchbox holders, quaint souvenir ashtrays and suchlike are still sold by hand at the village gyfte shoppe.

Yet time has not stood still in these pastoral backwaters. Though simple canned ale, lager drawn from the zinc and rough salt-'n'-vinegar-flavoured crisps remain the staple fare of the village inn, gone are the days when the traveller could expect nothing more imaginative than a humble ploughman's lunch of French bread and vacuum-sealed cheese.

No: these days he is just as likely to be offered ploughman's curry, ploughman's quiche, ploughman's foil-baked potato with choice of six fillings, or even ploughman's scampi in a basket.

Then there is the bounteous harvest of the countryside itself. 'One is nearer God's heart in a garden centre than anywhere else on earth,' a poet wrote. How pleasantly satisfying, as twilight descends and the voice of the blackbird gives way to that of the car radio, to wend one's weary way homeward with a sack of freshly-bought potting compost or a treasured barbecue kit on special offer.

What is this lure of field and lea, this urge of townsmen and women to head for the open motorway at the first flicker of spring sunshine or the first announcement in their local What's On of a Super Easter Air Show featuring the Red Arrows plus demonstration of free-fall parachuting?

What is the mad instinct that drives us to put ourselves to the inconvenience of stopping on a busy road to buy free range eggs, even when it means being overtaken by a stream of traffic? Whose is the siren voice that bids us to pick our own strawberries after leaving the kiddies in supervised play area at rear of caravan site?

My belief is that well over two hundred years after the start of the Industrial Revolution, we stubbornly remain a nation of country-dwellers at heart, and that it needs only the call of a drum majorettes team or the distant sound of a motor-cycle scramble to draw us as if by magnet back to our roots.

We are fortunate, of course, in having a rich and varied countryside – the envy of foreigners whose own bleak, featureless rural landscape is completely devoid of gymkhanas, sponsored walks, marathon runs, conducted tours, second-hand car auctions, and Sunday markets in disused aircraft hangars.

No wonder we treasure it. No wonder Englishmen abroad, at this time of the year, dream of wandering our gently rolling meadows with the old metal-detector kit, to the soporific hum of the bees and the model aeroplanes.

No wonder Browning wrote, 'Oh, to be in England, now that April's there, and whoever wakes in England sees, some morning, the annual Spring Fayre and car boot sale in aid of Friends of the Earth . . .'

A WORD THAT LOST ITS WAY

When you shut your eyes and think of England, what picture is evoked by the word 'community'?

I wouldn't mind betting that it's something ratty with corrugated iron in it. Strange, isn't it, how some words change their image over the years?

The dictionary defines a community as 'a social group of any size whose members reside in a specific locality and have a common cultural and historical heritage' – and at one time that's precisely what a community was. A school, a pub, a row of shops, a bowling green, a scout hut, a public library . . . here's the church and here's the steeple, open the doors and here's the people.

Nowadays a community is an acre or two of wind-blown nothing brooding on its problems from behind a plywood stockade.

Once community leaders were the preachers, the teachers, and the High Street ironmongers and corn merchants who were the councillors and magistrates of the town. Today's community leaders are the director of social services, the welfare rights coordinator and the multi-racial neighbourhood development training programme assessment unit administrator.

A community project once meant the annual flower show or the waste-paper drive. Now it's skinheads scrubbing graffiti off the bricked-up frontage of a vandalised laundry-room while an old lady with a black eye watches cautiously from a urine-etched breezeblock walkway.

From being a warm and beckoning and leafy word, community has become a barren one, as bleak and as cold as concrete. And yet, as a concept, it has never been more popular . . . among those who don't have to live in it.

Daily our worthiest and staunchest pillars of society argue the case for a period of compulsory community service – a kind of short, soft shock, I imagine – for the young. Daily our politicians, their eyes misting in wistful recollection of more ordered days when there was a place for everyone and eveyone knew their place, preach community values and community pride. Daily the concerned letters about community spirit or the lack of it flow into the offices of *The Times* from old rectories and converted oast-houses far from the battleground.

One of the most recent epistles – from nearer the front line – was signed by no fewer than eight urban bishops. 'Every young person must be able to feel he can contribute to the society in which he lives, even if he cannot find gainful employment ... Instead of paying people to do nothing, surely it is better to pay a little more to provide regular work for young people and help the community ...'

Signed: Hugh Birmingham, John Chelmsford, Kenneth Lichfield, David Liverpool, Stanley Manchester, Ronald Southwark, Jim Stepney, David Ripon. And Uncle Tom Cobbleigh and all.

And so the well-meaning flow of platitudes continues ... and no one seems to have pointed out its central absurdity: that having produced a lost tribe of no-hopers by systematically, brick by brick and beam by beam, dismantling the intricately-structured community from which they would have drawn a sense of purpose and a scale of values, we are now proposing to restore their community spirit by persuading them to clear up the rubble.

Perhaps the lost tribe will savour the irony of it all – leaving us greybeards to appreciate how infinitely pathetic are advertisements like this one for a community worker in an 'inner area priority zone' in Leicester: '... To be responsible for making effective contact in a defined area of the city and for assisting in the development and maintenance of recreational, cultural and social activities. This will include identifying community needs, planning and developing a programme to meet those needs and developing local community networks ... The successful applicant will also be expected to play an active role in developing community self-help, and organising and co-ordinating voluntary support ...'

There was a time when community self-help didn't need 'co-ordinating' – but that was back in the sunshine age when community meant what it ought to mean and not the broken-backed thing it has become.

FLY-BY-NIGHT TOWERS

I don't venture into London's West End much these days, for pretty well the same reason as I don't venture down the main sewer much these days.

When I did have occasion to scurry through that tinsel waste-land the other day, I emerged even more depressed than usual. For I had observed a hole in the ground where four years of my life used to be.

The building that once stood there possessed little architectural merit. It was on no preservation list and its destruction will have gone unmourned – except by some of those who used to work in it.

It was one of those gloomily ornate Victorian office blocks that until a few years ago were common in all our cities, and still are in some. They had names like Corn Exchange Buildings or Town Hall Chambers, and behind the frosted-glass panels of their rabbit-warren corridors there laboured a multitude of trades, some more reputable than others.

I had the attic. Or to be precise, a quarter of the attic, the other three-quarters being occupied by a one-man mail-order company selling items like nostril-hair clippers.

My rooftop perch was reached either by a clanking, lurching and probably condemned lift, or, if that was out of order (which it more often was than not), by six flights of stone stairs. This latter route, as well as being less hazardous, was more interesting.

To spiral laboriously up the core of this ramshackle edifice was to take a fascinating vertical expedition through the mercantile jungle. Each shabby landing was a plain from which to observe the enchanting, ever-changing ways of Mother Commerce.

Thus, on one floor, in an office so small that its claustrophobic occupant felt obliged to keep the door open, you might catch a glimpse of an authentic private inquiry agent, looking not so much like Philip Marlowe as like the principal of the correspondence college down the corridor, which indeed he was, since he ran both businesses.

On another floor, where a travel agency had sadly (and rather hurriedly) dissolved into oblivion, the rejuvenation of the species was assured by the prompt arrival of another travel agency – the transition being all the more smoothly engineered by the fact that it did not actually involve a change of managing director or staff.

This regeneration process was constant throughout the building. If an escort agency fell victim to hard times, a mini-cab service would have taken up the lease before the departing tenant's tears were dry on the worn lino. If an obscure import company failed, an obscure export company at once took its place. If the small, hopeless publication edited from a cupboard on the fourth floor could not pay its printing bills, another small and even more hopeless publication arrived to snatch up the ragged mantle of failure.

Not all the tenants found it convenient to announce their existence on the varnished directory-board in the ratty lobby, or even to paint their names on the doors of their offices. They were mysterious, telephoning, typewriter-pecking, floor-pacing silhouettes behind the frosted glass and I wonder what they all did. I expect they wondered the same about me.

What I did, over four happy years, was to potter up to my quarter of an attic each day and scribble or look out of the window at the rooftops. It was a good place to work, it got me out of the house and the rent was cheap. Before that I'd had a succession of other garrets in a succession of other buildings, similarly decrepit and similarly populated. They were all either pulled down or tarted up into 'prestigious' office suites beyond the reach of the little fly-by-night businesses who once scraped a living in them. And now this last landlocked ship of fools has sunk without trace too.

Where did they go to when the bulldozer moved in like a forty-ton bailiff, those flitting, raincoated figures I used to meet in the shuddering lift, riffling through their mail to judge which were the cheques and which were the writs? Do they, like me, work at home now, or did they move out to the suburbs, or did they just say to hell with it and take an honest job?

One thing's for sure. When the new glass tower with the revolving doors and automatic lifts and sliding room-dividers goes up where that seedy old office-block used to be, there'll be no room in it for the likes of small-fry inquiry agents or obscure import and export companies or one-woman typing bureaux or mail-order businesses or bucket-shop travel agencies. Someone will be the richer for their departure, but not the life of the city.

SAFE AS MARZIPAN HOUSES

Mother Mullins, would you tell the Planning Appeals Tribunal your profession and your present address?

I am a trained witch, and I reside at No. 4A Bat Caves, Haunted Hill, Gnomesford SG14 1NJ.

And you have been refused permission, have you not, to erect a property to be known as Marzipan Cottage at the end of Long Winding Path, the Magic Wood, Metropolitan District of Dwarfborough HE6 4NL?

Up to press, yes.

Would this cottage be for personal or business use?

Both, actually. I should live there, but the room over the broomstick-port would be a dispensary for casting spells. Also, there would be a stove fired by smokeless fuel for the parboiling of lost children for consumption off the premises.

And to what, specifically, did the Chief Planning Executive take exception?

Specifically, to being turned into a frog.

No, I mean as to the plans for the proposed structure in the Magic Wood.

Oh, I see. He objected on several so-called grounds. First he claimed that the materials detailed in my specifications – marzipan walls, chocolate doors, butterscotch roof, barley-sugar chimney pots and spun-sugar double glazing – fell short of the minimum standards required by the building regulations.

Then he cracked on that the Magic Wood is in the green belt, which is not what he said when allowing the woodcutter to build a hovel bang in the middle of a listed glade last year. And finally he said that the existence of a marzipan cottage would attract sightseers and hot-dog carts, thus causing traffic jams on Long Winding Path.

And did you offer to modify your plans in any way?

No, but I offered to turn the sightseers into frogs.

Did the Deputy Chief Planning Executive, who was by now processing your application in the absence of the Chief Planning Executive who was fertilising eggs in the bullrushes, express his concern that your choice of building materials might invite excessive condensation, giving rise to mildew; and also that the structure as planned would be in danger of erosion due to being licked and nibbled by passers-by?

Yes. He also made a big song-and-dance about my licorice waste-pipes, saying that while they would just about pass muster as sherbert dabs, no way did they measure up to the stringent requirements of the Land Drainage Act 1930.

What was your response to these reservations?

I turned him into a frog.

You didn't go back and instruct your architect to see if he could go some way to meeting the objections raised by the planning authorities?

I did, actually, but he said it was beyond his capabilities to draw fresh blueprints with webbed feet.

I believe your application next came before the First Assistant Planning Executive, and that he voiced some proposed modifications for your consideration?

I wouldn't say voiced. Croaked, more like.

And what was the burden of these proposals?

He asked if I'd considered employing less unconventional building materials such as shortbread or bun mixture. I told him he ought to get out of his nice cosy office and try living in a house made of cake for a week or two. You are vacuuming up crumbs from morning till night; not to mention the property attracting so many birds that the sky is just one solid mass of frogs.

You have actually lived in a cake house, have you, Mother Mullins?

Lived in one? I was brought up in one. Icing floor like a blessed skating rink, stale bedroom walls and an outside lav made out of Swiss roll. Then we moved to a council maisonette system-built out of digestive biscuits. It was terrible.

What was your experience there?

The rain came through those little holes that they have in biscuits, and ran all over the floor which as luck would have it was jerry-built out of custard powder. You have never seen such a mess. It was like living in a cheesecake.

And what was the First Assistant Planning Executive's response to your rejection of his suggested amendment to the plans?

Nothing, really. He just hopped away on to a lily pad.

The Second Assistant Planning Executive next came forward with a compromise proposal, did he not?

Yes, he said that if I would clad the outside walls with green Turkish delight, to meld in with the foliage, and could also see my way to curing his warts or better still transferring them to the end of his mother-in-law's nose, he might be able to swing my application with the planning committee.

And what was your reply to that, apart from converting the Second Assistant Planning Executive into a frog?

My reply was that if I wanted to live in a jellified igloo I would have waved my magic wand and made one. Added to which, I cannot be doing with all that powdered sugar. I am such a martyr to a bronchial condition that you might just as well sprinkle the house with asbestos dust and have done with it.

You then made an appointment with the Third Assistant Planning Executive, I believe?

Yes, but he hid in a cupboard. The Fourth Assistant Planning Executive climbed up a big tall beanstalk and wouldn't come down, and the Fifth Assistant Planning Executive – the same old cow who refused me an improvement grant for my treacle-toffee dinette extension when I was living in Gingerbread Terrace – had been granted maternity leave to look after her tadpoles. So I got on my broomstick and came to the Planning Appeals Tribunal.

And you are making this appeal on the basis that a marzipan cottage would enhance the neighbourhood, and that there are many precedents for persons engaged in witchcraft being domiciled in premises fashioned out of confectionery?

Yes. Also on the basis that it is not very nice being turned into a frog.

You don't feel that the erection of a residence such as is outlined in your plans would be to the detriment of the amenities of the Magic Wood?

What amenities? There is nothing at the end of Long Winding Path except a neglected fairy ring.

You are positive it is neglected, Mother Mullins?

It is now, yes. It is just a dump for old mattresses and frogspawn. Also, as regards recreational facilities for the kiddies, the Magic Wood is a disgrace. There is nothing for them at all. If I were allowed to build my marzipan cottage, I would regard it my duty as a responsible ratepayer to create a special adventure playground fully equipped with poison berries, swamp, wolf and picnic area.

And you have voluntarily entered into an undertaking as to possible nuisance caused by noise, have you not?

That is true. I have pledged that there would be no maniacal cackling outside normal business hours.

And what would you say to the objection that the high glucose content of the structure would encourage wasps?

I already have a firm arrangement with the wasps. They don't trouble me and I don't trouble them.

Thank you, Mother Mullins, you may step down now. And now with your permission, Mr Chair-frog, I should like to call several witnesses who will give evidence of the desirability of a marzipan cottage in the area. Hansel and Gretel, please ...

THE PING-PONG TRAIL

The idea of a minister of Free Time, with the brief of channelling the large quantity of leisure that is lying around into something useful like raffiawork, is so wholesome and sensible and public-spirited and thoroughly Swedishly depressing that I can't imagine why we didn't think of it first.

It sounds like the kind of notion that would appeal to the Social Democrats. If Shirley ever forms a Government, perhaps she will award the free time quango to some worthy life peeress with nothing better to do all day long.

In the event, it has surprisingly fallen to the French to blaze the ping-pong trail. I say surprisingly because I bet until their Minister of Free Time was appointed, the French didn't even know they had a leisure problem. They just lolled around in cafés piling up those little plastic saucers and thinking about nothing in particular, very loudly.

This turns out to be bad for the brain and is to be officially discouraged. 'We are charged,' announces their new Free Time Minister, M. André Henry, 'with helping people to conquer the fatalism of passivity faced with leisure.'

Now that I have copied that sentence out I'm not too sure what it means, but I suspect that whatever M. Henry is saying, it is the opposite of 'Have a good time.'

Aided and abetted by two junior ministers, who I suppose stand in for him on his days off, M. Henry is proposing to deal with the above-quoted mouthful by 'the development of regional cultural entities and a significant growth in cooperative and club movements.'

Methinks I smell raffiawork. Not to mention the unmistakable niff of the pottery class, the raw odour of half-baked street theatre, the brooding pong of yoga and the garlicky whiff of whatever is the French equivalent of Morris dancing.

How sad for the French. They vote for a glorious Socialist republic and they end up with a one-man Camden Borough Council who harangues them for using their free time 'negatively'.

My heart goes out to them. Ever since my youth club days, when I was subjected to enforced table tennis and compulsory chess, I have had a horror of organised leisure. Admittedly, I signed on voluntarily for night school – but only to meet girls. When I found it was possible to meet girls without at the same time learning to play the typewriter, I applied at once for the King's shilling.

Nowadays, when it comes to the municipalisation of life's idle moments, the night school and the youth club are of course only the tip of the iceberg or artificial ski slope. In every borough across the land there has sprung up, on some inconvenient acre of damp grass on the edge of town, a factory-like brick cavern which goes by the name of the Council Leisure Centre.

In this echoing pleasure tomb, squash and bingo are practised openly and evils such as basket-making are inflicted on the old and feeble under the chilly eye of the Leisure and Amenities Co-ordinator.

Local government can at last claim that it has a noble purpose in keeping the spirits of its ratepayers depressed with weak tea and subsidised ping-pongery, in that it keeps them from doing anything inflammatory with their spare time such as keeping rabbits without council permission or playing cards for money. But what are we to say about the commercial interests which have also taken up the deadening, bogus-sociological concept of 'planned leisure'?

At one time they didn't care what you did in your non-working hours so long as they got the kiss-me-quick hat concession. These days their computers monitor your every move in case you stumble across some means of enjoying yourself without spending money.

At one time you could go to the local Roxy and buy a choc-ice from the girl with a tray round her neck and then settle down to a rotten old movie made by Colossal Pictures Inc. These days you visit the Roxy four-in-one cinema complex where you buy your controlled portion of ice-cream from the kiosk run by the catering division of Roxy Leisure Ltd., and settle down to a rotten old movie made by the Leisure Division of the Colossal Oil Corporation Ltd. And the rotten old movie isn't only rotten, it's a ten-billion-dollar stinker.

At one time you could waste an hour in a pin-table saloon. These days you visit a Family Leisure Centre where not only are those bland and bleeping Space Invaders in full control but the managing director of the Japanese leisure outfit that imports them openly boasts: 'We would like to sanitise the business completely. We want to create a suitable environment.'

Sanitised leisure! Regional cultural entities! I think I will find the suitable environment of the nearest pub and spend my free evening getting ever so quietly drunk.

HOW NOW, BAUHAUS?

I grew up in the Thirties never knowing that there was a Bauhaus tram shelter at the top of our street, that the circular chrome-framed window of the Chocolate Cabin adjoining the Tivoli cinema was pure Art Deco, or that the Tivoli itself was built in 'jazz-modern.'

It never occurred to anyone in our street that architectural style had anything to do with our tram shelter or our Tivoli (pronounced Tivolly, to rhyme with brolly). Architecture, if we ever thought of it at all, was something with soot on it, statues in front of it and a big dome on top of it.

In the same way that you never find out you've been harbouring a valuable antique until you've given it to the jumble sale, most of us who were brought up in that period didn't notice Thirties design happening until it had already happened – by which time much of it had been blitzed, pulled down, thrown away, painted over, broken up or sold to the Americans.

It took us a long time to realise that it wasn't all bakelite and bent plywood (not that these highly versatile materials were to be despised). Even after the redevelopment holocaust in the 1960s, when we were poking about in the debris to see what was left, a surviving doorway or street-lamp or bit of glass or marble had to be Edwardian or earlier to be worth crossing the road for.

Hotels throwing out their red plush and gilt were vandalising: those dismantling their ocean-liner cocktail bars were only modernising.

Not until the Thirties were getting on for a safe half-decade distant, and were being written about by A.J.P. Taylor and suchlike as if they were real grown-up history, did it dawn on us that some quite pretty things must have passed through our hands during those tinny years. And we noticed it at last only because by that time they were being sold in repro in the gift boutiques of Carnaby Street.

We were aware in the Thirties, of course, that things were going on that had not gone on in previous decades. After all, it would have been difficult for the new Broadcasting House to have been built without anyone wondering what it was for. We registered vaguely that new buildings tended to be whitish and had rounded corners, and that the latest bedroom furniture was the texture of sucked toffee, with the dressing-table drawers arranged in tiers as if Fred Astaire meant to tap-dance up and down them. But that simply meant that some things were 'modern' while others were 'old-fashioned'.

This was, don't forget, an age when grandmothers still wore floor-length bombazine and shawls rather than pink trouser suits, and their spiders'-web parlours were crammed with elaborately-carved sideboards like Transylvanian family tombs, and horsehair sofas draped with antimacassars. When they attended one another's funerals, which they did regularly, they went in a horse-and-carriage. They were 'old-fashioned.'

We, if unlucky enough to fall victim to consumption or some other killer disease, made our last journey in the Co-op motor hearse. Here on earth we had the wireless and the pictures and our leatherette or uncut moquette three-piece suite, and our co-respondent shoes, and our cork-tipped cigarettes in a gun-metal cigarette case. We were 'modern.' (Our sisters, leafing through the new gravure women's weeklies while waiting for their pin curls to set, or powdering their noses over the electro-plated tea-things at the Kardomah, went even farther. They were 'moderne.')

What we didn't realise was that all this modishness had any shape or pattern – that there was any connection, for instance, between the speedcars hurtling round the track at Brooklands

('Ascot's keenest fashion rival') and the streamlining of the new factories on the Great West Road; or between the white flat-roofed semis of Metroland and the launching of the *Queen Mary*; or that when holidaymakers went to jeer at the Epstein sculptures on the concretely-functional Golden Mile at Blackpool, they were looking at one typical artifact of the Thirties contained within another.

In my home town of Leeds, visiting aunties from less prosperous (ie, more Depression-hit) areas were always taken on a conducted tour of all that was 'modern': the new, Flying-Scotsman-age railway station with its Mussolini-proportioned booking hall and concealed lighting; the Queens Hotel with its cinema-organ decor; Lewis's department store with its new-fangled soda fountain; the Portland stone Civic Hall and ornamental gardens (and can you imagine showing your relatives round any of your local new developments of the Seventies – or your relatives wanting to see them?).

The tour always ended up in our council flat (municipal Modern Movement, circa 1931) for a feast of John West salmon and Monk and Glass jelly and custard. Given that our boxlike, highly functional living room, with its fretwork pelmets, imitation parquet lino and mail-order coal scuttle in fancy art metal, was itself a monument to contemporary taste (though twenty years before 'contemp'ry' was all the rage), all the aunties needed was a catalogue and a guide in a peaked cap for them to have been able to boast that they had seen a splendid and comprehensive exhibition of Britain in the 1930s.

It is a pity that none of them has survived to see the equally splendid and comprehensive exhibition of Britain in the 1930s which the Arts Council has mounted at the Hayward Gallery on the South Bank. With less acreage to cover on their bad feet, though just as much to see, they might have noticed how all those seemingly disparate bits and pieces really slotted together, like the pieces in one of those giant competition jig saw puzzles that were themselves a feature of the Thirties.

The decade didn't produce a uniform, this-is-it style in the same way that – say – the Festival of Britain put its splay-legs-with-yellow-knobs-on trademark on just about everything that was manufactured in the Fifties. Architecturally, for example, the Regent's Park Zoo's futuristic penguin pool seems far removed from ribbon-development Tudor or the by-pass semi. Furniture design ranged between elaborate ebonised-mahogany-and-chromed-steel cocktail cabinets and the boxwood tallboy so plain that it could only have been a dress rehearsal for wartime utility. Ceramics veered between a Laura Knight 'Circus' dinner service and the kind of tea-set you won at shooting galleries (in my own household's case, it had been). There was a tremendous row going on – in an age that produced a surge of artists, Euston Road meant a school of realistic painting rather than a realistic traffic jam building up to the Westway – about whose style had most 'significance.'

'Most of us who enjoy Mr (Ben) Nicholson's paintings do so less as cosmic symbols than as tasteful pieces of decoration,' declared the future Lord Clark of Civilisation. (Evidently, unknown to me at the time, the conflict between 'modern' and 'old-fashioned' went far beyond the purlieus of my Bauhaus tram-stop.)

Wandering through the Hayward exhibition, all these contradictions and many others are apparent. Yet what comes over very clearly – like a dance-band concert heard through the sunburst-decorated soundbox of an Ekco 'wireless receiving station' – is a sense of unity, of this being a particular period and no other. The Thirties indeed, are of such a muchness that they deserved their own Great Exhibition in their own time, with a sun-roof Crystal Palace of chrome and Vita-glass.

The conecting link is *vigour*. Like the Victorian era, the Thirties was a period on the move. Despite – or was it because of? – the slump and the imminence of war, it was a decade of remarkable innovation, invention and progress.

As any reader of *Modern Boy* (2d, every Saturday) could have told you, land, sea and air records were being broken every day; £100 Morris Minors were hurtling down the Brighton Road at forty miles an hour, and the Coronation Scot clipped eighty minutes off the fastest service from King's Cross to Edinburgh. We were obsessed by transport in all its forms. Imperial Airways, the railway companies, the Cunard Line and the London Passenger Transport Board had, separately and corporately, the kind of image that nowadays belongs to Concorde and nothing else that moves. Their prestige was reflected in the progressiveness and confidence of their approach to design.

New industries meant not only new factories but a new kind of factory, centred on the ring roads of the south-east and Midlands rather than the Lowryesque north. (The Victorians built their factories like the temples of the Nile; we new Elizabethans build them like brick sheds, when we have occasion to build them at all; but those new Georgians built their factories to look like municipal casinos in the South of France.)

New factories meant new suburbs, with suntrap bungalows, labour-saving semis and cinemas even more splendid (or 'splendide') than our jazz-modern Tivoli. New houses meant new gadgets – vacuum cleaners, wireless sets and radiograms, electric cookers, portable electric fires – and new materials, some of them going by the odd name of 'plastics.' Thanks to the miracle of hire purchase there was, if you lived in the Hoover and Frigidaire belt, a consumer boom. The ever-expanding market for new things bright and beautiful gave designers a challenge they had not had since the reign of William Morris.

The Thirties saw the real dawn of mass-production – and the only time in mass-production's over-fertile life when it has been wedded to the arts. Elegant and original design went not only into the things you would expect to see elegantly and originally designed, like fabrics, jewellery and furniture, but into ordinary household appliances and gadgetry such as the new electric razors, into packaging (another new industry) and into advertising. (If the Tate Gallery wanted to be truly representative of British art at its best, it would devote a floor to the posters of the Thirties.)

Such was the towering, glowering reputation of the nation's Calvinist conscience, Lord Reith, that from this distance we tend to believe that the arbiter of 'good taste' in the Thirties was the BBC. To a great extent it was, as five minutes at the Hayward exhibition will show. But five minutes more will prove that there was an influence so unlikely, in today's context, as to sound absurd.

The London Passenger Transport Board, under the direction of Frank Pick, a design fanatic, virtually dictated the 'modernistic' look of the new, post-Industrial Revolution garden-suburb England. From its streamlined stations on the (rounded) corners of the new far-flung shopping parades, down to the litter-bin fixed to the Green Line bus stop, everything that London Transport touched was design-perfect.

The distinctive typeface evolved by Edward Johnston for its

posters and station signs is still in highly attractive use. Compare it with the dreary, featureless 'corporate lettering' that you can see plastered over any railway station, hospital or other public building, and see what was lost when great institutions stopped caring about good design. And compare today's Lego-brick 'prestige' office blocks with the magnificent Citizen Kane towers that went up when the great corporations had something to be really prestigious about. (They are hard to find in our own cities, but New York, San Francisco and Chicago have examples of High Art Deco so stunning and intricate and rich that you wonder there was any money left over to pay the lift attendants.)

From my Bauhaus tram shelter in Leeds to Arnos Grove tube station would be a very long ride but a very short step; the Chocolate Cabin next to the Tivoli has echoes of Tilly Losch's superb all-glass bathroom designed by Paul Nash; the Tivoli itself is related to the Odeon, Sutton Coldfield, which is related to the Odeon, Leicester Square, which is related to Broadcasting House, which is related to those abstractish scraperboard decorations in the pre-war *Radio Times*, which is related to *Picture Post*, which is related to the first (sixpenny) Penguin books, which are related to the Left Book Club, which is related to the stagnant industrial north, which is related to my Bauhaus tram shelter.

The Thirties evoke many images for me. The most vivid is one that is as foreign to my lifestyle of the time as riding a camel across the Sahara. It is of tootling through the leafy suburbs in my two-seater, munching a bar of Motoring Chocolate and smoking a De Reske or two before pulling in for a snifter at a roadhouse on the by-pass, then pressing on to Croydon Airport where I have a seat (a basket-chair, actually) reserved on one of Imperial Airways' Empire flying-boats to Paris.

I don't want to hear that flying-boats didn't leave from Croydon or that they didn't go to Paris. In this dream they do ... and dreams are just about all that are left of the syncopated, stream-lined, modernistic and on the whole rather delightful Thirties.

10

THE FLYING DUMPLING

THE PRICE OF CRUDE GOLDFISH

THE PRICE OF CRUDE GOLDFISH

The Lunacy Commissioners, fearing a run on the limited number of roadside strait-jackets available to motorists who have lost their marbles, have asked me to explain why the cost of petrol is going up again despite a world glut which has resulted in a fall in crude oil prices.

If it is all right by you, I think that to simplify matters we will pretend that instead of gallons of petrol we are talking about goldfish, and that a bowl of these goldfish is in the possession of that well-known character beloved of school arithmetic primers, Johnny.

Please smoke if you wish and do not hesitate to ask questions should you be in any way baffled.

To begin, then, at the beginning, or rather in the middle since we don't have all day, Johnny has a bowl of goldfish which he wishes to sell for chocolate pennies. However, owing to the fact that the price of crude goldfish has fallen, he has had to pay a higher tanker price for his goldfish than he would otherwise have ...

I believe someone has a question. You, sir – the gentleman with the steam coming out of his ears.

Thank you, sir. The explanation is that despite the price of crude goldfish having fallen, chocolate pennies have diminished in value as against Monopoly money. I need hardly remind you that crude goldfish is always priced in Monopoly money.

A gentleman signing himself N. Bonaparte has just sent up a note in shaky handwriting asking: 'In God's name, why?'

The answer, Your Excellency, is that the owner of the North Sea goldfish rig prefers to deal in Monopoly money, since unlike the unstable chocolate penny it does not melt.

I will take a question from that lady at the back – the one with the very attractive foam on her mouth.

The owner of the North Sea goldfish rig, madam, is none other than Johnny himself. He sells to the goldfish refinery in Monopoly money, but then fixes the pump price of goldfish in chocolate pennies, thus incurring a serious loss.

That gentleman swinging from the chandelier, waggling an

index finger over his lips in order to induce a gibbering sound – do you have a query of some kind, sir?

He wishes to know whether in the event of the chocolate penny rising against Monopoly money, the price of four-star goldfish would then go down.

On the contrary, sir. The price on the goldfish forecourts would go up again.

Because you have to remember, sir – would the two men in white coats please not remove the questioner until I have given him his answer? – that there is a world-wide glut of crude goldfish. So if Johnny has to pay himself fewer chocolate pennies, this can only diminish his already shrinking profits, and he will have to recoup his losses at the goldfish pumps.

However, there is always a bright side. If goldfish prices go so high that no one can pay them, they will have to come down again in order to reduce the profit-shrinkage incurred in putting them up. This arrangement will last until goldfish prices have to be increased again in order to reduce the profit-shrinkage incurred by bringing them down.

One last question from that gentleman in the third row – no, not the one with the celery behind his ears, the one being strapped into his chair by his attendants.

I'm sorry, sir, the fact that you are an arrowroot biscuit is not a question.

The meeting is now closed. Next week's seminar will show how European air fares make complete economic sense, if only you think of them as pounds of passenger apples.

PERKINS PULLS THE STRINGS

The merest wisp of a paragraph, buried away beneath all the chaos and crisis news like a snowdrop under an avalanche, has been intriguing me all weekend.

Here it is: 'A violin Gladstone gave to his butler was sold for £260 at Christie's yesterday.'

I find that riveting. It's not the price of the violin that interests me, or even that it was sold at all. It is the fact that Gladstone gave it to his butler in the first place.

It is my observation that the kind of people who have butlers do not, in the general run of things, present them with violins. Old suits, yes. Unwanted golf clubs, perhaps. Violins, no.

Several theories spring to mind. The front-runner is that William Ewart Gladstone, four times Prime Minister and our greatest statesman of the nineteenth century, was barmy.

Losing one's marbles takes many forms and it may be that in the evening of his life Mr Gladstone took to pressing his possessions on anyone who came into contact with him. I'm told this kind of behaviour is quite common among people of great age. Thus this kind of scene may have been enacted daily at No. 10:

'Will that be all, Mr Gladstone, sir?'

'Yes, thank you, Perkins. By the by, would you or Mrs Perkins have any use for a silver inkstand?'

'I'm sure we can find a home for it, sir. It'll go very nicely with that Louis XV bureau you kindly gave us this morning.'

But for this to hold water, the death of Gladstone's butler should have revealed a vast cache of diamond shirt studs, coal scuttles, calf-bound sets of Hansard, cutlery, cigar-cutters, busts of Palmerston and other loot. ('It was like Aladdin's Cave in there' – Inspector Lestrade.) As it was, they seem to have found only a violin. So we must look at the mystery afresh.

It seems unlikely that the violin was a formal presentation on the occasion of the butler's retirement. A striking clock would have been more appropriate. But it could have happened:

'Perkins, you have served me faithfully ever since you came to me as a pantry boy in 1824. Your loyalty is a shining example to all. When my motives for helping fallen women were misunderstood, you could have sold the story to the *Penny Dispatch* and cleaned up. But you remained aloof. I am forever in your debt, Perkins, and as a token of my esteem I would like you to accept this violin.'

'Thank you, Mr Gladstone, sir, and in reply may I say it is what I have always wanted and I look forward to spending many happy years learning to play it.'

No, perhaps not.

Did Mrs Gladstone have a hand in it? 'William, I am a patient woman. I have not complained when you have sat up all night with political riff-raff. I have put up with your bringing home women of ill-fame and giving them cups of tea. But I will not stand for you scraping away at that thing in bed. Either you give it away to the butler at once or I will leave you.'

That doesn't ring true either – but it does give us a lead. Gladstone gave his butler the violin because he had to. Now that's worth pursuing.

Of course. The Jeeves stories. Bertie Wooster is forever surrendering his favourite ghastly spats, plus-fours or whatever in exchange for Jeeves getting him out of a tight spot.

Suddenly it all fits. Gladstone's butler, like Jeeves, was the power behind the throne. It stands to reason, when you think about it. How could a man of eighty function as Prime Minister? Gladstone was only the front man. It was Perkins who made all the decisions.

Picture, if you will, the ga-ga statesman crucifying 'Pale hands I loved' on that infernal violin as Perkins shimmers in with the hot milk.

'Will that be all, sir?'

'Not quite, Perkins. What about that Home Rule Bill you were going to draft for me?'

'I fear, sir, that little progress has been made. As I had occasion to point out when I was preparing your Irish Land Act and you had taken up the drums, concentration is of the essence.'

A brooding silence.

'If I gave up the violin, Perkins, could you draft a Home Rule Bill that will roll 'em in the aisles?'

'I will endeavour to give satisfaction, sir.'

'Take the thing,' said William Ewart Gladstone, 'and auction it at Christie's.'

THE UKKISH WAY OF LIFE

A puzzled American came up to me in a pub the other day and asked me if I could tell him where the UK was. I told him he was standing in it.

He said that had rather been his impression, so in that case, what was the difference between the UK and Britain?

I trotted out the standard definition – that Britain is the United Kingdom of Great Britain and Northern Ireland minus Northern

Ireland. This leaving him none the wiser, I was elaborating the point with matchsticks when I suddenly realised that this is not the real difference between the two at all.

The fact is that the UK and Britain are not two slightly different territorial states – they are two entirely different states of mind.

There are people in these islands who, although foremostly English, Welsh or Scottish, will in fits of maudlin patriotism call themselves British. That is one class. There are others who always speak of their country as the UK and themselves as UK citizens. That is the other.

In what ways do the British and the Ukkish, as we shall call these UK denizens, differ from one another?

One difference is that for all that the British reside in Great Britain, they are little Englanders to a man. They never believed we should have gone into the Common Market and they are deeply gratified, with every example of EEC bureaucracy, extravagance or waste, at having been proved (as they would believe) dead right.

The Ukkish are Europeans through and through. Even when they oppose the EEC, which most of them don't, it is for the most boring of political reasons, rather than the proper one which is that foreigners are foreign. They live for the day when they'll get their exciting new foreign-looking European passports, and should a European currency ever come about they would make a bonfire of pound notes out of sheer bliss.

The British love pottering in the garden, washing the car, drinking real ale and slumping in front of the telly.

The Ukkish love tinkering with their microprocessors, repairing the car, drinking canned lager and slumping in front of the video.

True Brits are Fahrenheit. True Uks are Centigrade. True Brits read library books. True Uks read airport paperbacks. True Brits say 'Thank you very much.' True Uks say 'Cheers.'

It is Ukkish to keep a wire coathanger in your hatchback. It is also British – so long as you are using it as the aerial.

The BBC is British but it shows some pretty Ukkish programmes (Thorn Birds). ITV is Ukkish but shows the best of British (Brideshead). Cable TV is Ukkish. The Post Office is British, even though it doesn't call itself such. British Telecom, however, should be called Ukkish Telecom. British Rail tries to be Ukkish Rail but makes a hash of it. BL is UL.

Many people go round claiming to be True Brits who are True Uks really. Margaret Thatcher is an out-and-out Uk although she goes on and on about being British. Denis, on the other hand, would probably call himself an Uk when all the time he's a Brit. Mark Thatcher, the Brian Tilsley of Downing Street, is a complete Uk, but sister Carol is a Brit.

Neil Kinnock is a Brit, as is David Steel. David Owen is an Uk. Roy Jenkins makes Uk speeches but he is as Brit as Cheddar cheese (Lymeswold is Uk). The Queen, of course, is a True Brit but Prince Philip is a True Uk, as is Prince Charles. Princess Di is a Brit.

English cricket is a British game watched by Brits. English soccer is an Ukkish game watched by some right little Uks. Tennis and Bowls are Brit. Snooker and ice-skating are Uk. Pub darts is a Brit game which has been taken over by Uks. Pub video games are Uk. Pub pool tables are Uk. Pubs, however, remain stubbornly Brit.

So do vicarage tea parties and one or two other institutions I can't call to mind just now. But otherwise, the British way of life is rapidly becoming the Ukkish way of life.

THE OLD FAMOUS NAMES ACT

'What consideration,' asked Tory MP Cyril Townsend in the House this week, 'has been given to the retaining and bringing back of old famous names?'

Now here, I thought, is a man after my own heart – a politician with a true sense of priorities who wishes to bring back Motoring Chocolate, Gold Flake cigarettes, the GPO, the BBC Home Service, and film stars with names like Clark Gable or better still Betty Grable.

Closer examination of the text showed that Mr Townsend was limiting the scope of his inquiry to the new Territorial Army battalions announced by the Defence Secretary on Monday.

The question yielded fruit, Mr Heseltine indeed undertaking to consider reviving, for example, the Green Jackets and the York-shire Light Infantry (the Queen's Own Yorkshire Light Infantry, shouldn't that be?) though he stopped short at pledging that the Territorials would henceforth revert to their proper name of the Terriers.

Well, that's all right as far as it goes, but I fear Mr Townsend has missed an opportunity here. I thought he was talking about old famous names in general rather than in the militarily particular.

For one blissful moment I imagined he might be putting Parliamentary time to good use for once by introducing an Old Famous Names Bill. It would have had my full support.

The Old Famous Names (Retention and Restoration) Act 1984 would, at a stroke, give Yorkshire back not only its light infantry but its three ridings; it would resuscitate Rutland; and it would restore to all those counties like Avon and Cumbria which now sound like soft processed cheeses their proper, tangy, age-matured titles.

That's only clause one. Clause two would bring back a whole range of old famous names including the shilling and the florin, the office of town clerk, telephone exchanges (ACOrn and all that), the Ministry of Works, aldermen and BOAC. Before slaughtering the GLC, the Government would have to admit that it is really the LCC.

Under clause three, it would be an offence for institutions to alter or shorten their existing names in the belief that it makes them sound more efficient. Thus the North West Electricity Board would be fined £1000 for each day it continues to call itself by the hideous acronym of Norweb. British Rail – before it has chance to contract itself still further to Brit Rail – would be British Railways again. Should it choose to go the whole hog and resume the titles and liveries of the GWR, LNER etc, it would get a special improvement grant.

Grants would also be available for private firms deciding to revive such old famous names as Paramount cinemas, the Morris Minor, Captain Webb matches, and the Pickwick, the Owl and the Waverley pen.

As for impertinent councils which change the names of familiar streets, the best they could hope for under the Old Famous Names Act would be a battalion of the Green Jackets parachuting into Mandela Square.

SCHOOL FOR SHERBETS

I'd better explain my headline first. A sherbet, or sherbet dab, is a taxi-cab. And the reason I'm breaking out in Cockney rhyming slang is that the British Legion's Taxi Drivers' Training School is celebrating its golden jubilee.

I bet you didn't know taxi drivers went to school, did you? But where else would they take their 'U' and 'V' levels? (That's when they have to do a complete U turn in the face of oncoming traffic, at the same time giving the V sign to angry motorists.)

I have been privileged to see an end-of-term examination paper which all cabbies must sit before they are allowed to switch off their 'For hire' signs the moment the rain starts. Here are some representative questions and answers:

How do you address a fare?
I address a fare as 'Squire'. Know what I mean?

How do you greet a fare who flags you down?
I shake my head pityingly, and drive on. Know what I mean?

But if the fare stands in the middle of the road, so that you are forced to stop?
I caution him. I say: 'I am only going East.'

What do you do when a fare wants to go along Oxford Street?
I slump over the wheel with my head in my hands, as if I have just heard about the death of a loved one. I then sigh heavily and say in a martyred voice: 'Go on – hop in.'

What remark do you pass when held up in a traffic jam?
I pass the remark, 'Cuh!' sometimes adding, 'Come on – God Almighty – get an effing move on – stroll on – don't it make you sick – sod me.' Know what I mean?

How do you react when a fare gives you a fivepenny tip?
I hold it in the palm of my hand and stare at it with deep loathing, as if it were the Black Spot out of *Treasure Island*. Then I swivel my eyes to heaven, jerk my head back in a spasm of contempt, and drive off without a word. Know what I mean?

How do you react when a fare has nothing smaller than a five-pound note?

I inhale sharply through my teeth, as one does after stubbing one's toe on a brick. I then say to the punter: 'Can't change that, squire, I've only just come on.' Know what I mean?

What do you say when a fare points out that you are going the wrong way? I ask who is driving the bleeding cab, him or me? Know what I mean?

Thank you. You may now practise drumming your fingers on the steering-wheel and whistling tunelessly while the fare struggles to get his luggage on board.

(PS: to the next cabbie who picks me up outside the *Mirror* office. I'm only joking. Know what I mean?)

THREE WHOOPS FOR EUROPE

You know, many of my Euro-constituents in Home Counties Central have been saying to me, 'You know, why should we bother to turn out to vote today? After all, the European Parliament is only a glorified talking shop.'

Well, you know, it's easy enough to make that kind of sweeping generalisation. But you know, it isn't as simple as that. Nothing connected with the Common Market could possibly be as simple as that.

You know, no one's denying that there are some aspects of the Community we haven't got quite right. That's where your EuroMP comes in – to keep on reminding us there are some aspects of the Community we haven't got quite right.

You know, throwing money about as if it were going out of fashion is no way to tackle Europe's problems. But you know, it's no use just sitting at home on our backsides and moaning about it. We've got to go sit on our backsides in Strasbourg and moan about it there.

And you know, I'm on record as hotly opposing every aspect of waste and extravagance in the EEC except on EuroMP's expenses, which I believe must be kept in line with what they already are if we are to be taken seriously as a potentially powerful legislative body.

'Look here,' I'm on record as saying. 'All this wine lake nonsense has got to stop. It is not on,' I am on record as adding.

Now you know, some of you tell me quite justifiably that the European Parliament doesn't have teeth. But you know, there's only one way to get those teeth and that's to do something about it. 'Look here,' we should be saying, 'We haven't got any teeth.' And you know, that's what the Euro-election is all about.

But you know, it's also about something else, and this is why my colleagues in Westminster are urging you to go out in your tens and vote for us in Strasbourg. You know, many of you voted – probably unintentionally – for the wrong party at the General Election, and this Euro-election is a heaven-sent opportunity to say Whoops! – to put things right by voting for the party you didn't vote for before. Look on it as a giant MORI poll.

Supposing, for example, you're unhappy about the abolition of the GLC. By electing me your Euro-member you enable me to go to my colleagues in Europe and say, 'Now look here, my constituents aren't at all happy about this GLC business.' And you know, you'd be surprised at the feedback we'd get. 'Mein Gott, fancy that!' or 'Mon Dieu, you don't say!' I can imagine them saying.

And you know, there's another reason why your vote is vital today. You know, there is now a very real prospect of a new two-speed Europe that promises to be even more incomprehensible than the half-speed Europe we've got at present. When that day comes, you'll want our voice to be heard. 'Look here,' you'll want us to say. 'Just what the hell is going on?'

If I may end on a personal note: you know, for public figures like myself who have reached the cocktail hour of their days, it's a toss-up between the House of Lords and the European Parliament. I happen to think I've made the right choice. Now it's up to you to make yours. And you know, only by using your vote will you have a say in my future.

You know, you know it makes sense.

THE PONTEFRACT BRONCHOSAURUS

While there is rightly worldwide interest in the 124-million-year-old skeleton of a carnivorous dinosaur dug out of its last resting-place in a Surrey claypit, surprisingly little has been made of what one expert told *The Times* in discussing comparable finds.

This was to the effect that the few bits and pieces of meat-eating dinosaur hitherto discovered have all been in the south of England, since 'dinosaurs did not venture north of Watford.'

What are we to make of this? The standard jibe of northerners, when they wish to suggest that this or that public figure does not know how the other half lives, is that he has never been north of Watford. But this is the first time I have heard the accusation levelled at dinosaurs.

I do not know what Watford was like 124 million years ago – this would be before the by-pass was built, I fancy – but there must have been some very good reason why roaming dinosaurs, having got as far as the town hall, would chew a meditative oak tree or two and then amble back to Surbiton or wherever they came from (Thornton Heath, in the case of the one just excavated. A commuter, evidently).

The obvious explanation is that they were frightful snobs. These toffee-nosed dinosaurs would rather have been seen dead than live in Birmingham and suchlike unfashionable places.

Herein, by the way, may lay the answer to the mystery of why these prehistoric monsters are nowadays to be found only in bone form and can no longer be bought in pet shops. Having eaten everything that walked, swam, flew or grew in the Home Couties, they were far too stuck-up to get on their bikes and move on to the still-fertile Midlands. Being stupid as well as snobbish, the poor boobs didn't even think of the West Country – an acceptable enough address except in the holiday season – but simply flopped down on their suburban lawns and pined into extinction.

This explanation, however, although it has a lot going for it, is not the one I favour. I prefer to think that the reason dinosaurs wouldn't venture north of Watford was the same as why certain of the old music hall comedians wouldn't venture north of

Watford, and that was because they feared the competition.

Your Max Millers may have filled the Palladium but they would never play Blackpool if George Formby was in town. It was the same with dinosaurs. They may have gone over big in Thornton Heath or Croydon, but once beyond Watford and heading up the M1, they stood every chance of bumping into the tripe-eating Pontefract bronchosaurus – so-called because of its wheezing cough. They wouldn't have liked that.

The fact that the bronchosaurus had an endearing habit of putting its head on one side and winking, and that its bellowing cry of 'Ecky thump!' sounded much friendlier than the snooty 'Oh, I say!' of the effete Home Counties dinosaur, led the unwary into believing that it was as harmless a monster as ever clomped the Dales.

The truth is, I am afraid, that anyone rash enough to push his snout into the bronchosaurus's black pudding and mushy peas would feel the back of the creature's hand. Since the average bronchosaurus knuckle sandwich was about twice the size of Halifax Cloth Hall, the victim tended to wake up, if at all, in Lincolnshire.

The bronchosauruses were sporting beasts and despite their chesty condition would often run races for a bet. It was after a mass coughing fit during a sprint to Carlisle and back – last one home buys the drinks – in that foggy winter of 131,000,000 BC or thereabouts that they became extinct. No bones were ever found, since the carcases were apparently baked in an immense pie by the ravenous cavemen of Denby Dale; but blackened bronchosaurus teeth (they smoked a lot) occasionally turn up on Ilkley Moor, where they are nearly always mistaken for crags. The famous Cow and Calf rocks, on the edge of the moor, are in fact all that remains of a dental plate worn by an elderly hermit bronchosaurus which used to go for its Sunday morning walk in that direction.

And that's as much light as I am able to throw on why you would never meet a dinosaur north of Watford. Unless, of course, you care to opt for the one remaining but thoroughly mundane explanation.

Walking uphill made their paws sore.

THE URCHINS' OPERA

Your children have lost their Boswell. Peter Opie, the old-Etonian who spent much of his life recording their catchphrases, skipping rhymes and nonsense songs, and the Byzantine rules of their street games, died a few days ago.

I'll make a little bet with you. Think of some little gutter-jingle that you used to sing when you were about the height of a stick of rhubarb, such as 'Oh, Jemima, look at your Uncle Jim, he's in the duck pond learning how to swim.'

Now go to the library and look up two books by Opie and his wife Iona, *The Lore and Language of Schoolchildren*, and *Children's Games in Street and Playground*. You will more than likely find your street song there in one version or another.

It is rather unnerving in a way. I must say that when, in the abdication year 1936, I used to swagger along Middleton Park Grove, Leeds 10, bellowing the subversive ditty, 'Who's that walking down the street, Mrs Simpson's sweaty feet,' I had no idea that someone was writing it all down, otherwise I should have moderated my language.

The Opies scoured the country for these hitherto unrecorded gems and in doing so, I may say, proved Spuggy Parkin a liar. Spuggy (so called because potatoes were reputed to be sprouting in his ears) had something of a reputation as the street poet laureate, and he claimed the authorship of the elegant couplet, 'Oh me finger, oh me thumb, Oh me belly, oh me bum.' He would have collected royalties on it if any of us had had any money.

Yet here we have the evidence of this scholarly couple, in black and white, that the rhyme was current in Faversham, Kent, in the year 1910.

And therein lies a mystery. The Opies have never satisfactorily explained to me how these songs and snatches spread from one end of the country to the other. What fifty-dimension corporate intelligence is it that enables half the children in the land, as one child, spontaneously to announce to the other half, 'Diana Dors has no drawers'?

That there is such a network is beyond doubt. In one of their golden treasuries of playground ballads the authors quote some doggerel based on the old Dick Barton radio serial: 'Temptation, temptation, temptation, Dick Barton went down to the station. Blondie was there, All naked and bare, Temptation, temptation, temptation.'

Now this verse was heard in Kirkcaldy, Scotland, one January; in Swansea the same month; and in Alton, Hampshire, in the February – places four hundred miles apart. And the question is: how was it transmitted?

Since children do not operate fleets of long-distance lorries, have no access to radio wavelengths and are not in possession of clandestine printing-presses, there can only be one logical explanation. Word of mouth.

But the implications of that are mind-boggling. Are we to understand that from Penzance to Perth, from Liverpool to London, from Cardiff to Colchester, a great commonwealth of children are invisibly holding hands and in defiance of all the parents who want them to speak nicely, all the teachers who want them to learn their songs from books, all the playgroup leaders and organisers and social workers and qualified child specialists who want to purify and process and package their culture like Swiss cheese segments, are secretly passing one to the other like an Olympic torch, their mutinous anthems and Rabelaisian verses and private, haunting rhymes?

It is an awesome and frightening and beautiful thought.

And it is not only in distance of miles that the juvenile underground operates, it is in distance of years too. Adapted, corrupted, topicalised, some of these songs and sayings have been passed down from the reign of Henry VIII and earlier. (The child who cries 'Halves!' when his companion finds a coin, the Opies report, is perpetuating a custom that was known in Stuart times.)

And so the children's Odyssey continues. Next time you come across some snotty-nosed little pipsqueak chanting what might sound even to a professor of linguistics like gibberish 'Eeny meeny mackeracka ...' reflect that you are privileged to be eaves-dropping on a fragment of an aria from a mighty urchins' opera that, largely unheard by adult ears, swells across the land with a piping grandeur.

A PICTURE POSTSCRIPT

I see that a complete set of *Picture Post* is coming up for sale at Sotheby's who expect it to fetch £200. My bet is that it will fetch at least double. I really must stop using my own bound volumes of this famous photo-magazine as doorstops.

Not that I would ever want to sell them – and anyway, unlike the chap whose set is being auctioned, I don't own a complete run. The best I can offer is a mere twenty-nine volumes, covering the entire span of the war and hogging about a yard of bookshelf.

I bet you didn't know, by the way, that *Picture Post* was originally to have been called *Lo!* – which sounds as if it could have been dreamed up by Sir James Goldsmith, founder of that other exclamatory magazine *Now!*

Had it gone on the streets under that title and with its original slogan – 'Buy *Lo!* See and Know!' – I imagine that complete sets would consist of one slim volume.

Happily they got the label right and of course *Picture Post* was a roaring success until the late Fifties when it fell victim to wet management (who put the blame on television).

Picture Post really was as good as we now think it was (not always the case with golden-age institutions). Its campaigning reputation was well-deserved: there has never been any magazine like it for covering the great social issues of the day with courage and vigour. Browsing through my old volumes, however, I find that it is an altogether subtler quality that comes over the strongest.

What comes flooding out of those pages is the authentic atmosphere of England. This is a very difficult atmosphere to describe, unless you happen to be a George Orwell or an early Ealing comedy, but it's an easy one to recognise.

Just walk down a terrace street or along a suburban avenue on a spring Sunday morning, when you'll catch the whiff of a dozen roast beef dinners floating out from a dozen open windows. It is an essentially English aroma that somehow embraces a dozen other English flavours – pubs, allotments, Sunday papers, cricket, municipal parks ... and *Picture Post* managed to capture all this Englishness in black and white.

Not a bad trick – considering that the man who thought it up was a Hungarian Jew. (His name was Stefan Lorant, and another of his engaging inventions was the pocket magazine *Lilliput*.)

When I bought my twenty-nine volumes of *Picture Post* (at a fraction of what they'd cost today, I tell myself smugly – though my smirk fades when I note that the original price per copy was three old pence for eighty-eight pages) it was with the vague idea that it would be instructive to possess a complete pictorial record of the war years. So it is. But even more interesting: I find myself the keeper of a unique diary of everyday English life as we tried to live it then; indeed – where the planners and demolition experts have not stamped it out entirely – as many of us try to live it still.

What *Picture Post* did (brilliantly) was to explore the fascinating range of small social foothills – commercial travellers' dinner dances, anglers' outings, amateur dramatic nights, street parties, mystery coach tours, mock parliaments, flower shows, market days, jumble sales, pigeon races, whippet races, brass band contests, darts matches, tennis matches and all the rest of it – that, more than the Pennine chain itself, forms the backbone of England.

'Fashionable Birmingham has its lager and sandwich in the snack-bar of the Grand Hotel,' reports one caption on a page opened at random. Hardly world-shattering stuff but how else would we know what fashionable Birmingham was doing in 1939 – and how will anyone ever find out what fashionable Birmingham was doing in 1980?

It would be a brave editor nowadays who would devote four or five pages to a picture-essay on the subject of 'A Day In The Life Of A Fishmonger' (much less run a two-page article called 'The Drama Of Cement'). Yet it was, and still is, riveting stuff – the fishmonger's day, I mean, not the drama of cement which fails to grip.

Picture Post went under at just about the same time as they began to pull most of England down – maybe these two acts of destruction were not unconnected. Even with a management less like a hen running around with its head cut off, it couldn't have survived into the computer age – but I wish it had. We still need to be reminded, or do I mean reassured, what an extraordinary daily event is ordinary, everyday life.

MISUNDERSTOOD

Those of you who have nephews will be interested to learn that a batch of the Richmal Crompton's William books are being reissued, in nice time for Christmas.

Those of you who have been nephews yourself will recall that the idea of getting a William book for Christmas was so that your generous uncle could promptly borrow it back and read it himself.

There can be very few people reading this column who have not devoured a William book at one time or another. They sold in their millions. It will be a joy to see some of them again.

It was with the sole purpose of reading William books that I took up with Leeds Public Libraries at a few months under his own perennial age of eleven, having discovered him in a journal called *The Happy Mag*.

Within a week I had got through five William books – *Just William*, *Still William*, *William the Conqueror*, *William the Outlaw* and either *William the Good* or *William the Bad*, I forget which – and had been lectured by a stern librarian on the unwholesomeness of gobbling down books as if they were licorice allsorts.

Over the next few years I read every William volume then in print, sometimes crossing the city to track down an elusive title in some obscure branch library. I think the last one to pass through my hands was *William and the Brains Trust*, published at the end of the war; whereupon I snootily put away childish things, discarding Richmal Crompton (who I thought was a man) for the likes of Evelyn Waugh (who I thought was a woman).

What I didn't know, until much later, was that the William books were never intended to be childish things in the first place. Although lapped up by legions of children – I remember seeing two bullet-headed candidates for the reformatory, in all other respects sub-literate, actually fighting over possession of a library copy of *William and the Evacuees* – they were written for adults. Even when Richmal Crompton realised she had a huge junior audience, she made no concession to their limited general knowledge.

This may explain why, from first to last, there were some aspects of the William saga which puzzled me. For instance, Mr

Brown went 'up to Town' on a train every morning, but I had no idea where this town was or what he did when he got to it; nor why when William went to town (the nearby market town, which I assumed must be the same place) he went by bus.

Nor, since he lived in a big posh house every bit as grand as the bow-windowed semis near my local park, with a maid and a grown-up brother and sister who led lives of total idleness, could I understand why William went to the village school instead of a private academy; nor why he spoke even worse English than I did.

No matter: I and my friends worshipped him. While William and the Outlaws were pretending to be pirates or gangsters, we were pretending to be William and the Outlaws.

It was a matter of permanent and perpetual regret that we did not have access to an Ole Barn in which to stage our concerts or rig up our inventions or otherwise copy whichever particular William adventure had taken our fancy. There also seemed to be an acute scarcity of short-sighted old gents losing their way who were an essential element of so many of the William stories. But at least we had a dog we could re-christen Jumble.

It has always irritated me to read that William was the prototype mischievous boy. He was nothing of the sort – there was not an ounce of mischief in his stocky body. William was a deeply serious individual, a would-be Einstein among boys, who embarked on his adventures from the highest and most philanthropic of motives, only to be woefully misunderstood by his elders. It was his burning sense of grievance at the wrong construction put on his good intentions that struck a chord with young readers.

The William stories were repetitive, far-fetched in plot and peopled – apart from the immortal Outlaws themselves – with stock characters, and I do not suppose they would ever have been short-listed for the Booker prize. But it is nearly forty years now since I put William's exploits aside and they remain as fresh in my mind as ever. They must have had something.

THE MITTEN BOARD

Government health warning: Government health warnings can seriously damage your health.

Indeed, I fear they have already done me immeasurable harm. So jittery have I become as a result of repeated official injunctions to eat less, drink less and cut out smoking that last night I dreamt I was back on forty Capstan Full Strength a day.

Stress caused by excessive nannying, that's what that is.

I also suffer intermittently from impaired vision due to a red mist floating in front of the eyeballs. This is brought on by reading such news items as: 'The Government is to spend £100,000 on an advertising campaign to combat a big increase in unwanted pregnancies among teenagers.'

I can imagine the slogans. GOVERNMENT HEALTH WARNING: TOO MUCH OF THE OTHER CAN MAKE YOU GO BLIND.

Those who rule over us have become such fussbudgets that I am beginning to suspect there has been a secret Whitehall coup by a parachute corps of district nurses.

Why, after all, should any Government that is right in the head invest, of its own free will, large sums of taxpayers' money on advising those same taxpayers to send off for a free booklet that will tell them whether cheese spread has more fat than cheddar?

If, by the way, you fell for all those full-page advertisements by the Health Education Council and filled in the coupon, this is what they will be sending you:

One lapel badge (made in Holland) with the slogan LOOK AFTER YOURSELF.

One twenty-four page booklet entitled THE SMOKER'S GUIDE TO NON-SMOKING, including ready reckoner proving that if you stop smoking eighty a day for twenty years, you will save £20,454.

One wall-chart of daily exercises ('Raise both arms forward, upwards, backwards and sideways in a circular motion, brushing your ears with your arms as you go past').

One full-colour brochure of health tips ('Eat less meat. Try jogging. Bicycle to work, but always give clear hand signals.

Don't swim within two hours of a heavy meal. Bake your own bread. Eat more fibre. Weigh yourself once a week').

You also get the answer to the question that prompted you to send off for this costly drivel in the first place: the fat content of cheese spread is twenty-three per cent as against thirty-four per cent in Cheddar.

Digesting the Health Education Council's keep-fit kit over my accustomed breakfast of fatty foods this morning, I began worrying about what this fanatical quango is going to do for a crust (wholemeal, naturally) when it has finally, and expensively, got us all weaned off cake, built up our little legs, introduced Prohibition, and banished cigarette-smoking to officially-licensed tin shacks on derelict sites lately abandoned by reformed methsdrinkers.

After chewing meditatively on my cholesterol-rich fruit slice for a while, I came up with the answer. The Health Education Council must reconstitute itself as the Mitten Board.

The Mitten Board, by means of newspaper advertisements, television and cinema commercials, leaflets, free video-cassettes, demonstrations in schools, hospitals and Darby and Joan clubs, bumper-stickers, posters, T-shirts, hot-air balloons and any other means of communiction likely to add a few more noughts to the bill, will urge the nation never, never, ever to go out without wearing mittens, for fear of getting chilblains.

A winsome cartoon character, known as Charlie Chilblain, will brainwash toddlers from birth into believing that if they take off their mittens while out toddling, their hands will drop off.

When the entire population meekly and obediently has its paws encased in Shetland wool of the approved Fair Isle pattern, the Board will then use its considerable lobbying powers to talk the Government into passing a law compelling all mitten manufacturers to sew into each and every pair of mittens a label measuring not less than 4 centimetres by 2.5 centimetres, and carrying, in Roman letters not less than 3.75 millimetres high, the legend:

GOVERNMENT PIE WARNING: THE LOSS OF THESE MITTENS MAY RESULT IN THEIR WEARER HAVING NO PIE.

THE HORSE-SHOE NAILS SURPLUS

I should like to direct your attention to a historic event which is taking place this week – the very last of the great Ministry of Defence war surplus sales, or peace surplus sales as I suppose they have become by now, which have been going on without a break since 1946.

I know a scrap millionaire who will observe a two minutes' silence at the news – unless he chances upon a punter who is in the market for two unused minutes.

The last war surplus sale! The Defence Ministry, that cornu-copia of gas-capes and camouflage-painted bicycles, will continue to dispose of its surplus booty, but only in small local sales run by private auctioneers. It won't be the same. The days of those great Eastern bazaars on obscure disused airfields are over.

Thus there finally passes that glorious, ever-changing pageant of fleece-lined flying boots, oilskin waterproof gloves, tyres, binoculars, bolts of parachute silk, enamel plates, radio valves, cellular drawers, boots, bedsteads and bayonet frogs which runs like a silver thread – or should I say a coil of ex-Ordnance Corps detonator wire? – through the tapestry of our recent history.

The term 'war surplus', of course has always been a bit of a misnomer, suggesting as it does that this is what is left over in the quartermasters' stores in the way of tent-pegs, groundsheets, WAAF bloomers and field telephones after the dust of battle has cleared. My scrap millionaire goes further and supposes that the whole aim and object of a war is to create war surplus. But for myself I have always believed that war surplus simply generates itself, like yeast.

How else do you account for those great dumps of clothing and cutlery, those Everests of toggle-switches and teapots, that have been going under the hammer these thirty-seven years? They make the EEC's food mountains look like hillocks. I did part of my national service in an RAF maintenance unit and it is no infringe-ment of the Official Secrets Act – or perhaps it is – to reveal that we had more trousers, barathea, warrant officers for the use of, than there were legs in all the combined forces of the NATO alliance. I now realise that we were quietly breeding war surplus.

I did once go to one of these Ministry of Defence auctions, out at Woolwich Arsenal. I think I had need of a typewriter. Had I happened to have need of 6000 typewriters they might have been able to help me. But before leaving, I couldn't help noticing that they had twelve million horse-shoe nails on sale.

With the aid of an equestrian friend I worked out on the back of an envelope that this was enough to keep every horse, donkey and mule on the strength of the British Army in horse-shoe nails for thirty-eight years. My equestrian friend, reminding me that it was for want of a nail that the battle was lost, held that you couldn't blame the Army for being cautious.

All right: but twelve million horse-shoe nails are pretty useless without the horse-shoes to go with them. And horse-shoes were not on offer.

Intrigued, I rang the Ministry. Had they recently auctioned about a million horse-shoes? No. Were they about to auction about a million horse-shoes? No. Even more intrigued, I called the War Office. Was the Army hanging on to about a million horse-shoes? No. Had the Army ever, in fact, since say the Boer War, possessed about a million horse-shoes? No. Then what was the point of having accumulated twelve million horse-shoe nails?

'There is no point,' said the War Office. 'That is why we are getting rid of them.' There was no answer to that.

Chronicled in the pages of the *Exchange & Mart* and in those bargain squares of the Saturday papers, the war surplus story is really the story of that backyard England of allotments and tool-sheds which has remained virtually unchanged since the days of Kipps and Mr Polly. There is no ex-WD item so obscure or esoteric, from a hydraulic aircraft jack to a left-handed morse tapper, that it will not come in handy one of these days.

But I would like to know who found a use for those twelve million horse-shoe nails.

The silly sickness

Following the demand by a Swansea theatre's Mrs Mopps to have gay actors banned from their stage, and the boycotting of gays by tattoo artists, a fresh outburst of the very silly disease AIPS – AIDS-induced Panic Syndrome – has been reported from an unnamed London borough.

There, town hall cleaners have gone on strike for rubber-glove money because they fear that councillors handing over generous grants to gay workshop co-ordinators without gauze pads over their mouths may have become AIDS carriers.

The council wishes to remain anonymous in case potential industrial investors in the borough are put off by rumours sweeping through AIPS-affected areas that you can catch AIDS from sitting on park benches.

AIPS was first detected in San Francisco three years ago when hitherto sane citizens began boycotting restaurants allowing gay waiters to handle the lettuce. The Silly Sickness, as it is known, is believed to have been transmitted to this country on a souvenir menu.

The first notified case in Britain was in August 1984 when a man addressed as 'you little saucebox' by a camp actor came out in psychosomatic boils within a week.

AIPS is believed to be transmitted orally, usually by gullible or excitable persons coming into contact with persons of a similar disposition and filling their heads with rubbish.

There is as yet no firm evidence that it can be contracted from reading the *Sun* newspaper.

As the AIPS plague spreads, leaders of the very silly community fear for a level-head backlash against known idiots. They insist that the so-called Silly Sickness is not, as is widely thought, endemic to the very silly and that there have already been several cases of quite intelligent people catching it.

Doctors stress that vulnerable persons such as prison officers and hospital workers who take sensible precautions against AIDS are unlikely to be suffering from AIPS unless they have experienced the telltale initial symptoms of running around like a scalded cat crying, 'A friend of my brother's has heard of a top secret report which admits that it can be spread by sneezing and it's only a matter of time before we're all dead and the Government can do nothing about it, apparently.'

Though there is no known cure for AIPS, some health authorities are working cautiously towards the theory that making information freely available may be a way of quelling the virus-carrying tittle-tattle which is believed to be the Silly Sickness's main cause.

WHEN OUR NUMBER'S UP

More nuclear survival news. A declassified Home Office circular reveals emergency plans for the telephone service in the event of the Big One dropping.

It seems that the telephone exchanges are able to throw a switch disconnecting all but essential subscribers – that is, the planning officers and other bureaucrats who will be conducting our affairs from their regional bunkers.

They have it all nicely worked out and you will be relieved to know that when that gigantic mushroom cloud appears on the horizon, your local VIP fall-out shelter will be able to put a call through to the fire brigade without let or hindrance.

Unless, that is, our telephone service runs true to form ...

'Hello?'

'Yes? Who is that?'

'I'm ringing in response to your advert in the newsagent's window. Big chest for sale.'

'I think you have the wrong number. This is the Emergency Powers Controller, Blue Zone ...'

'... Hello?'

'Blue Zone here. Could you let us have fifteen thousand stirrup pumps, fairly urgently?'

'I'm afraid the manageress is buried under some bricks at the moment, but I don't think we sell stirrup pumps.'

'Isn't that the Director of Essential Supplies, Green Zone ...?'

'No, this is Dorothy's Cake Shop ...'

'... Hello?'

'Oh, good morning. This is Ned. I'm a first-time caller, and what I wanted to ask, Brian, was what you think about all these coloureds coming over here and jumping the queue for council bunkers. I mean to say, ours used to be a very nice street but now we've got nineteen Arabs living in one bomb-crater, Brian ...'

'This isn't Brian, this is the Director of Essential Supplies, Green Zone. We have a crossed line, I'm afraid ...'

'... Hello?'

'Here is General Raskolnikov, Fourth Omsk Rifles, Peace-loving Red Army. Please to speak with Emergency Powers Controller.'

'There's no one of that name here, deary. This is Dawn, model, big chest for sale. Can I be of assistance ...?'

'... Hello?'

'Operator, this is the Emergency Powers Controller, Blue Zone. Could you give me the number of the Director of Essential Supplies, Green Zone?'

'I'm sorry, caller, that number is ex-directory.'

'But I have to get my hands on fifteen thousand stirrup pumps as quickly as possible.'

'Have you tried Yellow Pages ...?'

TEETHING TROUBLES

While these are trying times for all of us, I believe it can do nothing but good to reflect occasionally that on any given day the times are more trying for some people than for others.

I therefore invite your attention to the plight of Mr John Ayland, a Liverpool driving examiner, who found himself in the front passenger seat of a car – the make is not specified – careering down a steep hill with a dead body at the wheel.

I can do no better than to take up Mr Ayland's own account of this awkward moment, as recorded in Saturday's *Daily Mail*:

'I thought there must be something very wrong.' (Got his wits about him, you see.) 'He was completely incompetent even before he died and I'd been thinking of calling the whole thing off.

'I was pulling on the hand brake with one hand and pulling out his false teeth with the other, because I'd read that was what you are meant to do.

'I managed to stop the car just before it went over a junction. A policeman arrived and when I told him what had happened he fainted.'

Now one obvious question arising out of this unhappy business is what has happened to the calibre of the Liverpool police force, which has not hitherto endured a reputation for cissiness? But that is no affair of mine. What I am most interested in is exactly where Mr Ayland read that if you find yourself hurtling downhill with a dead body, you should take out the deceased driver's false teeth as well as pulling on the handbrake.

Well, I mean to say, it could happen to any one of us, couldn't it?

The obvious source was the Highway Code. But I have gone through it from start to finish and while there are sections headed The Road User On Foot, The Road User On Wheels, and so on, there is no section entitled The Road User Pops His Clogs. (What I did discover, though, is that there is no recognised hand signal for 'I am about to meet my Maker.' Surely this should be rectified?)

I next turned to the British Leyland handbook's section on Automatic Transmission which I would have thought covered the activities of dead drivers. However, under the heading Descending Steep Hills, it recommends only that second gear should be used, nothing about removing false teeth whatsoever.

It then occurred to me that this advice about what to do in the event of finding oneself being chauffered downhill by a stiff was very likely not aimed at the general public at all, but was specifically meant for driving examiners, for whom it is probably a recurring professional hazard.

Where Mr Ayland must have read it, then, was in his official manual: 'Should the candidate expire before completing any portion of the test, the examiner at his own discretion may (a) gently apply the hand brake, (b) remove the candidate's false teeth, (c) signal his intention to crash through a shop window, and (d) mark the deceased's licence application "Failed".'

That is the obvious explanation. It leaves, however, one puzzle outstanding, which is as follows:

Why?

Why are driving examiners required to remove the false

gnashers of any dead L-plate drivers in whose company they may chance to find themselves? Are they supposed to take them back to the office, to prove that they did not fail the candidate maliciously but merely because rigor mortis set in before he could successfully manage a three-point turn? In that event, what if he still has his own teeth? They are not advised, I hope and trust, to pull them out with pliers?

I am afraid that having raised these questions, I am completely unable to answer them. But my purpose, as I said at the beginning, was only to demonstrate that there is always someone worse off than ourselves.

Mr Ayland could argue that in the dilemma outlined above, there was no one in the whole of creation worse off than himself, with the possible exception of the toothless corpse by his side. Perhaps. But things could have been blacker.

Supposing that, in the very act of removing the learner-driver's false teeth and wrapping them in his handkerchief, Mr Ayland had discovered that he wasn't dead after all? How would he have explained *that* to the fainting policeman?

THE FLYING DUMPLING

They are not all as gentle and harmless as Arthur Scargill in Barnsley. I see that a colliery official up there has been fined for giving his wife a black eye after she served him up an unsatisfactory Yorkshire pudding.

Now I know that I am walking on eggshells here. Giving the old woman a fourpenny one is but comic-postcard euphemism for wife-battering, which is not a proper subject for levity.

Yet notwithstanding the crunch of eggshell underfoot I have to confess that I was as bemused by this news item as I would have been to learn that mill-girls still wear clogs.

I was at once wafted back, on wings of disbelief, to a long-lost era when the ceremony of Throwing The Sunday Dinner In The Fireplace was as familiar a feature of northern life as whippet racing and the Whitsun Walk.

There were Sunday dinner-times, just after pub closing-times, when our street gave the impression of having a dress rehearsal for one of those traditional Greek weddings where they smash all the crockery.

Passing an open window on a pleasant Sabbath afternoon could be a chancy experience. One minute you would be full of the joys of summer and the next you would have rabbit gravy streaming down your face and a suet dumpling lodged up your nostril.

If the census forms of forty years ago had had a supplementary question, 'State the exact position of your Sunday dinner at 2.30 pm on Census Day,' a majority of householders in my neighbourhood would have been compelled to reply, 'In mid-air.'

Spouses of either sex were eligible for dinner-hurling – and there could be any number of reasons for the tendency of meat, roast potatoes and two veg in our little community to fly like a bird and sting like an eyeful of mustard.

One was that men who'd sworn they were only going to the pub for the one came reeling home having had the one over the eight. Another was that domestic discussions touching on the women-folk not having had a new frock for ten years just happened to reach their climax when savoury missiles were at hand. A third was epicurean in character.

The colliery worker hauled before the beaks in Barnsley had taken issue at his wife's Yorkshire puddings being too thin. I have known fastidious diners hurl their Yorkshire puddings into the fire, or at the ceiling, or at the cat, on the grounds that they were too thick, or over-salted, or not properly crisp at the edges.

One neighbour of ours was a gourmet of such sensitive palate that he hardly seemed to eat at all. Was the cabbage too watery? *Crash*. The string beans a little too stringy? *Crash*. Given a better start in life, he might have become Editor of the *Good Food Guide*.

I had always supposed that the custom of slinging one's victuals into the fireplace instead of down one's throat had died out in the war, with the onset of rationing. That snippet from Barnsley suggests, however, that passions still run high come Sunday dinner-time. Maybe dinner-throwing is not one of the lost arts after all.

Passport to Puzzlement

Looking for my passport the other day (I'm not going anywhere – it's just that every so often I wake up at three in the morning thinking, 'Oh my God, where's my passport?') I unearthed one of those leaflets the bank gives you when you buy foreign currency.

You've probably seen it. It's called 'Notice To All Travellers' and is printed in important-looking red type. It tells you what you can do and can't do – when you take money abroad, or 'within or outside the Scheduled Territories' as the Bank of England prefers to call foreign parts.

I have never actually read this document and I only read it now to put me in a calm frame of mind so I could remember where my passport was when I saw it last. (In my raincoat pocket. Yes, but did I take it out before I sent my coat to the cleaners?)

It contains, as I suspected, nothing of interest to anyone – except in the paragraph that begins, 'Do not present yourself at an airport or seaport with more notes than you are allowed to export.' The last sentence reads: 'In particular, unless you hold special permission, you may not take out any gold coin, bullion or postal orders.'

Postal orders?

I have, of course, a suitcase full of postal orders, mostly in small denominations such as thirty-three pence and one pound and seven pence, together with some dog-eared five-bob issues of Billy Bunter vintage. I intended scattering them discreetly about the restaurants of Paris as soon as my passport turned up. (Could it be in that old airline bag? I sincerely hope not, because I gave the old airline bag to the jumble sale.) But now the risk seems too great.

Now, I can readily understand why the Bank of England does not wish me to export my vast reserves of gold coins and bullion. If we all stuffed our pockets with bullion every time we left the country it wouldn't half cause a run on the pound, not to mention making the cross-Channel ferry turn lopsided. But postal orders?

Why would anyone want to export postal orders? And having exported them, what would he do with them upon reaching Calais and extracting them from the false bottom of his valise?

Is there an international syndicate cynically trading in British postal orders? Did the flight from the pound a few months ago happen because Swiss financiers were swapping their British postal orders for Italian lottery tickets and Tristan da Cunha triangular stamps?

I was so intrigued that I rang the Bank of England and asked why they won't let me take my postal orders abroad.

'Can you hold a second while I think?' the man said.

There was such a long silence that I though I must have reminded him that he hadn't seen his passport lately, and he was rummaging in his desk for it.

At length he came back with: 'I think possibly because, er –'

He then went off the air for another spell. 'I don't know. That's the answer,' said my informant finally. But he was kind enough to make inquiries and later he rang back in what sounded to me like triumph. 'The reason you cannot take postal orders abroad without special permission is that there is no necessity to do so.'

Of course, I should have thought of that in the first place.

My passport, by the way, was in the dressing-table drawer as usual.

THE LISPING COCKROACH

Browsing through a list of the micro-processed miracles in store for us in the Orwellian Eighties, I was reminded of the advertisement columns of the pre-war boys' papers.

Those of you who remember those ads will recall that the big selling-point for every product on offer, from invisible ink to the multiplying billiard ball, was that it would AMAZE YOUR FRIENDS.

You could amaze your friends by growing taller overnight and becoming an accomplished pianist simultaneously. You could astonish them by throwing your voice. You could stupefy them by demonstrating your ability to see round corners with the aid of the Wonderscope.

I am here to tell you that the Wonderscope is as nothing compared with the scope and wonder of the technological grotto now opening for business.

You will, in the Eighties, be able to amaze your friends with your pocket telephone and your flying bicycle (unless, of course, your friends amaze you first with their pocket bicycles and flying telephones).

You will be able to amaze not only your friends but your enemies with a computerised death-ray. (For this, you will need to be an army.)

All things improbable will be possible. There will be wrist-watch TV with eighty channels. There will be memory pills (amaze your friends by remembering their names). There will be synthetic petrol. There will be solar air-conditioning.

But of all these wondrous developments, the one that impresses me most – and will doubtless amaze my friends when I have sent off my postal order for full details, money back if not delighted – is the Great Cockroach Breakthrough.

As any cockroaches among my readers will shortly learn to their peril, thirty years of dedicated research into their beastly social habits has at last paid off for the scientists, who have discovered a way of making the cockroach confused.

Now, given the choice between a cockroach with a puzzled frown and any of the other marvels on display here today, I suppose most of you would settle for wrist-watch TV or the multiplying billiard ball.

You wouldn't, however, if you lived in New York, where cockroaches are an even greater public menace than joggers and encyclopedia salesmen. Anything that throws the little blighters into a tizzy will be Nobel Prize material so far as New Yorkers are concerned.

What the scientists have succeeded in doing is – I quote – to synthesise the female cockroach's sex excitant. Male cockroaches need only one whiff of this come-hither hormone and they go bananas. Apparently they will screw any insect in sight and I have no doubt that the seedier male cockroaches will finish up sending off for inflatable rubber female cockroaches under plain cover.

The most significant side-effect, however, is that if there is no female cockroach on hand – not even a fat, ugly female cockroach with thick legs – the male cockroaches *will mount each other*. This is what makes them confused and it is what, ultimately, will be their undoing because – as I am sure you realise – two male cock-roaches, however much in love, will never hear the patter of tiny antennae.

I see, friends, that you are still not amazed. Let me tell you why I, on the other hand, am.

Modern science dates from four hundred years ago when Francis Bacon pulled together all the tattered strands of knowledge stretching back to the ancient Greeks and published *The Advancement of Learning*. Meanwhile Galileo was inventing the telescope.

Along came Sir William Harvey and we learned about the circulation of the blood. Along came Sir Isaac Newton and his apple and we learned about gravity.

Leeuwenhoek identified the red corpuscle, Halley observed his comet, John Clayton demonstrated coal gas lighting, Fahrenheit invented the mercury thermometer – and still science marched on.

Faraday died, Alexander Graham Bell was born. Darwin published *The Origin of Species*. Now science was not marching but running. It gave us the motor car and antibiotics, the aeroplane and heart transplants, the photo-copier, the Polaroid camera and the bomb.

It hurried us into an age where the computer, the man-made satellite and the laser beam are everyday objects.

And what, having been to the moon and back and with its vast data-bank of accumulated knowledge, does science promise as its next achievement as we come within sight of the threshold of the twenty-first century?

A lisping cockroach with one hand on its hip.

Amazing.

JENNY'S BIRTHDAY

Somewhere in London there is a girl called Jenny. Or, to adjust that statement slightly, possibly not.

Somewhere in Paris, or in Spain, or in Tangier, or in Cornwall, or on the golden road to Samarkand, or perhaps only in the next postal district from where she used to live, there is a girl called Jenny.

I know Jenny as well as anyone can know her – which is to say, not much. She is mercurial, tranquil, impetuous, steady, gregarious, lonely, open, secret, generous and I think she has a small mean streak. In short, an interesting contradiction of herself.

She is a restless, mobile spirit who hankers to grow roots, and a homebody who strikes camp at dawn without leaving a forwarding address for the laundry or her friends. She was in love once.

She is an early riser who gets invited to late-night parties by people who ask for Jen baby. She is a night-owl who is well-acquainted with brisk, efficient secretary-birds who ring her first thing after they have brushed their teeth and ask for Jennifer.

Jen, Jennifer or Jenny has a friend called David who rang her belatedly – several months belatedly – to thank her for the cuff-links.

She has a friend called Bernie who once required her now, this very instant, to come on over and talk about some past mis-understanding. At four am.

I don't think David knows about Bernie. I don't think Bernie knows about David. I don't think either of them knows about Harry. We'll come to Harry in a second.

Some of Jenny's friends ring at eight in the evening expecting to find her in. Others ring at half-past midnight and they are not surprised to find her gone.

They never call back, and we'll come to that too. It doesn't much matter, because there are plenty more friends where they came from.

I call them friends because that's what they call themselves, and probably Jenny would fool herself, if she needed them as we sometimes do need friends, that that's what they are. Or were. Acquaintances would be a better word. People she's met. People who don't exist except in other people's address-books, and at other people's parties. And who only come alive when telephones ring.

I know about Jenny because I take a lot of her calls.

She's always been a bit of a roamer but at one point in her life she settled down sufficiently to get a place of her own and probably she shared it with Harry. Or Harry shared it with her, which is more likely, because the telephone was in her name.

She met a great many people and gave them all her phone number. She told them they could ring her day or night, whenever there was any fun going on. Perhaps she told some of them that if

Harry answered they'd better hang up the receiver, because that is what some of them still do.

One day for a reason I do not know anything about, Jenny packed her bags and went. To the next postal district. Or Paris, or Spain, or Tangier, or Cornwall, or the golden road to Samarkand. Or back home.

Perhaps she told Harry she was leaving but she didn't tell anyone else – except the Post Office. She said she wouldn't be needing her telephone any more.

The reason I know all this is because when Jenny's line fell vacant, it came to me. And for months and months and months I've been getting her phone calls. At five in the afternoon. Nine in the evening. Midnight. And two, three or four in the morning.

Yesterday, at a respectable hour, a lady called my number and asked if Jennifer was there.

I said that Jennifer was not.

'Is that Harry?'

I said it was not Harry.

There was a sort of silence that women go into only when they're protecting other women from the consequences of follies that they wish they were committing themselves.

'Did I say Harry? I meant Bernie.'

'No, it's not Bernie either,' I said. 'You've got the right number but the wrong person. Jenny doesn't live here any more.'

'It doesn't matter,' she said. 'I only wanted to wish her a happy birthday.'

Now I'll tell you an odd thing. The phone didn't ring again yesterday – at least, not for Jenny. Out of all her friends, only one remembered, or knew about or cared about her birthday.

Happy birthday, Jenny. Wherever you are, and whoever you are.